Dr Aric Sigman is an Associate Fellow of the British Psychological Society and has conducted research on a range of subjects, from the use of psychosurgery, to the effects of hypnosis on the brain and autonomic nervous system.

Dr Sigman has worked on health education campaigns with the Department of Health and acted as advisor to the Institute of Personnel Management on health and psychology issues. He has written and presented scientific documentaries for BBC1 and Radio 4 on the scientific basis of faith; the biology of hypnosis; and the effects of too much choice, and for *Dispatches*, Channel 4, on the hidden detrimental effects of moderate dieting. His health and psychology book *Getting Physical* won *The Times Educational Supplement*'s Information Book Award in 1993.

Dr Sigman travels abroad frequently to observe the influence of television on various cultures, including Bhutan, Tonga, Myanmar, Iran, Korea, Vietnam and Bolivia. He is American and lives with his wife and four children in England.

REMOTELY CONTROLLED

CONTROLLED

How television is
damaging our lives
– and what we can
do about it

DR ARIC SIGMAN

Vermilion
LONDON

Copyright © Aric Sigman 2005

Aric Sigman has asserted his moral right to be identified as the author of this work in accordance with the Copyright, Design and Patents Act 1988.

First published in the United Kingdom in 2005 by Vermilion, an imprint of Ebury Publishing Random House UK Ltd. Random House 20 Vauxhall Bridge Road London SW1V 2SA

Random House Australia (Pty) Limited 20 Alfred Street, Milsons Point, Sydney, New South Wales 2061, Australia

Random House New Zealand Limited 18 Poland Road, Glenfield, Auckland 10, New Zealand

Random House (Pty) Limited Endulini, 5A Jubilee Road, Parktown 2193, South Africa

Random House UK Limited Reg. No. 954009 www.randomhouse.co.uk Papers used by Vermilion are natural, recyclable products made from wood grown in sustainable forests.

A CIP catalogue record is available for this book from the British Library.

ISBN: 0091902606

Designed and typeset by seagulls

Printed and bound in Great Britain by Mackays of Chatham plc, Chatham, Kent

The author and publishers have made all reasonable efforts to contact copyright holders for permission, and apologise for any omissions or errors in the form of credit given. Corrections may be made in future printings.

CONTENTS

Acknowledgements

I would like to thank my literary agent Sara Menguc for her unstinting belief in the need for an urgent reconsideration of television. Amanda Hemmings, for originally seeing that there was a book to be written and a debate to be had. My editor, Julia Kellaway, whose objectivity, good judgement (and timely praise) ensured that I wrote about what I promised I would write about. Copy editor Michele Turney, for ensuring it made sense. My brother Nicholas, for drawing my attention to several key studies concerning children and television, thereby arousing my suspicion to begin with. Steve Trawley, for his valuable contribution to my understanding of the role of dopamine in ADHD. Lucy Lowe, for additional literature on the biology of faith and common experience. Christian Hill, a television documentary producer and friend, with whom I had many highly constructive discussions on the telephone during the writing of this book. And Katy, who not only endured daily – sometimes hourly – telephone calls asking for her opinion on a paragraph or two, but then had to endure even more of the same when I returned home in the evening.

Man had given no clear indication that he could use wisely the power that already lay at his command; to multiply that power hundreds or thousands of times over by scientific and technological means, without a concomitant growth in wisdom, would be to make the world a far more dangerous place than it had been in less enlightened times.

John Adams

PREFACE

Whether writing on the history of dried fish or the hidden effects of television, authors are consumed by an interest or concern in a subject and are driven to tell others. I am no exception. It has been 80 years since John Logie Baird transmitted an image for the first time. This was an invention more profound than that of the light bulb for it has unleashed a worldwide cultural force equalled in history only by religion. In addition to its influence, however, I have come to see the amount and type of television we watch as being nothing short of the greatest health scandal of our age. Several personal experiences have conspired to draw my interest and concern, especially travelling and fatherhood. There are two incidents in particular.

Two years after I first visited it, I returned to a tiny provincial village in the far northwest of Thailand, near the Burmese border. I had terribly fond memories of it and how it seemed so far removed from my life in London. Just as I remembered it, the sights, smells and sounds were reassuringly alien as I sat down in front of a tea and soup shack on the dusty main street and immersed myself in the Oriental way. People floated past in a Buddhist mist, conical rice paddy hats on their heads and soft gentle cotton gowns flowing from their slight frames. They seemed so graceful. Their gait, cadence, their entire demeanour was engagingly different from purposeful Western Man.

Then, suddenly, a figure appeared on my left. It was a young Thai man dressed in a brightly coloured polyester shell suit and wearing a baseball cap backwards. His face was covered in a light powder making his skin seem more Caucasian in tone. But it was his body language that was most striking. This local young man from the remote hills of northern Thailand began to vibrate and quiver, then his arms, neck and head started to jerk in spasmodic waves. Next, he was diving to the dusty ground, rolling and spinning around on his back, then flipping on to his front, back and forth, becoming dirtier and dustier in the process. Finally he jumped to his feet, and for no particular reason shouted 'Yo'. I realised that this wasn't a public seizure but an impromptu bout of break-dancing triggered by my presence.

I got the impression it was this local man's way of showing me that we had some common cultural points of reference. Yet I found it difficult to hide my disappointment, because I hadn't flown thousands of miles to see this particular type of cultural exhibit. As he dusted himself down and shuffled away in a funky un-Buddhist slouch, I began to wonder: how could this sudden change in behaviour have occurred in the space of a mere two years? How had this man picked up his dance moves? I discovered he'd never been to

New York or LA – in fact, he'd never even been out of his village. He'd never seen anyone break-dancing in his life.

He had, however, seen newly arrived television images via the satellite dish that had been installed within the past year. It was as if a form of visual voodoo had taken control of this man's body and compelled him to quiver and jerk as he fell under the influence of a transmitted cultural spell. How, in a space of only a year, could remote images from such a distant culture change the way these local people dressed, moved, walked and sounded? And what other more subtle inner changes did these images bring?

Back in England, I began to find visual voodoo at work in my own home in ways I hadn't expected. My wife and I began to notice that our two-and-a-half year old daughter's light and endearing laugh was being replaced by what I can only describe as a coarse, middle-aged man's cackle with the crude facial expression to match. How did this happen? Who had turned my baby girl into Sid James? We soon discovered that our daughter was waking up before us and had found a video of *Carry on Again Doctor*.

When I was a student I didn't have a television for 10 years. This was not borne out of any ideological objection to television; rather I preferred sound, music and radio, and I was very busy enjoying my guitar, motorcycle and lack of responsibilities. However, because I was unused to seeing a television set, friends would remark that when a television was on in their sitting room, I inadvertently became mesmerised by it. At the same time I began academic research on attention and hypnosis and became aware of television's power to draw and hold attention. Later I would occasionally be interviewed on television to briefly explain psychology or health studies. I noticed how other interviewees – ranging from cabinet ministers to the actors of *Baywatch* – would, with the help of an entourage, prepare themselves with great effort to make the most of the screen time they were afforded.

While these experiences made me aware that television was powerful, the new generation of very recent medical studies have caused me to see television as a major health issue. My interest isn't merely academic. After carrying out the research for this book I have stopped my younger children from watching any television until more is known about its biological effects. Our society urgently needs to have a serious debate about the sheer amount of television we are watching and the crucial activities that have been displaced as a result. It's time television was brought to book, and so the following is intended less as a 'how to' and more as a 'why to' book.

I hope that this book makes you think about the role of television in your life. If you have children, I hope it makes you think twice.

Aric Sigman, East Sussex, May 2005

INTRODUCTION
THIS IS YOUR LIFE

'Bitch or whore? Bitch or whore? Bitch or whore? Bitch or whore?...'

The studio audience is chanting as the two main 'guests' – the wife and the mistress – square up to each other over an errant husband. Then, in the new expression of on-air hostility, they strip naked and scream more obscenities before lunging at each other like two 16-stone animals, trading punches. The crowd's rhapsodic chanting reaches a crescendo of ecstatic cheering...

This isn't *Jerry Springer the Opera*; this is *Jerry Springer* the daytime television show.

The content of today's television would have shocked viewers only a generation ago, but it isn't merely the content that has changed in recent years.

For that generation, colour television was a luxury to be enjoyed by the few – a television 'console' cost as much as a brand new car. A television was a special feature in a house akin to home cinema. But what was at one time a bit of a treat has become our society's staple diet. The sheer amount of time people spend watching television is astonishing – it has become the industrialised world's main pastime, taking up more of our time than any other single activity except work and sleep.

We spend on average four hours a day doing nothing but watching television – that's more than one full 24-hour day a week. By the age of 75, most of us will have spent more than twelve-and-a-half years of 24-hour days doing nothing but watching pure television.[1]

Children now spend more time watching a television screen than they spend in school. At this very moment, the average six-year-old child will have already watched for nearly one full year of their lives. In fact, most of our children now literally have more eye contact with television characters than with their own parents.

The same is true of our eye contact with one another as couples. Modern couples spend precious little time in one another's company and, according to the Government, what time they do have together is now spent predominantly in front of the television. Even the normally reserved Government Office for National Statistics was moved to comment on this new development in British romance, venturing to suggest, 'The main shared activity – watching television – might be regarded as a passive rather than an active way of spending time together.'[2] Market analysts now issue reports describing a 'telly-addict culture where staying in is the new going out'.[3] Interestingly, this is all taking place at a time when British and American couples are having less sex and less satisfying sex, while in the 1950s – half a century before *Sex and the City* and *Oprah* – married women were having better sex and more of it. The birth rate is dropping significantly, down to 1.7 children per couple, perhaps not so surprising when the Government study also reveals that couples spend even more time watching television alone.

Television has become not just our favourite pastime; it is our prime time, our main source of common experience. When you add to this picture our use of the Internet, computers, DVDs, videos and interactive mobile telephones, the total time we spend in front of a screen each day is set to overtake even the amount of time we spend sleeping. This is your life: if you work in front of a computer screen, you are actually watching a screen for more hours per day than you spend sleeping and eating combined – four months of 24-hour days of screen time every year. Even those of you who spend less than the average amount of time in front of a screen should take stock, as you are still spending literally years of your life in front of a screen.

Life is short, but with television it's even shorter, and in more ways than one.

In an age when we complain of time poverty, we urgently need to reconsider precisely what we are doing with our most valuable resources: our time and our children. It isn't merely a case of television taking up a great deal of our time; watching television is actually doing things to us – psychologically, politically, neurologically, even metabolically – that we are quite unaware of.

In an essay, 'Say No To Teletubbies', two eminent academics at Harvard Medical School state, 'Television viewing is exactly the opposite of what toddlers need for their development...young children's television viewing should be postponed as long as possible...'[4]

While everyone acknowledges the existence of the couch potato and many people live with one, I have yet to meet anyone aware of the Harvard findings that the act of watching television actually slows down a child's metabolism. He will burn fewer calories watching television than if he sits and does absolutely nothing.[5] Nor Stanford Medical School's conclusion that 'television viewing is a cause of increased body fatness'.[6] Or that government agencies across the world now brusquely describe television as 'an independent factor for obesity'.[7,8] And although I hear plenty of debate about 'copycat violence' and how television 'numbs us' to the true effects of real life violence, I have yet to meet anyone who has heard of the long-term international studies on television and violence published in the *Journal of the American Medical Association*. These found that 'If, hypothetically, television technology had never been developed, violent crime would be half of what it is.'[9,10]

What I find most interesting about these studies is that they aren't referring just to the effects of violent programmes, but to all types of television programming. They believe the medium of television actually leads to half of all instances of murder, rape and grievous bodily harm in the industrialised world. Perhaps it's not surprising that some people respond to these findings as if they are the product of journalistic sensationalism or the most extreme exaggeration.

Watching television is also implicated in another increasingly global theme, depression. This is at the highest levels ever witnessed for both adults and children, and increasing. The World Health Organization reports a deepening global health crisis, an epidemic of clinical depression.[11] It seems that a TV nation becomes a Prozac nation.

We are constantly subjected to the drip, drip, drip of arguments and concerns in the media about specific aspects of television. Perhaps you read last week about a new connection between television viewing and obesity; today you may hear of another controversy about television violence; tomorrow a study looking at the effects of television on our social skills will be published. But debate has focused on the narrower and in many ways safer issue of the messages relayed by television as opposed to the wider issue of the medium itself. Yes, we may be watching the wrong sort of television and yes, we are watching too much, but there's far more to this issue that we're not aware of.

To some, this devotion to television means simply that people enjoy watching television and make a conscious decision to watch it. Nowadays this is couched in the inviting language of 'lifestyle' and 'choice'. But if this is true, why is it that so many people experience misgivings about how much television they watch? Researchers in Japan, the US and the UK have even identified a middle class guilt arising from knowing that you watch too much television instead of doing something more productive.[12]

To consider television as habit forming is an understatement. Why does Columbia University Professor Jeffrey

Johnson, who has published a number of key studies on the effects of television, declare that 'television is highly addictive'?[13] Why would anyone consciously choose to watch a television screen for 12 years of their life? If our relationship were with a substance as opposed to a screen, we'd be talking in terms of abuse, overdose and going cold telly. Even so-called sex addiction is a more readily accepted concept. We wouldn't watch this much television unless there were powerful physiological mechanisms at work. Is the cosy-sounding expression telly addiction really an overstatement?

Reconsidering the role of television in our lives is inconvenient. We like to slob out after a hard day and we use television to occupy our children in order to buy us some time to ourselves. However, unlike straightforward health debates, à la *Fast Food Nation*, where additives, contaminating agents and hidden fats can be revealed and blamed directly for causing cancer, heart disease and food poisoning, television's route to harm is more covert and hitherto difficult to explain. Yet another problem in evaluating the effects of television is the sheer lack of control groups to provide a point of comparison. It seems that everyone's gone to the movies.

Perhaps the biggest obstacle to having an honest look at the effects of television is the simple fact that we enjoy watching it. Criticising our main waking activity, aside from work, tends to bring about a selective deafness, along with an inclination to shoot the messenger. Yet if we based our health policies on how much we enjoy things, hospital waiting lists would be even longer than they are now. Whether it's sunbathing, drinking alcohol, smoking in the family sitting room or eating junk food, we enjoy lots of things that are, after a certain point, bad for us or for the rest of society. That's precisely why we've come to recognise concepts such as units of alcohol, sun cream SPF factor, cholesterol levels, passive smoking and body weight. And I can envisage a time when we will finally talk in terms of recommended limits for hours per day of screen time.

This state of affairs is reminiscent of how the tobacco industry managed for years to claim that people enjoyed smoking and that there was no definitive proof that cigarette smoking actually caused lung cancer – that there was only an association between the two, not a causative relationship. The industry's scientists were also pressured to cover up the findings that nicotine was addictive. In a similar way, the sugar industry is successfully funding and pressuring World Health Organization scientists to issue international guidelines and reports that cover up the strong link between refined sugar and diabetes, obesity and death.[14]

The most influential arena of all – television – is hardly likely to broadcast bad medical press about itself and contribute to its own demise.

There is a survival instinct within most powerful industries with predictable responses to those who question their virtues: '…this is merely speculation – there's no definitive proof'. Those who do advise a better-safe-than-sorry approach are predictably referred to as being alarmist, overreacting or jumping the gun. A stock answer is: 'it's too early to conclude…there's no empirical basis for these assertions'. The most popular refrain is: 'This presents a one-dimensional analysis of television as the cause of so many problems – it's too easy to blame one thing for society's problems...' It's reassuring to accept this type of soothing balm as it excuses us from having to change a comfortable and fundamental part of the way we live.

There is also the gritty reality of academic funding and image. There's little money, funding and public gratitude in looking for the negative effects of the television screen. It's far easier and safer to explore avenues that seem to acquit television or, better yet, seek out its virtues. Centres for media studies, which produce most of the research about television, seem curiously prone to sitting on the fence, so it's hardly surprising that the incriminating research concerning television comes from outside their jurisdiction. It is often studies that focus upon health rather than television that happen upon worrying links between the two.

Yet enough evidence now exists to say better safe than sorry. There is simply too much at stake not to be responsibly decisive now. In short, there's nothing to be lost by watching less television but a great deal to be lost by continuing to watch as much as we do. The intention of this book is not to cause alarm about little-known dangers of television. Equally important is our understanding of how television is displacing many vital positive things that really do make individuals and societies happier, sexier, slimmer, healthier and more fulfilled, just like the smiling people revered on the television screen. As is often the case, things that are good for us have few benefactors or lobbyists – after all, has anyone heard of an Association for the Greater

Understanding of Broccoli? – and so the second part of this book, *Un*televised, will identify those crucial things we're missing out on.

Finally, there are other reasons why we haven't had the big debate yet. Television is a cultural force equalled in history only by religion, so should we be surprised that the media and government have stood in the way of a forensic examination? After all, both need us – the bewildered herd – to continue to take our cue from the screen. They conduct society's main discourse through television.

Television is The Establishment. It is such a central part of society's infrastructure – our culture's central nervous system – that its use and relevance transcends the divides of political left and right, bohemian and conventional. Consider the fact that both Chairman Mao's Chinese Communist Party and the American right's Republican Party promoted television ownership and use. Both understood the power of television. And like the building project which is costing three times more than expected, too much is now invested to pull out. It's simply too late.

Media analyst Marshall McLuhan's maxim, the medium is the message, is even more pertinent today. He knew 'a medium is not something neutral – it does something to people. It takes hold of them, it massages them'. Nowadays our culture is receiving quite a rub-down.

PART 1
TELEVISED

ONE
ARRESTED DEVELOPMENTS
What Television is Doing to our Children's Brains

From organic baby foods and factor 30 child sun creams to educational toys, good parenting is now treated as a fine science. Even the practice of smacking has undergone rigorous re-examination and attracted tremendous concern from Her Majesty's Government. What is conspicuous by its absence, however, is any mention of television as a major health and developmental issue. In its latest White Paper, proposing radical measures to improve the health of the nation, the British Government whitewashes the role of television into oblivion. The normally more progressive American government is curiously even muter on the subject. We should take note of a few names for future reference when it's time to apportion blame. Given the mounting credible evidence that television damages children, the Government's role is nothing short of a motivated negligence.

The link between watching television and physical and psychological damage is neither a concoction nor an exaggeration. Rather, the reverse. Highly respected medical bodies have voiced clear concerns, and the normally conservative mainstream medical and scientific journals have published worrying associations between television viewing and health. In surveying the response by politicians and the media to this evidence, Peter Preston, former Editor of *The Guardian* newspaper, wrote, 'It is, all things considered, a scandal of cowardly silence.'[1]

The Link between TV and ADHD

In August 1999, the American Academy of Pediatrics (AAP) issued guidelines clearly recommending that children under the age of two watch no television or any screen entertainment at all, and that children of all ages should never have a television in their bedroom because television 'can negatively affect early brain development'.

This startling announcement has just been added to by the latest study of 2,500 children published in their medical journal, *Pediatrics*.[2] About seven per cent of our children now suffer from attention deficit hyperactivity disorder (ADHD), and the rate of this neurological disorder appears to be increasing. In the United States, it is now the most common behavioural disorder in children. Although genetic inheritance accounts for some of the prevalence of ADHD, and despite decades of research, little thought has gone in to the potentially crucial role that early childhood experiences may have on the development of attentional problems. The authors of the study wondered if there is an omnipresent environmental agent that is putting children at risk of developing ADHD. Critics have wrongly argued that ADHD is a convenient label that simply medicalises the behaviour of difficult American children for the benefit of exasperated parents, teachers and pharmaceutical companies, and that Ritalin is a profitable 'chemical cosh'. Yet new research at London's Institute of Psychiatry concludes that ADHD is a real problem, and brain-imaging evidence shows it has a biological basis. The parts of the brain that we use for controlling our impulses are found to be underactive. Moreover, 10 years later, boys with ADHD are four times more likely to have developed mental illness.[3]

The authors of the study in *Pediatrics* believe that '...early exposure to television during critical periods of synaptic [brain cell] development would be associated with subsequent attentional problems'. And it looks as if the researchers are being proved right. They found that 'Early television exposure is associated with attentional problems at age seven' which 'are consistent with a diagnosis of ADHD'. Children who watch television at ages one and three have a significantly increased risk of developing such attentional problems by the time they are seven. For every hour of television a child watches per day, there is a nine per cent increase in attentional damage. The scientists suggest that their findings may actually be an understatement of the risks to children. They speculate that even if there is some educational benefit to be had from the actual programmes watched, this benefit may have covered up the even greater damage to the children's attentional systems that would occur if they watched programmes that had little educational benefit for them. Banning all screen time during the formative years of brain development, they believe, 'may reduce children's subsequent risk of developing ADHD'.[4]

There is now growing concern that watching television distorts the wiring in the developing brain, which is undergoing rapid growth during the first few years of a child's life. The advice now is that children should not start watching television before the age of three. The American Medical Association is now notifying its paediatricians to assess viewing habits when treating all hyperactive children.

Our Shrinking Attention Spans

When it comes to the link between our television culture and attention 'spans', there are wider concerns than children developing ADHD. While ADHD is the most infamous label in attention pathology, attentional damage and attention itself are enormous subjects that we are just beginning to understand. Attention – the act or faculty of applying one's mind – may be something we take for granted, but capitalist boardrooms and the advertising industry certainly don't. *The Harvard Business Review* and Harvard Business School Press are beginning to publish articles and entire books on the 'attention economy'. Observations within the book entitled *The Attention Economy* include business mantras such as 'Like airplane seats and fresh food, attention is a highly perishable commodity,' and '...there's a cash market for human attention, the most coveted commodity of all'. The business authors are even fully aware of the medical evidence of the role of television in affecting attention: 'The American Academy of Child and Adolescent Psychiatry suggest that children who watch a lot of television have lower grades in school, read fewer books, and exercise less. There is only so much attention to go around...' And perhaps in a piquant twist of irony, they maintain, 'Just as attention deficit disorder is diagnosed with increasing frequency in individuals, organisations can suffer from "organisational" ADD.' They even go on to provide a checklist for the Symptoms of Organisational ADD.[5]

I've always felt that naked capitalism is a most revealing scientific method in that it is willing to recognise anything that will make a profit. So it seems that our society's poachers have a greater appreciation of the importance and vulnerability of children's attention than our gamekeepers do. For the wrong reasons.

This approach to attention fits in neatly with consumer behaviour. We are sensation-seeking organisms living within an economy and culture that is increasingly stimulation-rich. Television in particular is highly effective in coaxing our attention towards the external as individuals and as a culture. But our attention needs protection.

Attention is the prerequisite to what we consider being alive. Whether you want to recite Proust or dial a pizza, you have to be able to pay attention to things in order to experience them. Once your attention is damaged, then everything that comes from it is compromised. Learning language, reading, school work, exams, job performance, relationships, having an orgasm and even one's sense of identity can all suffer. It's like damaging the focus control on your lens that looks out on life. In damaging your attentional system, you have damaged the prerequisite to experience, your hard drive.

Yet attention is not merely confined to everyday descriptions such as 'concentration' or 'attention span'. For example, it's being able to notice things on the periphery of awareness out of the corner of your eye, versus being able instead to diminish your peripheral awareness and focus and concentrate on one narrow thing. While this version of attention refers to attending to external things, there are also forms of attention to internal matters, both physical and psychological: inner awareness. The search for the G-spot is, in many ways, a misguided search for regaining long-lost control of inner-directed attention, not a physical spot.

Many of the unusual images we have of the East – walking on hot coals, Tantric sex, hari-kari, meditation – we associate with an exotic inner awareness, a greater mental control somehow instilled or inherent in easterners. Now we in the West seek techniques or secrets to unlock or gain access to this dimension. 'Richard Gere staying up there before...Demi Moore too!' my Bhutanese guide told me as he pointed to a temple on a remote hillside outside Thimpu. Both Hollywood celebrities had come to this Himalayan kingdom not merely to seek reclusion, but also to develop an inner awareness. And those who can't travel to Buddhist kingdoms pursue different routes to this inner landscape.

Reading Deepak Chopra, meditating and many new age pursuits are attempts to gain an inner awareness and a 'mental control'. It seems that we are born with a capacity for inner-directed attention which our culture then erodes.

And so a pressing question is how can we regain our attentional skills that were lost, damaged or eroded during our formative years? Most importantly, how can we preserve and cultivate them in our young children? You could say that these Hollywood stars are in attentional rehab. This is one of the few aspects of their glamorous lifestyles that we should emulate.

At one time I was involved in academic research on attention. I soon realised, like many who came before and after me, that there are different types of and aspects to that everyday term, attention. As a postgraduate, I was involved in an exchange of academic journal articles over what we thought attention was and how we thought we could measure it in humans.[6,7] Years later, I'm left feeling that there are some aspects to or types of attention that defy labelling. And new brain-imaging studies are finding that different parts of the brain deal with different types of attention, and so there can be different types of attentional damage.[8] Even within ADHD, one scientist now claims to have identified six different types of attentional damage.[9] So, in looking at the link between television and attentional damage, there are many more opportunities for different types of damage to emerge in future.

After trying to piece together possible explanations as to how a child's attention is actually damaged by watching television, I can understand why this vital area has been overlooked by society. The sequence of events is complicated and the evidence often comes from unrelated areas of science and has to be pieced together. It isn't as simple as explaining the way cigarette smoke causes lung cancer. And, like a cumbersome television programme with too many characters and an overly complex plot, most people simply switch off. Please don't.

The Developing Brain

There is great truth in the adage, 'Give me a boy until the age of seven and I'll show you the man.' A child's brain is 'plastic' in that it is constantly being physically shaped in response to what environmental experiences the child has. And, like a clay sculpture, it ultimately 'sets'. This is why children below the age of 11 can speak multiple foreign languages without an accent. This is also why feral children, or young children locked in basements or cages for years before being rescued, can never be taught to speak. Their formerly plastic brains have missed the boat. And this is also why we as adults cannot learn foreign languages as easily, nor ever speak them without an accent.

Psychologists often refer to these limited learning opportunities as critical periods of development.

A child's brain is literally sensitive to exposure in the way that a child's skin is to sunburn – only three sunburns before the age of 18 can lead to skin cancer. But, perhaps because a child's brain is out of sight, we don't perceive it as a physically sensitive organ. Repeated exposure to any experience will have a powerful impact on their mental and emotional development by either building specific brain circuitry in relation to that experience or by simply depriving their brain of other experiences. The types and degrees of stimulation the child receives from his environment affect the actual number and the density of his brain cell connections. This process of moulding, which affects both the brain structure and function, appears to influence brain cell development and the regulation of the brain's chemical messengers (neurotransmitters). A good example of this is the finding that learning a musical instrument by the age of 12 will actually make a part of a child's brain larger, in particular the left temporal region. This gives them a better verbal memory and vocabulary years later when they become adults.[10] However, a child's brain is also affected by being exposed to other environmental experiences at a young age, especially watching television.

Television is unique, the perfect medium to produce strong rewards for paying attention to something.

So what is so powerful about this reward? Compared to the pace with which real life unfolds and is experienced by young children, television portrays life with the fast-forward button fully pressed. Rapidly changing images, scenery and events, and high-fidelity sounds are overly stimulating and, of course, extremely interesting. Once you are used to food with monosodium glutamate flavour enhancer, real food doesn't taste as interesting. Television is the flavour enhancer of the audiovisual world, providing unnatural levels of sensory stimulation. Nothing in real life is comparable to this. Television overpays the child to pay attention to it, and in so doing it seems to physically spoil and damage his attention circuits. In effect, television corrupts the reward system that enables us to pay attention to other things in life.

How Television Grabs our Attention

Before television can arrest your attention, it has to grab it. In the first instance, television triggers what Pavlov first described as the orienting response, our instinctive, built-in sensitivity to movement and sudden changes in vision or sound. Our survival once depended upon this response to protect us from predators. As a boy growing up in the United States, I remember the bewildered soldiers returning from their tour of duty in Vietnam with horror stories from the forests and jungles. One soldier told me he now had to drink a bottle of vodka every day 'to stop seeing Vietcong hiding in the trees downtown on Main Street'. Every minute he spent carefully trekking through the jungle with his platoon, his orienting response had been pushed to the absolute limit. 'There were times I'd turn around and find my buddy behind me lying dead, but I didn't hear a thing and it happened in a flash. They'd come from nowhere and disappear into nowhere. I had to pay attention to everything, all the time!' Back home, he ended up firing live rounds of ammunition from his own Colt 45 at imaginary Vietcong in the trees on Main Street, his orienting response hijacked by the post-traumatic stress syndrome that had engulfed him.

The orienting response to television is apparent almost from birth. Dafna Lemish of Tel Aviv University has recorded infants of only six to eight weeks attending to television. Other scientists have documented infants who, when lying on their backs on the floor, craned their necks around 180 degrees to watch. This is how couch potatoes are made. Almost 20 years ago, studies began to look at whether the medium of television alone – the stylistic tricks of cuts, edits, zooms, pans, sudden noises, not the content of the programme – activates this orienting response to the television screen. By watching how brain waves were affected, researchers found that these stylistic tricks can indeed trigger involuntary responses because we are biologically programmed to detect and pay attention to movement, something television has in abundance. They believe 'It is the form, not the content, of television that is unique.'[11]

What Makes Us Keep Watching?

Scientists are now publishing studies with titles such as 'Attentional Inertia in Children's Extended Looking at Television'[12] and 'What Holds Attention to Television?'[13] There is a lot of money riding on the answers to questions like this. The science of attentional inertia looks at life after the orienting response, and involves finding out precisely what, after television grabs our attention, makes us continue to pay attention to it. Most of our stares at a television screen are actually quite short, lasting less than three seconds. And during that first three seconds, our stare is highly prone to 'termination'. But as we continue to stare, our stare becomes progressively less fragile – its existence gains a powerful 'inertia' after about 15 seconds. Attentional inertia was designed by nature to enable a child to keep attending to a source of information, such as a conversation between his parents, even when it becomes incomprehensible to him. This ability to stick with it ultimately enables the child to pick up words and their use, and may expand their general understanding as they process dialogue they might normally ignore as boring. So it seems attentional inertia is absolutely essential for learning, both formally and informally. One recent study involving 12 scientists firmly concluded that it is not the viewer but the *television* screen that controls attentional inertia.[13] So, after hijacking our orienting response, television hijacks this primitive attentional mechanism too.

Other scientists working for the media are publishing the recipe for gaining that 'strategic attentional inertia' in the television viewer. For example, a study of the rate of edits – camera changes in the same visual scene – finds that increasing the rate of edits actually increases physiological arousal. Television directors will be pleased to hear the conclusion that 'edits can increase attention to and encoding of television message content'.[14]

And this recipe has been brought to market. In a study of 'The Formal Pace of Sesame Street Over 26 years', the square-eyeballed researchers discovered that the number of editing cuts on this popular educational children's programme shown on non-profit public television actually doubled during this period: '...producers may have come to believe that a higher pace in television programmes is necessary to attract viewers, in particular younger ones'.[15]

Others have compared the attentional demands of children's programmes made in the public and private sectors, i.e. BBC and commercial television. The duration of a typical scene in a public children's show such as Sesame Street lasted over 70 per cent longer than in a commercially produced show such as Scooby Doo. These researchers found that children's television programmes, especially commercially produced ones, corrupt a child's attention because they 'demand constant attentional shifts by their viewers but do not require them to pay prolonged attentional shifts to given events'. And they're now asking 'Is it possible that television's conditioning of short attentional span may be related to some school children's attentional deficits in later classroom settings?' To hear scientists voicing the following concerns is worrying: '...the recent proliferation of attention deficit disorders of school age children might be a natural reaction to today's "speeded-up" culture...we live in an attention deficit culture...'[16]

And artists have noted the same thing. When Norman Mailer was recently asked to write an essay 'If you could do one thing to change America for the better, what would it be?', he wrote, 'With the advent of television, the nature of concentration was altered.' He points out that in the early years of television, there were relatively uninterrupted narratives. Then commercials began to interrupt. 'Soon enough, children develop a fail-safe. Since the child knows that any interesting story will soon be amputated...the child also comes to recognise that concentration is not one's friend but is treacherous. I believe that television commercials have got to go.'[17] Nowadays the 'conditioning of short attentional span' occurs during typical fast-paced programmes on non-commercial channels and is merely accentuated by the interruption of advertisements on commercial channels. So for those who might say 'I watched a lot of television as a child and I'm OK,' it's important to recognise that the medium of television is not at all what it used to be. Television is now putting pressure on young attentional systems in an unprecedented way.

The Dangers of Rewarding Attention

The attentional damage of children with ADHD is typically described as 'distractibility' and trouble with 'sustaining attention'. In clinics, the problems with sustained attention occur only in situations when the things a child has to pay attention to are widely spaced in time or uninteresting. Their attention to something needs to be frequently rewarded (reinforced) or they soon lose concentration. The reward systems for paying attention in these children cost more to run – they are, in effect, corrupt and need to be paid off early and often to avoid distraction. In behavioural terminology, they are described as having a shorter delay-of-reinforcement gradient. By the way, the same is found in studies of the rodent counterpart of the ADHD child: the Spontaneously Hypertensive Rat.[18] It may well be that all three symptoms of ADHD as well as the behaviour of the Spontaneously Hypertensive Rat – deficient sustained attention, overactivity and impulsiveness – are due to one factor: a shorter delay of reinforcement gradient. Their attentional scale of pay has suffered from hyperinflation and now it simply won't work for less. Bribery and over-tipping has upped the brain's minimum wage and it can't be bothered to pay attention to anything for very long – unless you make it worth its while. Television has just the assets to bribe and over-tip.

The actual currency used to pay off and corrupt the reward system may come in the form of the brain's chemical messenger, dopamine. The release of dopamine in the brain is associated with reward.[19] In particular, dopamine is increasingly seen as rewarding us for paying attention, especially to things that are novel and stimulating. Dopamine helps us pay attention to the information we need to stay alive. It tells us what is salient and shouts 'pay attention to this!' It seems that attending to new information is closely tied to the brain's pleasure mechanisms. What the brain really 'wants' is new information: brain cells exist to process information, and they're chemically rewarded for doing so. And looking at information on a television screen causes our brain to release dopamine.[20]

However, it is increasingly clear that ADHD is linked to a change in dopamine functioning. Dopamine gene polymorphism has been shown in ADHD, and dopamine underfunctioning is found in Spontaneously Hypertensive Rats too. This underfunctioning of dopamine probably causes the brain's attention cells to feel unrewarded, underpaid, so they won't work effectively. This is the true meaning of corruption in our main institutions, our brains. Modern television is the main suspect in this case of bribery.

And so it's interesting to discover that adults with attention deficit disorder whose brains are 'bribed' by taking dopamine-boosting Ritalin before doing a maths test find it easier to concentrate. This is partly because the task seems more interesting, so they feel more motivated to tackle the problem.[21]

We urgently need more research that looks at the extent to which this reward system involving dopamine (and other neurotransmitters) is 'set' in childhood by exposure to electronic media such as television. And how this relates to dopamine also being strongly implicated in a range of addictions, from cocaine and nicotine to binge-eating and gambling.

As children's programming has expanded and the pace of editing and event changes, as well as other stylistic techniques, has increased, children's attentional systems have shown growing signs of damage. An article in the American Academy of Pediatrics journal points out that 'Approximately three decades ago, teachers of young children at all socioeconomic levels began to report troubling changes in their students, mainly centering on decreasing abilities to listen, pay attention and to engage in independent problem solving. Frequently, the teachers blamed the advent of fast-paced, attention-getting children's programming for this trend. Now that the trend is viewed nationally as an "epidemic" of ADHD, perhaps it is indeed time to…consider that pediatricians may have yet one more job to do in early parent education about placing limits on screen time.'[22]

Other Health Problems Associated with Television

We shouldn't focus solely on ADHD. Given that there are different types of or aspects to attention, television may in future be linked to other forms of attentional damage. For example, the insistent noise of television in the home may interfere with the development of 'inner speech', by which a child learns to think through problems and plans and to restrain their impulsive responses. More than a third of children live in homes where the television is on all the time and they are far less likely to be able to read at the age of six.[23] And the *Journal of Genetic Psychology* is reporting children's television viewing 'resulted in an eventual decrease in their academic achievement'.[24]

Now, a new crop of medical studies is finding that television viewing among children under three seems to damage their future learning abilities. Scientists report 'deleterious effects' on mathematics ability, reading recognition and comprehension in later childhood. Along with television viewing displacing educational and play activities, it is suspected this harm may be due to the visual and auditory output from the television actually damaging the child's rapidly developing brain.[24a] Children who have televisions in their bedrooms at ages eight and nine achieve the worst scores in school achievement tests.[24b] And a 26-year study, tracking children from birth, has just concluded 'television viewing in childhood and adolescence is associated with poor educational achievement by 26 years of age. [And] may have long-lasting adverse consequences for educational achievement and subsequent socioeconomic status and well-being'. The doctors found a 'dose-response relationship' between the amount of television watched and educational damage which has 'biological plausibility'. Significant long-term damage occurred even at so-called 'modest levels' of television viewing: between one and two hours per day. They also wrote 'the overall educational value of television viewing was low...These findings offer little support for the hypothesis that a small amount of television is beneficial'.[24c] On reflection, watching television is a very poor investment in your child's future.

Also, according to a five-year study by the Broadcasting Standards Commission and the Independent Television Commission, television has become 'the background noise' for a generation of children who no longer regard radio as required listening – like 'a noisy light bulb' that is never switched off. Most children kept the television on while doing their homework. 'Just like a light bulb, the television is always on. It tends to be put on first thing in the morning when the household wakes up, and is often on last thing at night,' the report said.[25]

This new television generation can look forward to other medical damage quite unrelated to their brain's attentional circuits. A 26-year study of the 'Association Between Child and Adolescent Television Viewing and Adult Health' was recently published in the medical journal *The Lancet*, involving 1,000 children born in 1972–73. It found that children who watched more than two hours of television a day between the ages of five and 15 suffered serious health risks many years later, at the age of 26. The study concluded that 15 per cent of cases of raised blood cholesterol, 17 per cent of obesity, 17 per cent of smoking and 15 per cent of bad cardiovascular fitness were linked to the television viewing that took place years before when the adults were children. This link remained, irrespective of other factors such as social background, body mass index (BMI) at age five, parents' BMI, parental smoking and how physically active the children were by the age of 15. Dr Robert Hancox, who led the study, described these as 'well established risk factors for cardiovascular illness and death later in life. Our results suggest that excessive television viewing in young people is likely to have far-reaching consequences for adult health. We believe that reducing television viewing should become a population health priority'. He recommended an absolute maximum of less than an hour a day for children over five years old.[26] In an accompanying article in *The Lancet*, Dr David Ludwig of Boston Children's Hospital at Harvard Medical School wrote: 'Ultimately, parents must reclaim from television the responsibility for educating and entertaining their young children.'[27]

Getting the Message Across

One main reason why parents haven't reclaimed this responsibility is that they are either unaware of these studies, because they're certainly not mentioned on television, or unmoved by the way the studies are described. Here is an example of exactly how they are described. On 19 July 2004, *The Lancet* study above appeared in the Health section on the main BBC News website. But, because the BBC also happens to be one of the world's largest television broadcasters, one immediately suspects the BBC of having an agenda. It used classic newspaper layout techniques to ensure the reader was left feeling doubtful about the significance of this profound study. At two points on the BBC page, large coloured highlighted boxes appear out of nowhere, containing presumably key news statements in bold print in enormous blue quotation marks. The first contained the predictable phrase in these situations:

> '...we should sound a note of caution about looking for a single factor [TV]...'

In small faint print below, the statement is attributed to an unnamed 'Children's BBC spokeswoman'. Why is she unnamed?

The second box on the BBC News page contained:

> 'What difference is there between sitting in front of the telly for two hours or reading a book for two hours? I don't see anyone suggesting children read fewer books!'

This learned statement came not from someone in any way associated with either the news story or even the subject matter. In small faint print, the source of this wisdom appears in the form of 'Alan Montegue from Aylesbury'. In the printed version, the size and boldness of the letters used to display his quote is three times that of any of the scientists quoted in the very tiny unboxed text within the main article, so presumably Alan of Aylesbury is a man of substance. And yet it turns out, without ever being made clear by the BBC, that Alan of Aylesbury is merely an ordinary English television viewer who emailed his 'viewer feedback' to BBC News in order to 'Have Your Say'. And the BBC thought it natural to promote the – only in my opinion, of course – ill-informed view of Alan of Aylesbury while not highlighting or drawing attention to any of the statements made by the man who created the news story: Dr Robert Hancox.

Finally, further down the BBC page, the large bold words 'Common sense' in single quotes suddenly appear for no apparent reason. No one in the text had used those words or expressed that sentiment. So what on earth did it mean? One can only assume that it was thrown into the mix, along with the prominent highlighted statements, as a subliminal soothing balm intended to assuage public concern about watching television. 'Common sense' implies that the reader should perhaps take the findings of the study with a pinch of salt and lashings of English sensibility about unwelcome news. My point is that the way these important studies are either reported or under-reported is part of the health issue. The medium is not the medicine it should be.[28]

Newsweek magazine has quite a different approach to educating parents about the effects of television. On 11 November 2002, it actually ran a front cover story entitled, 'Why TV is Good for Kids'.[29] Why, against growing evidence to the contrary, is *Newsweek* trying to convince us that television is good for our children?

Well, one reason might be that *Newsweek* is owned by the Washington Post Company, which reportedly owns a sprawling cable company and six broadcast stations around the country.[30]

This tiny detail is curiously missing from the story. And what brand new evidence does *Newsweek* report to convince us 'Why TV is good for kids'? They interview an 'expert'... who simply says telveision is good for kids. By the way, he was also a consultant to a variety of television networks and related interests, and involved in the development of several television programmes for children. His clients include: Nickelodeon, Universal Pictures, NBC, CBS, Sony and General Mills.[30]

The article reports that television is beneficial because children learn from it, and parents are 'looking for TV to help them do a better job of raising kids'.

While the BBC, along with the Cartoon Channel, Nickelodeon and others, may broadcast entertaining children's programmes, they are far from being arbiters of children's health. You may be interested to hear that the BBC executive who acquired *Teletubbies* says the programme is good because the characters move around and teach children 'spatial awareness'.[31] As a result of her explanation, I'm now an enlightened parent. So when I saw my 18-month-old son crawling around the house this morning, I immediately grabbed him, restrained him in front of an episode of *Teletubbies* and said to his mother: 'That'll teach him how to move! You see, darling, according to the BBC, babies are supposed to learn about space and distance not from crawling around and picking things up, but from sitting and watching BBC1. So what have you been doing to our son all these months? What the hell were you thinking – letting him roam around and explore the real world like that? He'll never get into Oxford now!' On the other side of the Atlantic, the advice from ABC Television's senior vice president of advertising and marketing was 'TV is good...it becomes a babysitter for their kids'.[31]

Would you want these people to babysit your children? You'd understandably place more trust in Ozzy Osbourne.

Television and Eyesight

Television has been linked to damaged eyesight. International research published in the *American Journal of Human Genetics*, which reviewed 40 studies, found dramatic increases in myopia (short-sightedness), including extreme myopia, which can lead to blindness. This was previously put down to genetics, but this new study finds no evidence for a genetic cause. Instead it blames lifestyle factors, in particular television. Countries where children watch more television and look at computers more often have a far higher incidence of myopia. In Singapore, 80 per cent of 18-year-old men recruited for the army are short-sighted. This compares with only 25 per cent just 30 years ago. The scientists have warned that we in the West are now on the cusp of a similar explosion in myopia: 'As kids spend more time indoors on computers or watching telly, we are going to become just as myopic.'[32]

Sleep Problems

Researchers at Oxford University recently found that children who have televisions in their bedrooms are being deprived of up to a month's sleep a year. They claim that this is affecting the physical and mental health of up to a million children of primary school age. Their school and exam performance is also adversely affected, as one in five of them are having between two and five hours less sleep a night than their parents did.[33,34] Belgian research now shows that children with a television set in their bedrooms go to bed 'significantly later' and that children who watch more television are significantly more tired.[35] Children who sleep poorly are more than twice as likely to end up smoking, drinking and using drugs at ages 12 and 14.[36]

In the United States, the situation is probably even worse. The American Medical Association's *Archives of Pediatrics and Adolescent Medicine* report, 'Young people in the United States are in the throes of a glut of wakefulness,' putting them at risk of problems with their immune system, metabolism and clinical depression.[37] Moreover, an accompanying study at Columbia University found that young adolescents who watched three or more hours of television a day ended up 'at a significantly elevated risk for frequent sleep problems' as adults.[38] Remember that this amount of screen time is actually less than the average. On the other hand, those 'adolescents who reduced their television viewing from one hour or longer to less than one hour per day experienced a significant reduction in risk for subsequent sleep problems'. It seems that conditioning your brain to be able to sleep properly is a skill that can either be enhanced or – with the help of television – damaged in childhood and not recover. And the implications are serious.

Stanford University Medical Center has found evidence that a lack of sleep may disrupt hormone balances and make someone more vulnerable to cancer.[39] Sleep quality can seriously alter the hormone balance in a person's body. This can happen in two ways. Disrupted sleep can cause the body to produce less of a hormone called melatonin, an antioxidant that cleans the body of damaging free-radical compounds. Melatonin is also sleep-promoting. As it grows dark and you begin to get sleepy, your melatonin levels rise and help facilitate sleep. But all our modern-day exposure to artificial light might be wreaking havoc with levels of melatonin.[40] New studies are showing that this prolonged exposure to artificial light – and subsequent less exposure to darkness – can affect our sleep and overall health. Additionally, these reduced amounts of melatonin may result in a greater chance that cell DNA will produce cancer-causing mutations. Disrupted sleep patterns may also affect the hormone cortisol, which normally reaches peak levels at dawn and then declines during the day. Cortisol helps regulate immune system activity, including a group of immune cells that help fight cancer. Television, particularly in bedrooms, is central to modern-day sleep deprivation and disruption.[35,41]

A good night's sleep is a foundation for health. Researchers in Germany found that people who got a good night's sleep had almost twice the immune system antibody level to the hepatitis A vaccine – even a month later.

According to Jan Born, researcher at the University of Luebeck, 'Our results are amazing in that they show a decrease in antibody titer [concentration] after only a single night of sleep deprivation.' One reason may be that hormonal changes during sleep may help immune function. He noted that sleep boosts the release of prolactin and growth hormone, two hormones that lab experiments suggest enhance the immune response.[42] This may all sound rather technical and abstract, but it is the unseen dimension of the act of watching television.

One of the less sensational findings of the Oxford sleep study is that children with televisions in their bedrooms are often irritable and drowsy the next day, and this makes them more difficult to cope with. So the half-hearted notion that television will make parenting easier is a false economy. And parenting is made even more difficult because of what children watch on television.

Links to Early Puberty

One of the more oblique and intriguing links with television exposure is that of premature puberty in girls. There is considerable international evidence suggesting girls may be maturing earlier, including a study by professor Marcia Herman-Gidden of 17,000 American girls, and a British study at Bristol University that tracked 14,000 children, and found one in six girls with signs of puberty by eight years old, compared to one in 100 a generation ago.[43] Explanations have included hereditary and dietary factors, exposure to certain chemicals in the womb acting as hormone disrupters, and the presence of a new stepfather's pheromones. But now television is under suspicion.

It is now suspected that the increase in images of sex on television actually fosters sexual maturity among prepubescent girls in the way that food stimulates salivation. Research in adults has found that watching sexually graphic material causes hormone releases in the body. Marcia Herman-Gidden believes 'Obviously what we see can affect our physiological functions. So therefore, we can look at children who are exposed to an incredible number of sexual materials and knowing that it can affect sex hormones in adults, it would make no sense to assume it has no effect on kids...This is a serious public health issue.'[44,45] In a study of girls aged between six and eleven, those who matured earlier were more depressed, aggressive, socially withdrawn and had more sleep problems. Another found that earlier menstruation was linked to drinking, smoking, drug abuse, lower self-esteem and suicide attempts.[46,47]

The Effects on Child Development

There is now evidence of the way television actually stunts many children's development. In the last five years, there has been an explosion in television media for babies and toddlers. And we are now reaping the consequences. Researchers at Britain's National Literacy Trust have concluded that television is stunting children's ability to speak. Young children cannot really understand what they are watching, and even 'educational' programmes such as *Teletubbies* may cripple their language skills. James Law, Professor of Language and Communication Sciences at City University, reported, 'The idea that shoving a child in front of a television is going to teach them anything beyond movement of sound and light is silly. They get mesmerised by it, and it is too chaotic for them. Parents think that because they may use the medium to learn about things, children can take from it in the same way. But it takes a level of sophistication that children don't have. Young children need social interaction.'[48]

The same message is reiterated in an essay, 'Say "No" to Teletubbies', by Dr Alvin Poussaint, one of America's pre-eminent child psychiatrists at Harvard Medical School, and his colleague Dr Susan Linn. As it happens, Poussaint was a script consultant to *The Cosby Show* while Linn is an award-winning producer and writer for children's 'educational television'. Yet, when it comes to the prospect of television for young children, they point out the obvious that few others dare to mention. Just because young children like *Teletubbies* doesn't, by any means, indicate that it is good for children: 'TV viewing can be addictive. TV viewing is exactly the opposite of what toddlers need for their development...we feel strongly that young children's television viewing should be postponed as long as possible...'[49] Just because *Teletubbies* was launched on wholesome public broadcasting networks BBC and PBS and was highly publicised as 'good' for young children means nothing. In retrospect, the programme consisted of unnatural figures with television sets built in to the front of their stomachs, engaging in unnatural high-speed body actions and unintelligible speech. Entertaining, yes, but there's no reason to assume that it confers any benefits what-soever. It may cause attentional damage as well as displacing vital behaviour for a child's development.

The *Teletubbies* saga is reminiscent of the Ribena Toothkind blackcurrant-flavoured children's drink. Children do love the drink. The manufacturer claimed, and many parents believed, that Ribena Toothkind's special formula with added calcium countered the impact of fruit acids on the teeth and minimised erosion. The British High Court forced them to remove these claims and backed the Advertising Standards Authority, which maintained the drink was simply less harmful than other sugary drinks, rather than not harm-ful at all. Perhaps a name like Ribena DL – The Damage Limitation Drink would have been more suitable. It's a shame we haven't reached the same level of health claim legislation for children's television yet.

Television has also been implicated in an interesting report by the Basic Skills Agency. Fifty per cent of children in Wales are not ready to start primary school at five because of their inability to speak sufficiently, a pattern reflected across England. This marks a huge decline in language skills among millions of children. The report describes how young children are now speaking in grunts, a trend increasingly arresting their academic progress. The agency spoke of these effects as the result of 'the child sitting in front of the TV, the child sitting in front of the home computer...'[50] And Ofsted's chief inspector of schools has recently attacked parents who use the television as a babysitter, creating a generation of children whose speech and behaviour are at an all-time low. Many children don't even know how to use a knife and fork or to fasten the buttons on their shirt. Parents should 'talk to their children and give them a whole range of stimulating things to do, and not just assume that the television, or whatever, will do that for them'.[51]

It's not merely that television is usurping the time children would have spent being socialised by talking and interacting, especially at the dinner table. Television is actively filling this socialisation void with faulty replacements.

The New Role Models

You only have to look at old films and television shows to see the kind of behaviour once projected as ideal. But since the golden age of television, Britain continues to go through something of a reckoning with its long-standing class system. One of the ways being used to redress centuries of social inequality is not only to ensure that lower-class behaviour is represented on television but to actively elevate it to being more desirable than behaviour associated with being educated and middle class. In the United States, the analogy is a collective white guilt over slavery, allowing and actively promoting violent gangsta rap culture on television and other media. In the way Britain has tried to make up for the perceived wrongs of an upstairs/downstairs society, this has been naïve, middle-class America's distorted way of supposedly giving black people a voice and representing their culture. Or, as one British professor, who is black, describes this portrayal, 'Gold chains and no brains'.[52]

In Britain, this form of social inclusion has bypassed the

casting couch and gone straight to screen. In many influential programmes, what most foreign observers would describe as 'thick, common' people and behaviour are often portrayed as being in some way more authentic, worthwhile, virtuous and ultimately more desirable than educated, middle-class or polite people. And, as of late, even hopelessly middle-class fully grown Englishmen have been pretending they're a bit cockney: better a lad than a gent.

A century ago, an Englishman aspired to be 'a gentleman', with each echelon looking up the social ladder for inspiration. However, this century has, for the first time in history, seen a complete inversion to different role models as seen on television. Social historians will record the late 20th and early 21st centuries as a time when educated middle-class people became socially chameleonic. As Britain has developed the largest middle class it has ever had, and is now the fourth richest nation on earth, a new study has found that an increasing proportion of traditional middle-class people now claim they are working class and proud of it.[53] Some of this has been attributed to a fashion for working-class chic symbolised by television personalities such as Ben Elton, Jamie Oliver and Jonathan Ross. Sociology professor Richard Scase points to a growing fashion for appearing working class, regardless of wealth or occupation: 'It has become chic to appear working class – to have a London accent, and drop your Ts, the way Tony Blair does when he's on popular chat shows. It may be that current fashions give positive cultural connotations in being working class, which don't exist for the middle class. After all, we never hear about middle class heroes.'[54] In fact, the Prime Minister, Tony Blair, has been identified as lowering his standards of pronunciation chameleonically. Professor John Honey has observed the Prime Minister compromising his educated accent in favour of gratuitous elements of Estuary English, or watered-down cockney.[55] And it's astonishing to think that only a few years before him, Lady Thatcher worked tirelessly through elocution lessons to perfect her vowels in order to rise from Grantham grocerine to presiding over this country with regal utterances such as 'We are a grandmother.'

What I find most interesting, however, is the way in which the middle classes have not only accepted but actively promoted poor enunciation and vocabulary through their influence in the media, education and politics. It's as if middle-class guilt has embraced a form of linguistic relativism as a means of removing the source of their guilt and protecting their identities in the process. Other cultures would see this quite differently. Instead of elevating standards and expectations in the way people speak, or simply being more accepting of different accents, the solution in Britain is to descend – or, perhaps, condescend.

All cultures judge people by the way they speak. Even in the 'classless' United States, linguistics research at the University of North Texas has found that job interviewers make hiring decisions based upon their subconscious feelings about the job applicant's accent.[56] And Stalin would be bitterly disappointed to find that 75 years of ardent Communism and social uniformity have failed to dislodge Russians' snobbery over their accents. All regional accents are considered inferior to those of Moscow and Saint Petersburg, which, in turn, have superior and inferior grades of accents. Like America, southern accents in Russia are deeply non-U. The metropolitan intelligentsia laughed privately at Mikhail Gorbachev because of his southern twang: instead of dropping his H's, he dropped his G's and replaced them with Slavic-sounding H's.

As the present climate emphasises social equality, perhaps it's not surprising to find that on television there has been both an unconscious and a concerted move towards overcoming our inclination to make value judgements based upon the way someone speaks. What is surprising is the direction this has taken, ironing out our social differences by encouraging those who are well spoken to adopt what would be considered lower forms of speech in any other culture. Meanwhile the well-spoken Englishman appears on television not as a symbol of authority and privilege, but as a figure of fun, nice but dim, or eccentric with a capital E. This trend is in stark contrast to that of other cultures I've observed.

A couple of years before I visited China, a fortune cookie I opened in a Chinese restaurant advised me that verbal precision can be a source of great power. If Professor Higgins were Chinese, he would be overjoyed. The young people I spoke to in China had a clear desire to speak 'good' Chinese. And while I found a difference of opinion in the exact Model Citizen accent they considered being standard Chinese and ideal for television broadcasting – Langfang versus Shendang – I had the distinct sense that half of the world's population actually cared about how well they spoke. Moreover, people were not uncomfortable about saying this. China is now the largest market for learning English so I was interested in knowing if they had any preferences in the type of English they heard and spoke. I found the answer to my question in a back alleyway.

Lost in a maze of narrow medieval backstreets in Beijing, unable to pronounce my intended destination, I spotted a passer-by, pointed to my map, grunted and gesticulated. The young woman told me in English that I was heading in the right direction and asked where I was from. When I told her England, she was impressed. 'So you speak BBC English?' She was completing a master's degree in English and considered Received Pronunciation to be a benchmark of clarity and tonal elegance. For a moment, I actually felt proud to be a virtual Englishman. Wanting to draw out her admiration of me for as long as possible, I felt disinclined to tell her of my colonial origins. I explained that nowadays, perhaps her admiration was not exactly shared by those in charge of the BBC itself, that in fact the BBC was now trying to avoid employing presenters on both radio and television who spoke the kind of English she so admired because it was considered elitist. She found such logic as incomprehensible as I found Mandarin.

A new television proletarianisation has displaced aspirations to behave and speak well, robbing many children of the opportunity to learn the necessary social skills to simply get on in society. Drawing attention to the way children speak and behave is neither a stylistic consideration nor encouraging snobbery. Returning to the expression 'Give me a boy until the age of seven and I'll show you the man', a child's mind is highly impressionable because his brain is malleable; it's in transition. And the habits and characteristics we establish during childhood often stay with us throughout our lifetimes. We, as impressionable children, don't acquire just our language or grunts from our main influences, but our body language as well – slack jaw, gormless gaze, gum chewing, manner of laughing, and more. These are not mere social fashions that can be picked up and dropped as we see fit.

The behaviour promoted by television has led to terms such as 'civilised' and 'polite' to be considered by many as being somewhat loaded, preoccupied with minding one's p's and q's, awfully genteel. But beneath the finery lies a core element of the social skills of self-discipline, respect and consideration. It isn't a question of returning to obsequious, deferential overtures, but of a considerate way of interacting with others that makes society run reasonably smoothly. This could reduce fights and save lives.

George Gerbner, who has spent a lifetime studying the effects of television, is old enough to realise that 'For the first time in human history, most of the stories are told to most of the children not by their parents, their school, or their church, but by a group of distant corporations that have something to sell. This unprecedented condition has a profound effect on the way we are socialized...'[57] Both the Broadcasting Standards Commission and the Independent Television Commission consider 'the television is almost like a member of the family in its own right'.[25] And Lord Dubs, chairman of the BSC, said, 'I am taken aback [by these findings]...It's a comment on what a change there has been.'[25] If during key stages of their development children are being tutored in elocution, deportment, facial expressions and conduct by the casts of *EastEnders*, *Big Brother* and *I'm a Celebrity Get Me Out of Here*, and street-cred in-yer-face children's television presenters instead of their own parents, should we be surprised at the outcome?

In the end, television harnesses and amplifies our children's developing tendencies and desires. In Freudian terms, modern compelling, highly spiced television stimulates our child's id, the department of instant gratification and pleasure-seeking impulses, the bargain basement of the three-tier structure of our personality. But in doing so, it turns inclinations into expectations and distorts their development. By focusing on the exceptional, the out of the ordinary, by normalising the abnormal, by elevating the normally-not-allowed to the must-be-seen, television gives permission to the id. This, however, is a role that should be performed by the ego – the rational, reasoning unit – and the superego – the conscience – after timely and considered moral and ethical development within a social and parental, not a broadcast, context. Through default, the development of the child's superego has been unknowingly out-sourced to the values of television, the new electronic conscience.

If you don't rear your children, someone else on a television screen will. And it's unlikely to be Mary Poppins.

Maybe the most critical argument against watching television is that it affects the three characteristics that distinguish us as human beings. In the first three years of life, a child learns to walk, to talk and to think. Television keeps us sitting, leaves little room for meaningful conversations and seriously impairs our ability to think. And when children do walk, talk and think, television can have a decisive influence on how they do it.

I'm not writing this to make parents feel guilty or to make their lives more time-deprived, harassed and inconvenient. And I'm not preaching an idealistic strategy to help parents raise virtuous, organic children. But few people are aware of the range of influence that television levies. If your child's environment doesn't provide the necessary nurturing and protections from over-stimulation, then certain potentials and abilities cannot be realised. Your infant is born with 100 billion nerve cells, which are then capable of forming thousands of interconnections extending to other regions of the brain. This potential for development ends around the ages of 10 and 11 when the child loses 80 per cent of these neural connections. It appears that what we don't develop or use, we lose as a capacity. An enzyme is released within the brain and literally dissolves all poorly used pathways. Like politicians vying for the affections of floating voters, many influences in your child's everyday life are trying to woo and enlist his brain cells to connect in given directions. A child's brain cells are literally up for grabs. Plasticity is political in that there is a constant battle for your child's neurons to quite literally develop in a certain way. Therefore, we need to have a far better understanding of the overwhelming lobbying power of a television screen. Again, content aside, the medium alone causes powerful irreversible changes to a child either directly or by displacing other critical experiences, which have sell-by dates on their consumption.

Once upon a time, a child's bedroom was furnished with little more than a toy box, a book shelf and a few posters. Today it has become an entertainment centre, a den of excess lined with technology:

- ❑ In the United States, 25 per cent of babies and toddlers from six months to two years now have a television set in their own bedroom. In fact, 10 per cent of them actually have a television remote control designed for just their age group.[23]
- ❑ The average three- or four-year-old watches television for around five hours each day.[58]
- ❑ More than half of three-year-olds now have a television set in their bedrooms.[58]
- ❑ By the time they're six, this rises to two-thirds.[59]
- ❑ Between the ages of eight and sixteen, nine in ten have a television set in their bedroom.[60]

And now scientists are witnessing compound effects. Children and teenagers are spending an increasing amount of time using 'new media' like computers, the Internet and video games, without cutting back on the time they spend with 'old' media like television. Instead, because of the amount of time they spend using more than one medium at a time (for example, going online while watching television), they're managing to pack increasing amounts of media content into the same amount of time each day.[61]

As the price of televisions has crashed and their physical size has shrunk, children are spending more and more time watching a screen. Television is a major health issue. Now, even the United Nations Convention on the Rights of the Child 1989 seems hopelessly out of date. Article 13 Freedom of Expression gives the child the 'freedom to seek, receive and impart information and ideas of all kinds...through any media of the child's choice'. How do you feel about this?

And it is particularly disturbing to still hear some academics urging 'caution in interpreting these studies' and warning of 'the risk of over-reacting'. They appear so open-minded, their own brains seem to have fallen out. How can you over-react to exposing young children to television? What harm could possibly result from preventing very young children from watching television and from drastically reducing the amount of television for those over three years of age? It's as if by over-reacting, we risk harm to the television industry...and perhaps media studies departments as well. This prevailing stance reveals a most bizarre set of priorities and a shameful instinctive bias in expressing great concern over the welfare of television. A more rational perspective might be: 'let's pause for thought before continuing to expose children to this type and amount of television'.

There is the classic defence of 'we should sound a note of caution about looking for a single factor' or 'you're blaming television for everything'. Implicating television in medical and social problems is neither too simplistic, one-dimensional nor attributing these to a 'single factor'. These responses are intended to undermine the fact that while television is not a single factor, nor are its effects simple, television is still a main issue that has eluded the scrutiny it warrants. Unlike other factors that influence a child's health – such as genetic predispositions, poverty, death or divorce in the family – exposing your children to television can be controlled entirely: it has an on/off button and needn't be bought and put in a child's bedroom. Isn't it high time television took its place in the queue of blame for damage to our children?

While we've been preoccupied with the effects of the single-parent family, we've failed to notice the presence of an additional intimate family member firmly ensconced in our homes. The term 'electronic babysitter' is, on reflection, beginning to sound rather flattering. Given the tone of the emerging evidence and the implications, haven't we got things the wrong way around? Shouldn't the burden of proof now be on advocates of television to demonstrate that the way we use it is harmless?

TWO
WALKING THE TV WALK, TALKING THE TV TALK

How Television is Making the World's Behaviour the Same

A friend told me how, when in Japan, he ended up in bed with a local woman. One of the most romantic and exotic aspects of his personal anthropological quest was that neither could speak the other's language. They had to rely on body language and instinct to communicate. However, as the woman reached orgasm, she began shouting 'Yes!...Yes!... YES!' My friend lay back on the futon, luxuriating in the self-satisfaction that there was no need to look up the translation for 'How was it for you?' in his Japanese phrase book. It was only later that he became curious as to how, in a moment of such complete abandon, a woman in such a provincial part of Japan could utter such a formulaic sexual response. Was she faking it?

No, she wasn't. It transpired that, like the rest of us, she too had watched Meg Ryan enjoying her lunch at the diner in *When Harry Met Sally*...on television. My friend had inadvertently gathered evidence of globalisation's bedside manner.

One way of assessing the true power of television is by stepping back and using the world as a laboratory. Looking at the effects of television from the top down reveals how a small screen creates mass international changes. It's similar to a public health study that traces a disease trend by following it from source or tracing it back to its roots, or a radiographer who injects a tracer dye into the patient to follow its path. Tracking Western, and particularly American, television, along with any changes in behaviour that coincide with it, tells you a great deal about the nature and power of the medium.

Globalisation is thought of by most people in terms of multinational conglomerates, logos and mass tourism – the Coca-Colafication of a culture. From the Internet to cornflakes, from face-lifts to whitened teeth, from Starbucks to Nike, the face of globalisation is seen in terms of what stands out. Yet for all their high visibility, these products are merely industrial relics. Most globalisation is not the result of industries and tourists being physically present but of flimsy electronic images beamed in from afar, true invisible imports.

I travel abroad frequently, particularly to countries that have remained remote from Western media such as Bhutan, Laos, Burma and Iran, as well as countries such as northern Vietnam and China, which have more recently been exposed to it. As a psychologist for me the true value of travel lies in providing an oblique second opinion on my assumptions

about our feelings and behaviour. Travel is a way of reviewing the norms and values of the day in my culture, by being
very far away from it. As a devotee of street anthropology, I
watch people in cultures from Tonga to Timbuktu and relish
their otherness, differences in the way they dress, move,
walk; in their gait, cadence, deportment and sound, along
with differences in their bodily and facial reactions to things.

How the Globalised Screen is Changing the World's Emotional and Behavioural Landscape

I've witnessed how the real influence of globalisation has
gone far deeper, to the way people in very different parts of
the world feel, behave and organise themselves socially. I've
seen with my own eyes people in the most remote places
behave and talk in ways that could have been derived only
from videos and television images beamed in from abroad.
Even the most intimate and personal aspects of their existence, and your existence – from your body language, hopes
and dreams to your pillow talk – are undergoing a cultural
convergence as the direct result of mere television images.
The picture emerging is that of a global village of behaviours
whereby each culture is getting in touch with someone else's
emotions (usually America's) instead of their own. To me this
is a far deeper indication of globalisation than a baseball cap
and a pair of Nike trainers. For the most part, globalisation
engenders a change in mindset with the most far-reaching
consequences.

Aside from my selfish objections as a tourist looking to observe the exotic, yet increasingly finding the familiar, there are lessons to be learned. And this personal qualitative form of study has – more than any other form of learning – afforded me the best insights into television's influence and the concept of so-called 'free will'.

From Kilburn to Kyoto, people are walking the television walk and talking the television talk. There are constant little reminders. Yesterday in Oxford Circus, I heard two 20-something English women chatting behind me. In mid-conversation, one of them exclaimed, 'It's like...Oh. My. Gaaahhhd! I'm soooo outa here' – phraseology absorbed straight from Rachel in the American sitcom *Friends*. In Belper, Derbyshire, I've seen locals greeting one another with high-fives. Even Prince William has exhibited funky moves from the television screen.

I leave this country to visit others, hoping to find a more foreign experience. But on holiday in Feteyeh, southern Turkey, my daughter and I are confronted by a grinning Turk salesman trying to endear himself by stating very matter-of-factly, 'Lubbely jubbely, lubbely jubbely', a well-worn phrase from British television's *Only Fools and Horses*. I try to put him off by telling him I'm not English but American, only to be met with 'OK, then, buddy – see you later, alligator, see you later, alligator.' Later that day we pass through a local town to find two pubs, The Rover's Return and The Queen Vic, doing a brisk trade. And The Crossroads Motel was full. You can begin to understand why the North Koreans have a ban on all foreign television.

Television's Influence on Perceived Beauty

In countries such as Japan, Vietnam and Thailand, I've discovered, too, how many people are now undergoing cosmetic surgery to widen their eyes so that they will look more Western. And as they become more affluent, Chinese women are seeking more Western television looks by altering the shape of their eyes and noses. Patients now even hand their plastic surgeon the particular Western television role model they want to look like. Strangely, the reverse doesn't occur back here on Harley Street.

Skin 'whitening' cream sales are soaring all over Asia. In Thailand, the whitening lotion segment accounts for more than 60 per cent of the country's annual US$100 million facial skincare market. On the island of Java in Indonesia, exposure to television has led to sales of facial whitening cream and powder, such as Estée Lauder White Light Brightening Treatment Lotion or Brightening Essence, rivalling those of the shades of make-up that match the natural Javanese skin colour. While L'Oréal moisturisers developed for the Indonesian market have all had whitening agents added to them recently. The company now sells a 'triple whitening repairing lotion' (part of its White Perfect range), which it says has been made available 'after years of research on Asian skin'. Extraderm even sells an underarm whitening cream. Many beauty salons are suddenly offering 'full-body bleaching'. And while here in the West a nose job means reducing the size of your nose, in Indonesia women are saving their money to have their noses appear longer and narrower to look more like the white Westerners they see on television.

In many of these countries, high-profile role models such as actors, pop stars and television presenters look racially unrepresentative of their culture, in other words distinctly Western. Bolivia has the highest proportion of indigenous people in South America. Most people in Bolivia are short and dark skinned. They look, as we expect, like South American Indians. Only five to ten per cent of Bolivians are of European extraction. Yet the main soap opera is Argentinian, looks as if it's set in California, and stars blonde-haired, blue-eyed characters and other racial types that certainly look very un-Bolivian. The Bolivian newsreaders don't look particularly Bolivian either.

Uyuni is on Bolivia's Southern Altiplano, described by the *Lonely Planet* guide as 'climatically challenged...a harsh, sparsely populated wilderness of scrubby windswept basins, lonely peaks and glaring, almost lifeless salt deserts...indeterminable distances and an overwhelming sense of solitude – the air has teeth. Many live at the ragged edge of human endurance...A world and lifestyle that's harsh beyond imagining'.[1] This is the legendary area where the outlaws Butch Cassidy and the Sundance Kid were probably rather relieved to meet their untimely deaths. This is the same tough culture that managed to withstand efforts by the Inca to assimilate it into the empire, rejecting the Inca language and culture. They were the only conquered tribe to get away with it. 'Fiercely proud and stubborn, they may well seem as harsh and cold as the land they inhabit; this attitude is spawned by a deep suspicion of foreigners.'[1]

But where the Incas failed, television is succeeding. With a population of eight million with 650,000 television sets, most of the programming is foreign.

A Tale of Two Restaurants

My first two evenings in Uyuni are a Tale of Two Restaurants. The first restaurant is very basic and family-run. Television is inescapable – there's one at either side of the room. It's news hour and the pretty long-haired presenter is taking calls on air. She looks deeply un-Bolivian, more like a northern Spaniard or even Irish. Her presentation style is somewhere between CNN and MTV video jock. She nods and bobs her head while raising and lowering her eyebrows as any American newsreader does. Even her voice modulation, inflection and prosody seem to come from another culture – Washington, DC. Over on the other channel is a variety performance-type dance trio beamed in from the capital, La Paz. As the prima ballerina twirls and twirls, her short skirt rises centrifugally to reveal her underwear. I can see the other women in the restaurant staring in fixated unease at the difference between their rounded indigenous Indian looks and the slender, entirely European-looking Bolivian dancer on the screen. Their self-esteem is further pulverised as the young waiter's eyes fixate on the dancer's bottom. All eyes are on the screen and there's little interaction between anyone in the room. Ten feet away in the other family-run restaurant where I'm eating the following night, there's no television set.

Couples look at one another – and talk. And there is people-watching. Women can compare themselves with and bitch about other patrons who are actually in the flesh and serve as more realistic points of comparison.

The first Bolivian scene is one I see increasingly throughout the world. Walk into any café or shack in China and, unlike 10 years ago when they'd look at you as well as at one another, all eyes are now on a television screen. Mao Zedong may have said 'Political power grows out of the barrel of a gun' but he actually preferred the power of the screen. That's why his aim was to ensure there was a television set 'in every home'. The change in television set ownership in China is among the fastest in the world's television history; 97 per cent of Chinese homes now have one. Mao's wish has been all but fulfilled. And in most countries, after watching for a couple of years, people change not only their appearance, but their minds as well.

Disappearing Cultural Differences

For me, the great pleasures of experiencing foreign cultures are found in subtle things, the small-scale finery of difference to be found in mannerisms, such as the way people walk. The Burmese all seem to have attended a school of deportment; they don't walk but rather glide mystically. Maybe there's nothing like walking with a three-storey stack of pots on your head to ensure a steady, elegant gait and cadence. The women seem so very foreign precisely because of the way they sway in the most graceful feminine way. And, by and large, their body language has so far resisted Western influence. This is partly due to the fact that Burma remains one of the world's most secretive and hard-line Communist states, cut off from the rest of the world by heavy censorship enforced by the military regime.

Bhutan – a Unique Perspective

Another posturally intact culture is in Bhutan, where men walk with an upright dignity that seems distinctly un-Western. Yet with the sudden introduction of television, I have seen the change in body language start to appear right before my eyes.

For centuries, Bhutan remained in self-imposed isolation from outside influences, and it is its undiluted culture that attracts the few tourists who have been allowed in since it cautiously opened its doors 30 years ago. The King of Bhutan emphasises the importance of retaining cultural integrity and promoting national identity, traditional values and the concept of One Nation, One People. Most important is the ideal of gross national happiness. If there is a Shangri-la, this truly is it.

In June 1999, Bhutan became the last nation on earth to introduce television.

Bhutan's political and geographical isolation, coupled with the suddenness with which its people have been exposed to 46 cable channels, has made it the perfect social laboratory.

The Bhutan Broadcasting Service (BBS) provides 'a local educational and cultural service'. It consists of an hour a day of amateur-quality religious footage directly from a Buddhist temple. I managed to see some of it and marvelled at how quaint and wholesome it seems. During my visit to Bhutan, the Ministry of Health held a small conference attended by the country's main health officials, and it happened to be in the dining room of the small hotel I was staying in. I was invited to the conference dinner, which was to be followed by traditional dancing.

During the conference, I talked with a number of doctors about the differences in health concerns between Bhutan and Britain and the United States. There was, for example, discussion and great concern about the link between the Bhutanese penchant for eating raw chillies and the prevalence of stomach cancer. I reciprocated by talking of the mounting Western health issues of stress-related diseases and depression, and caused raised eyebrows when I elaborated on new forms of elective surgery such as liposuction and the 'trout pout', before moving embarrassingly on to penis enlargement and the lunch-time boob job. I was, however, intrigued by their view of how the introduction of television might affect the health, well-being and gross national happiness of Bhutan. They didn't seem particularly concerned about the effects. In fact, I sensed an innocent but enormous gap in their comprehension of what television would do, not only to their culture, but to the health of the nation as well. It seemed that while the government had thought that tourists in the flesh would lead to irreversible changes in their country, ephemeral electronic images delivered from afar didn't feature very highly as either a cultural or a health issue. I said to them, 'Don't you realise what Western television will do? Do you have any idea how influential it is?' They listened politely, but I honestly don't believe they understood my point.

The next day out on the street there are glimpses of the influence of globalised television. I recognise the ever-so-slight American swagger-cum-lazy funky shuffle that heralds the change from Eastern cruise to Western strut. As more people are able to access Western music video television, MTV body language is spreading through the younger generations. The globalised screen is teaching them how to party.

Shortly after I return home, I am shocked to read that Bhutan is experiencing its first crime wave – murder, fraud, drug offences. While it was television-free, this country had never experienced serious law-breaking before. But now 18 people are jailed after a gang of drunken boys broke into houses to steal foreign currency...and a television set. A middle-class boy in the capital, Thimphu, is serving a prison sentence after putting on an American-style bandanna and shooting at the ceiling of a local bar. Six employees of the Bank of Bhutan have been sentenced for embezzlement. Police can barely control the fights at the new hip-hop night on Saturdays. Buddhism strongly influences all aspects of life but now the Royal Bhutan Police are searching the provincial town of Mongar for thieves who vandalised and robbed three of the country's most ancient shrines. Greed, avarice, selfishness and impatience are on the rise. Bhutanese academics have conducted an impact study and reported that television has caused 'dramatic changes': increasing crime, corruption, an uncontrolled desire for Western products, and dramatically changing attitudes to relationships. One third of girls now want to look more American (whiter skin, blonde hair). More than 35 per cent of parents prefer to watch television than talk to their own children, while nearly 50 per cent of children watch up to 12 hours of television a day. The Minister of Health and Education, Sangay Ngedup, is one of the only members of the government now willing to openly express his concerns about television. 'You can never predict the impact of things like TV...'[2]

Mali and Timbuktu – Television in Rural Africa

Mali in west Africa is the fourth poorest country on earth and, for me, the most unusual-looking culture I've seen. Despite the fact that 25 per cent of children die by the age of five and those who do survive die by the time they're 48, the dignity and civility of the Malians reveals the behaviour often found within our Western cultures to be nothing less than barbaric and inexcusable. The landscape and the elegant curved mud mosques and houses are truly alien and surreal.

It is so isolated that when I visit one small village, Sekoro, just the sight of me prompts an 18-month-old baby to cry spontaneously. He is terrified because I am white and ghost-like, they tell me. He's never seen a Caucasian, or the Cartoon Channel. Four hundred miles northeast along the Niger, on the remote southern edge of the Sahara, lies the fabled ancient city of Timbuktu. The local transport is donkey; by comparison, camel is considered rapid transit. Part of Timbuktu's allure has been its sheer distance and inaccessibility. Self-described as 'a city in the middle of nowhere', it looks organically medieval. 'It is a city unsullied by the worship of idols, where none has prostrated save to God the Compassionate…' But at sunset, from the roof of the ancient Sankore Mosque, I see in the distance a competing religious symbol, a satellite dish. The worship of idols other than God the Compassionate is slowly under way. It isn't until the following day that I identify the new idols being worshipped – Snoop Doggy Dog, Nelly and R Kelly. A couple of young men walk along the side of the road wearing baseball caps, their funky body language looking quite out of place compared with that of the other locals. I ask about this, and am told quite innocently that they currently enjoy the newly arrived television images of urban music, rap and hip-hop artists. My 18-year-old guide at the mosque actually says, 'There's a big change in the way some of our young people who see the television are walking, and they behave differently too – even their beliefs are changing.' When I have a chance to examine some of their home-grown talent on television, I find Malian rap acts dressed in traditional robes yet gesticulating and moving in ways that are an obvious direct and unnatural emulation from an LA street video. The local young men confirm that they have never seen a Western person dressed like a hip-hop artist in the flesh, and so it seems that their change in body language and behaviour has occurred without their conscious awareness. Timbuktu's teenagers are enamoured, their minds in a sense colonised by these exciting, foreign, realistic-looking images.

Back in the capital, Bamako, my young African guide, Mohammed, from the Bambara tribe, makes clear his disdain for this kind of televisual influence. 'This type of rap-man is not good for our culture. His behaviour is disrespectful and immoral. He would not be welcome in my village.' At the same time, however, I am hearing reports of young Malians suddenly beginning to copy some of the gun culture they have seen on the globalised screen. And when I see the Malian television programmes, as with Bhutan's Broadcasting System, it's clear that they don't stand a chance in the face of the glossy, slick, high-spice Western alternative shows.

But is this really merely an African version of what has happened to so-called Afro-Caribbean culture here in Britain? While white middle-class males engage in high-fives, wear baggy hip-hop trousers and ostentatious jewellery as seen on television, the children and grandchildren of Jamaican immigrants have all but turned their backs on their own cultural heritage in favour of a black American television version. And their black British role models – television presenters, actors, singers and athletes – have helped in this process by adopting fake American accents with matching phrases and foreign body language, nothing more than cultural echolalia. 'Respect!' 'Don't diss me!' 'I'm the Man.' Mohammed Ali did it with irony; nowadays they're deadly serious.

British programmes incorporate and reiterate this American version of black culture in their own drama programmes. For example, when recently launching their new urban music radio station 1Extra, the BBC repeatedly broadcast their advert involving young British black men on a council estate dressed and behaving just like 'African-Americans' 'in the hood', pushing each other aggressively and starting a fight. Despite the BBC's pretentions to appear like

New York, it was actually more Neasden. This piece of ghetto reconstruction had not the slightest hint of British-Caribbean culture about it.

This can be dismissed as in one eye and out the other, pop media simply reflecting transient style and fashion, but there is more to it than that. Television is filling a dangerous cultural and emotional void. There are tangible, measurable consequences to these globalised media images. Not only is the level of murder by gunshot becoming distinctly trans-atlantic, so are the actual choice of gun, method of aim, pretext and context.

Television in Tonga and Fiji

Half a world away, I arrive in Tonga, on the International Date Line, where day and night are the absolute opposite of the time zone I left behind, and so are the body politics. Tongans look like goddesses and warriors: they are big, natural people. They carry themselves with a lack of self-consciousness. In fact, one of the Peace Corps workers on the small island of Vava'u that I visited explained how Christianity has failed to control the Tongans' natural sexuality. Dating does not really take place as Tongans may marry within hours or days of fancying one another. They also have sex in a hurry because they live communally with little privacy; they enjoy stolen moments in the bushes. Foreplay doesn't exist. The women have names like Fi and Sessie. They have big feminine hips and walk with a noticeable lack of self-consciousness, which is also apparent in their lack of concern about their body shape and size. The national beauty contest is a potpourri of full-figured chunky contestants, and the winner is big. When I boarded a tiny 16-seater aeroplane to fly between islands, the women, most of them heavier than me, showed no embarrassment at being publicly weighed with their baggage on an enormous set of weighing scales for all to see.

But the arrival of American DVDs in the year 2000 has changed their bodies and their language. The new generation of girls are suddenly showing signs of change in a Westerly direction. They tell me they want to be slimmer like the women they see on the global screen. A more global gait and cadence is starting to appear, while both sexes are beginning to change the way they move their eyebrows. As a sign of agreement or recognition, Tongans traditionally raise their eyebrows twice in rapid succession – first to mid-raise position, then to fully raised. This is very disconcerting and foreign when you are in mid-conversation with one of them. But now more Western facial gestures are beginning to appear instead.

About 500 miles to the west, in the Fijian islands, the effects of television on a foreign culture are truly laid bare. Television has gone beyond changing body language to causing actual bodily changes. A poignant study by the American Psychiatric Association shows what happens when Western television arrives in another culture. In Fiji, the ideal body weight for females has always been very full, while going thin – as Fijians refer to weight loss – is a cause for concern, not admiration. However, in 1995 television arrived, and within three years all of this suddenly changed. Dieting among healthy Fijian teenagers who started to watch television increased dramatically, and the rate of self-induced vomiting to control their weight, which had been rated as non-existent before television arrived, leaped to 11 per cent of that population. In addition, the effects of television were dose-dependent, that is, girls who watched television three or more nights a week were 50 per cent more likely to feel 'too big or fat'. Almost two-thirds had dieted in the past month. The girls openly cited thin female characters in American programmes such as *Beverly Hills 90210* and *Melrose Place* as inspirations for changing their bodies. 'We try to lose a lot of weight to become more like them.' The researchers describe the 'dramatic increase' in eating disorders and 'an extraordinary cultural shift given the previously enduring strong cultural sanctioning of robust attitudes and body size among Fijians'. Writing in the *British Journal of Psychiatry*, Dr Anne Becker and colleagues from Harvard Medical School said: 'The impact of television appears especially profound, given the long-standing cultural traditions that previously had appeared protective against dieting, purging and body dissatisfaction in Fiji.'[3]

Back on Vava'u in Tonga, I interview Police Chief Inspector Ashley Fua about the effects of television on criminal behaviour. His response is typical of what I've been hearing in many corners of the world: 'Soon after American television and DVD arrived three years ago, crime among young men increased dramatically.' But what lends a forensic authority to his observations is this comment: 'This is especially apparent in house break-ins. The actual method of breaking in to houses indicates they learned these techniques

directly from American DVDs, particularly those that
portray hip-hop culture.' Break-ins have now become a form
of entertainment and risk-taking, whereby young men
compete with one another: 'How many have you done? Yeah,
really? Well, I've done three more than you!' Inspector Fua
describes this as a new social style that he attributes directly
to the newly arrived Western television images. The problem
for the island, he tells me, is that there are no juvenile courts,
jails or criminal justice system, and the police are suddenly
having to cope with a new problem for which no one has
been prepared.

The Demise of British Reserve

There are, however, countless examples of television's effects
on behaviour closer to home. Until recently, the British were
considered one of the West's most physically reserved
cultures. It wasn't merely upper lips that were stiff; entire
torsos were locked in cultural rigor mortis. And being owners
and masters of their 1,000-year-old mother tongue, they had
the language's infinite shades, nuances and subtexts to
convey anything without resorting to shrugging, grimacing or
waving their arms about. Unlike their Continental neighbours, the British didn't indulge in gesticulation as an aid to
conversation. But, in less than a decade, all of this has
changed. Grand gestures and assertive statements along with
general extroversion come across very well on television and
have consequently rippled out across the nation's behavioural
and emotional landscape.

The British are now practitioners of the grand physical gesture. Watch any documentary film of the public from 20 or 30 years ago and they appear positively mummified compared to the wide arm movements and hand gestures of today. As the result of the sitcom *Friends*, Rachel's exaggerated facial expressions, hissy huffing and rolling of eyeballs in exasperation, coupled with Joey's Italian-American posturing, open arm movements and innocently confused expression with wide eyes going from side to side in fake blamelessness, have transformed non-verbal communication in Britain. This has been authenticated by British attempts to emulate shows like *Friends* in which home-grown characters communicate in a foreign body language. Younger generations now communicate in a televisually driven pantomime.

Even elite news correspondents have begun to shake, rattle and roll on screen. The BBC's Political Editor has been described as 'flapping his hands like hyperactive pink kippers even when relaying the most ordinary news item from No. 10 Downing Street'.[4] And so the process continues and reinforces itself.

Remember English reserve? That, too, has undergone a transformation, re-emerging as conspicuous emotion. The indigenous veils and layers of personal revelation that have defined this culture have been rapidly stripped away in deference to a new culture of openness and transparency. And these public examples of emotional openness have now changed the way people who are not on television behave. The footballer Paul Gascoigne wept and hugged his teammates on television; now it's common practice. That never happened in Bobby Moore's day. And recall the concept of private grief? Just a few years ago, the British chortled at television images of grief-stricken Americans mourning the 20th anniversary of Elvis Presley's death; two weeks later, they find themselves doing the same for Diana, Princess of Wales, except it is Elton who is providing the soundtrack, available on CD literally as seen on television. The scene in front of Kensington Palace was described by one British historian as 'a holocaust of flowers'.

Television has provoked a conspicuous compassion, which at times borders on recreational grief. The globalised screen feeds a modern enthusiasm for living life through visible gestures. We use the death of someone we never knew to express our own pain, or simply to feel something intensely at the same time as the rest of society – to re-establish a sense of common experience, some connectedness, to feel in some way alive. Has television actually sapped our capacity to truly process our own emotions in a healthy way? Has our desire and ability to experience a genuine sense of connectedness been subverted by a simple electronic device?

Beyond reserve, what's become of Britain's world-renowned modesty and self-abasement? An American televisual model of 'learning to love yourself' has changed the way that British respond to their own successes and failures. Globalised television images of modern emotional responses have led the British to embrace themselves enthusiastically, through self-applause and self-aggrandisement. Just a few years ago, the protocol was that the audience applauded the contestants; now the contestants applaud themselves too, often with no particular justification. And an achievement in front of the camera is increasingly expressed through a graphic exaggerated arm-waving triumphalism, accompanied by a self-congratulatory 'YYESSS!!!' This, too, is now appearing off-screen on the streets of the UK. From tennis at Wimbledon to boxing, fair play in sport – where modesty prevailed and the actual sporting achievement spoke for itself – has been influenced by ubiquitous images of world-class athletes arrogantly boasting of their prowess and their right to be the champ, and openly challenging the rules of the game. Television has also eroded team spirit by highlighting a few personalities and encouraging them to think and behave more individualistically. John McEnroe's behaviour undoubtedly made tennis more televisually exciting but legitimised and amplified the cocky behaviour now commonplace in sport and in a society that reveres sporting celebrities.

Television has created a culture where greater emotional literacy has become a form of public graffiti. The broad brush strokes used mean that people don't express their emotions; they impose them. What television has brought about is more accurately described as a lack of impulse control: imposing one's momentary stream of consciousness on others.

Influences on Sex

The tendrils of globalised television have begun to embrace sex, which until recently afforded the formerly reserved British an arena of the unspoken in which to express themselves spontaneously and intuitively. Yes, the English had a wonderfully bestial way of conducting their sexual liaisons. Aside from a few drunken obscenities muttered into the pillow, British sex was a far more silent and savage affair than its Continental or American counterpart. It was actually a case of *Would You Kindly Keep it Down During Sex Please, We're British*. The globalised screen has, however, made British copulation a far more verbose affair. Glamorous role models in the throes of passion started to provide, for the first time, strong graphic mainstream points of comparison. Expressions of passion as seen on television, along with hammed-up verbal underlining of every bump and grind, are now available to all. Also, in the same way that television has had a profound effect on women's body image, so too have television and film held forth a 'right' way to respond sexually.

In Japan, the simple act of kissing seems to have been introduced as a more common private behaviour through television. Public displays of affection are very rare in Japan; the Japanese don't kiss in public. Even in the late 1960s, a kissing scene in a Japanese film was exceedingly rare. It seems that it was only when American films and television shows containing kissing scenes became widely available for Japanese viewers that it became more acceptable.

The Cult of the Individual

Perhaps the most fundamental effect of television on the various countries I've visited is how it quietly seduces a culture away from considering the effect of one's behaviour on others, glamorising the importance of expressing oneself.

Because the screen is most engaging when it focuses on individual faces and voices as opposed to groups, it is the individual, not the group, who rises to prominence. This simple electronic principle has tipped the balance between the individual and the collective. We have never before had complete strangers becoming instantly up-front and personal. The fine details of a television face, the pupils of the eyes and the voice seeming as if they are right before us, create a false intimacy. We see and feel things through this individual's eyes and actions that are reinforced by the reactions of others. Television is the pictorial version of the individual over the collective. And while the me, me, me society has often been attributed to the free-market economic policies of Thatcher and Reagan, it is the television images of me, me, me behaviour that have really changed minds. It's as if Reaganomics provided the finance and television provided the script on how to be more self-centred.

I saw this principle played out in a single television advert in Thailand, and have never forgotten it. A large group of young Thai people are milling around in the street on a hot sunny day when one Thai man starts to 'go for it'. He begins to wave his arms around in a triumphant mock-rebellious pop culture way. With his eyes wide and his mouth open, he shouts 'Yeah!' in a Western exaggerated way. Music playing, he suddenly makes a break for it, leaping onto the bonnet of a car and, with his head turned up towards the sky, greedily guzzles the advertised bottle of soft drink. The camera focuses on his Adam's apple gliding up and down with each enormous gulp, the beads of sweat glistening in the sun as he publicly satisfies his immediate craving. In 60 seconds, the advert graphically depicted the transition from a culture that considers others to the glamour of 'Look at me! I'm going for it!'

I've subsequently seen variations on this television theme within adverts, drama and music television, and also international football, where Western players act out their complaints, fight with the referee and stamp their individual personalities on the screen, behaviour shown on television in many countries where it is completely at odds with the way the local people behave. In fact, in the Far East, much of the foreignness resides in this basic difference: a lack of conspicuous yearnings, urges and cravings, cultures where modesty and the importance of maintaining public face have generally prevailed.

Modesty and maintaining public face do not, however, make for good television. Television is more compelling when faces are more animated. It's as if television is giving assertiveness lessons to the world. Yet this trend is eroding people's sense of self-restraint – their impulse-control – and is, in turn, undermining societies that think more collectively. In Freudian terms, television is giving permission to the id, the department of instant gratification where pleasure-seeking impulses reside and beastly inclinations lurk, the bargain basement of the three-tier structure of our personality. By focusing upon the individual, television amplifies our tendencies and desires, undoing much of the good work carried out by the ego, the rational, reasoning unit, and the superego, the haughty, grand department of consideration,

morality and ethical behaviour: the conscience. More powerful than any psychotherapy, television successfully shifts from
the collective to the individual, and from consideration to
gratification. This is what globalisation really means.

By linking the direction of television programme-making
from the United States outwards to changes in behaviour that
coincide with it, I've learned a great deal about the nature
and power of the medium that would never have been possible through existing orthodox means. The influences I've
seen and described are a large-scale example of how television has influenced us and our children as individuals and
collectively, and will continue to do so. If this approach seems
unorthodox, consider the growing similarity in some basic
behaviours I've described throughout the world – the way
people walk and talk, the style of cosmetic surgery they
prefer, the sudden appearance of mass dieting and eating
disorders with the arrival of television, high-fives, hip-hop
behaviour and the changes in gesticulation and body
language – and then try to identify some changes within your
own local community. Ask yourself: how could this picture
have emerged at roughly the same time in history in such
unrelated, distant places? Where do you think these changes
in body language and behaviour have come from? Is it possible that it is natural evolution through the gradual cultural
exchanges that have always occurred over time?

Cultural and behavioural influence in previous eras was
conducted in person. Either foreigners would visit or invade

your country, or you would visit or invade theirs, and return bearing their influence, which you would pass on. But in only a few decades, global television has changed this most profound dynamic of history. If you think about it in imperialistic terms, cultures and minds can now be colonised remotely, without a single shot being fired or a missionary landing on their shores, purely through the images sent to them on a television screen. It's called soft power and it is unprecedented. Formerly known as propaganda, soft power lies in the ability to attract and persuade other cultures of the validity and desirability of your own. Whereas hard power – the ability to coerce – grows out of a country's military or economic might, soft power arises from the attractiveness of a country's culture. So to dominate, you don't push, you pull. It's as if a nation uses its feminine side to influence another.

When I visited northern Vietnam, I was surprised to see my 50-year-old rickshaw driver wearing a baseball cap made entirely from Coca Cola tins and to discover, late one night, the staff at my hotel furtively watching a smuggled video of the Eagles singing *Hotel California*. Even in a hut in the mountainous rural area near the Chinese border, I saw a man wearing a strange fur hat with a tail, eating what I believe was a grilled fox and singing Sinatra's *My Way* through a karaoke microphone. Am I right in thinking that America lost the war in Vietnam? I've ultimately come to believe that CNN, HBO and Disney have succeeded where napalm failed. Perhaps *Apocalypse Now – The Sequel* is playing out on the streets of Hanoi as young Communists can be seen eating M&Ms while watching Eminem.

Dreaming the Television Dream

To most so-called developing countries, Western-style television offers a perceived modernity. To pull up your cultural drawbridge is to miss out on modern economic life. A country feels it must either embrace the global screen or remain primitive and disconnected from the world outside. Yet, because of the Western type of television that dominates, it's as if there is only one version of modernity.

Being modern the Western way is increasingly reinforced by what is going on behind the scenes in boardrooms across the world. Instead of the explosion in television technology providing the world with greater diversity, the result turns out to be fewer and fewer media giants buying up and controlling the world's television channels and production companies. These vertical integration mergers are thought by some to be a liberating and enlightening force, having a progressive impact on culture, especially when the global screen enters countries that have been tightly controlled by corrupt crony media systems (as in much of Latin America) or those that have significant state censorship over media (as in parts of Asia). And it's certainly true that the global commercial-media system is radical in that it will respect no tradition or custom, on balance, if it stands in the way of profits.

The reality is, however, a picture of global media companies distributing non-controversial entertainment and infotainment programmes. This strategy is funded by multinational corporations wishing to sell their products to ever-expanding markets. The commercial media companies use their control of broadcast network systems to limit access to alternative programming, especially with local content and alternative, non-capitalist values. So, with thousands of channels available, viewers come to accept the illusion of choice within a narrowly defined range of possibilities.

Meanwhile, as the world's public broadcasting systems try to compete, including America's PBS and the BBC, the citizens who are immersed in commercial media gradually embrace the values of selfish individualism and materialism. They tend to disengage from their local communities and aspire to global images, values and lifestyles – as seen on television. A study at Cambridge University identified this in Britain where, until recently, 'people set their aspirations for their standard of living by their own social class and the people around them. Television and other media has broken down those barriers, and people are increasingly setting their aspirations by people who lead a luxurious life'.[5,6] People are not only walking the television walk and talking the television talk, they're now also dreaming the television dream. People are being very remotely controlled. The study found, as is the case in other cultures, that these new screen-led aspirations have made British people more unhappy.

PBS and the BBC are both perpetrators and victims in this. A preoccupation with ratings, global co-productions with media conglomerates and the hiring of two BBC Director Generals, John Birt and Greg Dyke, from commercial television are obvious reactions to these vertical integration mergers. And ongoing debates about 'dumbing down' and the plethora of lifestyle, infotainment and

celebrity lifestyle shows are, in reality, the visible consequences of global mergers on screen. The political scientist
Benjamin Barber sees this as the gentle homogenisation of
culture on a planetary scale and the choking off of variety,[7]
while in their book *American Dream: Global Nightmare*, the
authors, Sardar and Wyn-Davies, define television's job thus:
'...show business is the business of colonising all minds and
undermining all imaginations'.[7]

But quite apart from the deluge of global values rushing
across the world's landscapes, it is the speed, scale and intensity of international cross-pollination brought to you by
television that marks it out from anything that has gone before.
And this delivery system does strange things to all cultures.
Television's preoccupation with all things new gives us an
exaggerated sense of perpetual change. But instead of appreci-
ating the wonderful variety and freshness of faces, scenarios
and news items brought to our sofas every night by innovative,
hard-working television producers, we are left unsettled.

Humans and societies are not designed to cope with a
sense of rapid change.

Television also deceives us into feeling that, by watching
major international events or interviews with the stars in
LA, we are in some abstract way part of a larger world
community, connected within a bigger scheme of things. We
begin to define ourselves globally. But thinking in such a
large-scale way erodes the consideration we have for our
own geographically real communities. Furthermore, this
new sense of omnipresence – where information is transmitted around the world in nanoseconds, depicting events,

people, values and lifestyles we have little connection with and even less control over – adds to an ever-growing sense of impotence and inadequacy.

Television's endless novelty and unsettling news, entertaining and fascinating as it is, accentuates our sense of the world changing quickly. It makes us feel as if our world and lives are not under our control. In fact, given the ongoing changes already brought about by the effects of economic globalisation and computerisation in other areas of our lives, don't we need, if anything, greater sources of constancy and continuity, more of the resolute? Yet the global screen accentuates the sense that our lives are out of our control. Television makes people feel less secure.

This ability to influence from afar, to remotely control people's aspirations, the way their bodies move, to change distant cultures almost overnight has powerful evolutionary implications. Television has taken advantage of what seems to be our genetic predisposition to acquire behaviour and culture. Culture is an evolutionary survival mechanism which can be passed on far more quickly than genes. This allows us to change and develop far more quickly than if we waited around for the benefits of natural selection and genetic advantage. And television has made this cultural transmission exceedingly rapid, a stark departure from the conventions of the evolutionary game. Television transmission has literally become a high-speed evolutionary force.

How Different People React Differently to Television

One inspiring thing I've noticed by looking at the effects of television in various countries is that there isn't a simple linear relationship between television viewing and subsequent behavioural and emotional changes. Some cultures appear to be more immune and others more susceptible to the influences of the global screen. Furthermore, people within a given culture also differ in their immunity or susceptibility to television's influences.

While I've tried to work out a vague hierarchy or scale of different countries and the extent to which I sense they've succumbed to the behaviours and values in *Sex and the City* (England: high; Iran: very, very low), I've realised that it isn't a fine science. A combination of key variables seems to conspire rendering a culture more or less gullible.

A confrontation with a group of bearded young Iranian men in the highly religious town of Kerman helped me clarify my thoughts. Realising that I was a live Westerner, they indulged themselves in the opportunity to vent their political and cultural frustrations. In a very civilised and articulate way, they expressed their resentment towards the effect of not only Western political and economic interference in Persia, but also of an indirect moral and spiritual subversion of their mindset towards a Western model. They considered much of global television to be a morally outrageous imposition on their values and culture. They seemed exceedingly aware of soft power and I was very impressed. The lesson I learned was that a strong religious base seems to provide some insulation from the effects of global television. Religion offers a competing value system and a form of continuity.

The depth of television's influence is also dependent on the age and integrity of the culture, in particular whether the population has a true sense of shared culture to bind them. A country such as Britain, which has tried to shake off its class system, where aspirations and allegiances were stratified and people are irreligious, is fertile ground for the global screen. The popularity of global cable television among the lower classes, and their penchant for the portrayal of the American can-do society complete with level playing field, is not a coincidence. Nor is the desire to immerse themselves in a lot more television and to live more vicariously. The age and education of viewers unsurprisingly enables them to critically analyse incoming information more or less effectively.

The stage in a country's development at which television is first introduced seems to be central to its initial influence. The culture must acclimatise to these new conditions.

A medieval agrarian society, that goes from having few televisions to receiving today's state-of-the-art emotionally manipulative programmes and DVDs on cheaper smaller colour sets, may experience more impact than if they had the usual introductory 50-year apprenticeship of watching grainy black-and-white episodes of *Sergeant Bilko* and the like beforehand.

So how is it that an electronic image can colonise the world's minds and tamper with our evolution?

THREE
VISUAL VOODOO
How Television Affects our Thinking

BBC *Ten O'clock News*, 27 October 2004:

'And the headlines: the Arabic television station
Al-Jazeera has broadcast a new video of aid worker
Margaret Hassan, who was kidnapped in Iraq last
week. The video showed Mrs Hassan asking for
British troops to be pulled out of Iraq. The BBC has
decided not to show moving images of the video.'

The BBC1 news report continues with a still photograph of
Mrs Hassan. Why are the BBC mandarins so concerned
about the effect of moving as opposed to still images?

Above and beyond the rights and wrongs of the war in
Iraq is a postmortem on the role of television images as a
weapon. In the new warfare the power of television images
works both ways. One thing the West failed to understand

was the power of the ultimate smart weapon – the flimsy portable television image. With a blindfold and a cheap compact video camera, your enemy can wreak an emotional warfare quite different from the disinformation and propaganda of previous wars. Now everyone can be their own producer and director. Even al-Qaida has gone on a media training course.

The September 11 Effect

The September 11 attacks are considered by psychologists as 'psychologically special', because of their televisual value. In the age of spectacle, the growing link between seeing attacks like this on television and traumatic stress symptoms remains a cause for serious concern. A Special Report by 10 scientists in the *New England Journal of Medicine* found that 'People who are not present at a traumatic event may experience stress reactions. Forty-four percent of adults reported one or more substantial symptoms of stress; 90 percent had one or more symptoms to at least some degree.'[1] While the American Psychiatric Association measured the increase in 'psychotropic drug use after September 11, 2001: The attacks were unprecedented in scope, and Americans viewed them over and over again on television'. There was a significant rise in new prescriptions for antidepressants, antipsychotics and benzodiazepine tranquillisers. 'Thus it appears that even the indirect experience of a stressful event – on television and in other media – can produce significant symptoms of stress.'[2]

And as far afield as New Zealand, these television images had extraordinary effects. The medical journal *Tobacco Control* reported that 'Events of 11 September 2001 significantly reduced calls to New Zealand Quitline: There was an overall 35% drop in the total number of new callers per week. It appears that quitting "dropped off the personal agenda" for some New Zealand smokers. It seems likely that at this time of increased media publicity of global security threats, the quitting plans of smokers were eclipsed by other concerns. This was despite the fact that New Zealand is an island nation that is very far removed from international trouble spots. It was also despite the fact that international terrorism has historically posed only a tiny risk of death to the general public relative to that from smoking (which kills half of long term smokers).'[3]

Looking at it another way, have you ever noticed that in almost any given coup d'état or foreign invasion, the first place the tanks roll up to is the main television station? Why? Because rebels and invaders know that we believe what we see on television, and if we see a new military order appear on our screen, we believe they are in charge, thereby making the whole takeover process so much easier.

Television as Tranquilliser

Are you aware that the UK prison service has been involved in a secret 'in-cell television project'? As budgets and staff are cut and overcrowding rises, television's tranquillising effects have been discussed at the highest levels of the prison service as the cheapest and most effective way to subdue the prison population. The General Secretary of the Prison Governors' Association has been revealed as saying, 'It's the best control mechanism you can think of. You know what the British are like; shove them in front of the television and you won't hear a peep out of them.'[4]

Television is being used to make gorillas more passive too. The Dallas Zoo reports that their gorillas each have their favourite television shows. They all like Disney cartoons; *The Little Mermaid*, *The Lion King* and *Beauty and the Beast* are their favourites. One teenage gorilla 'Patrick' has a penchant for public television and National Geographic specials but is bored by sports. The zoo explained that 'They don't follow the story of course, they like the music, the colour and the movement.'[5] And ferrets are no exception. A study published in *Nature* describes how 12 ferrets watched the film *The Matrix* while their brains were monitored. The scientists observed that as Keanu Reeves' hand moved across the screen to deliver a karate chop, the ferrets' brain cells responded as if it were real.[6]

Animals are even hard-wired to share our fascination with celebrities. A study in *Current Biology* looked at how the brain processes visual information about social status. Thirsty rhesus monkeys were offered a choice: their favourite drink, in this case Juicy Juice cherry juice, or the opportunity to look at screen images of the dominant, 'celebrity' monkey of their pack. Despite their thirst, they chose to look at the celebrity screen images. 'What is celebrity for a monkey but their status?' said the author. Monkeys with status have food, power and sexual magnetism — everything the others crave.

The impulse to look at these 'celebrity' monkeys was so strong, it superseded thirst. Interestingly, the 'celebrity' monkeys were just as interested in their fellow celebrities in order to keep an eye out for any rising stars who might threaten their status. However, unlike humans, the monkeys were immune to the charms of reality television. They were not willing to give up the juice to look at screen images of lower-status monkeys. In fact, they had to be bribed with extra juice to watch the rhesus riffraff. And sexual imagery on television works on male monkeys who were also willing to pay (with more cherry juice) to see images of female monkeys' hind quarters. Monkey porn? The study after all is entitled 'Monkey Pay-Per-View'.[7]

What Gives Television its Power?

For man or beast, moving pictures have the most powerful emotional, physiological and political effects imaginable. But how and why does this work? What is the medium's allure? Do terms such as neo-opiate of the masses, the enemy in the corner, the plug-in drug, chewing gum for the eyes, the culture of the disinherited, have any substance beyond a general dislike of the values conveyed through television? Television is an interesting tool with which to re-examine our concept of free will.

Hypnotic Effects

It's now almost half a century since a little-known yet remarkable experiment was conducted in the UK in which members of the public watched a closed-circuit television programme showing someone being hypnotised. The effects were so pronounced that some of the viewers reportedly 'went into a trance'. Politicians feared the effect if it were broadcast to millions. Parliament instituted the Hypnotism Act of 1952, making it illegal to show anyone being hypnotised on television. And it is still in force today. The authorities were primarily concerned with the message on television as opposed to the medium. Little has changed.

Hypnosis sheds an oblique light on human autonomy. Part voodoo and part placebo, it occupies a unique position, straddling the divide between the empirical and the esoteric, the rational and the intuitive, the voluntary and the involuntary, the conscious and subconscious. Hypnosis offers us one of the few opportunities for a guided journey into our primitive animal ancestry whilst sitting comfortably.

As a postgraduate looking for an interesting area of mind/body science to study, I found hypnotism's air of illegality alluring. I went on to read in academic literature about a hypnotised man with a bicycle spoke inserted through his face (the journal showed a photograph) and of a man's bloody appendix being removed through routine surgery without any anaesthetic. However, despite my study and preparation, when I finally hypnotised my first subject, I was stunned. To witness someone – who only minutes before was highly alert and rational – change so markedly was extraordinary.

This sense of wonderment was recently rekindled when I began to ponder why people continue to watch so many hours of television and why the screen is so very influential.

Professor David Speigel from Stanford Medical School in California recently told me that he sees hypnosis partly as a lesson in free will as it 'teaches us something about our vulnerabilities as social creatures that we can take in ideas that we might consider alien and act as though they were good ideas'.[8a] What exactly is hypnosis? A form of sleep or sleepwalking, an altered state of consciousness, one mind dominating another – the hypnotist's 'will' replacing that of the patient? For many people, hypnosis conjures up images of a bony-faced man complete with goatee beard staring into the eyes of his patient and waving his lengthy fingers as he intones 'Your eyes are growing heavy.' Or perhaps the pendulous sway of the dangling Victorian pocketwatch. While these methods work perfectly well, the reality is often far more banal – you can ask your subject merely to focus on the sound of you tapping your pencil on your desk or to stare at the pattern of your unsubtle cardigan. And there are practical issues to consider such as your arm becoming sore from holding that pocketwatch, developing cramps from waving your fingers or a sore throat from intoning too much. One common feature of hypnotic induction methods is to urge your subject to focus their attention, to diminish their peripheral awareness. The rhythmic monotony of a pencil tapping or hypnotist counting backwards can be spellbindingly effective in changing your subject's attentional focus.[8b]

There are some striking similarities between the act of watching television and hypnosis. In fact, when someone asks what exactly hypnosis is, one explanation describes the situation of being deeply engrossed in watching television drama and unaware of the noises out in the street. But what is going on neurologically? At Imperial College School of Medicine in London, John Gruzelier, Professor of Psychology, has been carrying out research into the effects of hypnosis on the brain. I asked him how he defines hypnosis:

'It's a condition of highly focused attention, where once you have become focused you become more responsive to suggestions given to you by the practitioner. And as a result there are alterations in brain function...Our studies have been going on since the 1970s. We've had consistent results – interesting alterations in the frontal lobes, which become less connected to the rest of the brain and aspects become repressed. This makes perfect sense because the hypnotist is specifically asking you to stop analysing everything critically and go with the flow. Your frontal lobes are parts of the brain for critical analysis, and basically he's asking you to switch these off. My interpretation of hypnosis is that this is a clever way of achieving this...As a consequence, the organisation of the brain is altered, and there are shifts in the activity from one side to the other. We are mostly left hemispheric, and we shift into right hemispheric, but it depends on what you are asked to do when hypnotised.'[8]

Changes in Brain Function

A similar thing seems to happen when we watch television. Research by Professor Herbert Krugman found that within 30 seconds of turning on the television, our brain becomes neurologically less able to make judgements about what we see and hear on the screen. Our brain treats incoming information uncritically. Our brain waves switch to predominantly alpha waves, indicating an unfocused, receptive lack of attention. What surprised Krugman, however, was how rapidly this state emerged. Further research revealed that our brain's left hemisphere, which processes information logically and analytically, tunes out while we are watching television. This tuning-out allows the right hemisphere of our brain, which processes information emotionally and uncritically, to function unimpeded. 'It appears,' wrote Krugman, 'the basic electrical response of the brain is clearly to the medium. Television is a communication medium that effortlessly transmits huge quantities of information not thought about at the time of exposure.'[9,10] This was a long-winded way of saying that the medium of television brainwashes you. The advertising industry immediately ordered copies of this report by the truckload.

If watching television or hypnosis causes a shift in brain activity from our left to our right hemisphere we should be aware of what this means for 'free will' in everyday intellectual terms. Michael Gazzaniga has spent at least 40 years studying this very difference between left and right brain, and recently described this dichotomy. 'The left hemisphere has proved quite dominant for major cognitive activities, such as problem solving...The right hemisphere, meanwhile, is severely deficient in difficult problem solving.' Gazzaniga has found that the left hemisphere is always hard at work, seeking the meaning of events, constantly looking for order and reason and explanations. He believes 'Although both hemispheres can be viewed as conscious, the left brain's consciousness far surpasses that of the right.'[11]

It's very interesting that these left hemispheric qualities – such as problem solving and the persistent search for meaning, order and reason, along with the general ability to sustain attention – are affected when television arrives in a society for the first time. A classic naturalistic experiment was carried out in a remote Canadian mountain community in British Columbia that previously had no television. When cable television was introduced the researchers recorded how things changed. Over time it was found that both adults and children became less creative in problem solving and were less able to persevere at tasks.[12]

Television protagonists argue that this description of viewers is demeaning, reducing them to passive recipients remotely controlled by television. But again this focuses on the content and overlooks the effect of the medium itself. If advertisers believed that we are spilling over with independent thought and critical reasoning, and that we are vigilant and discriminating, rational beings as we stare at the screen, would they risk paying up to $5 million per minute (plus the same amount again in production costs) to help us believe that beauty creams will destroy cellulite and lift sagging thighs, or that an insipid lager will make a man out of an insipid mouse? Why is the amount of money spent on political television advertising generally considered the most important part of an American presidential race?

We may prefer to think of ourselves as free thinkers but we're not. A British study, 'Right about others, wrong about ourselves?' shows how very pompous we are. Researchers at Keele University investigated the third-person effect – the belief that others are more influenced than ourselves by media messages. They found that while we are fairly accurate at estimating how much others are persuaded by media messages, we're in denial about our own autonomy. We report that attitude change occurs in others, but not in ourselves. The authors see this conceited disposition as our 'motive to maintain positive self-esteem and a feeling of control over negative influence'.[13] In reviewing the study, another psychologist wrote, 'See yourself as a truly independent thinker, unaffected by the news? Believe advertisers are wasting their money because you just glaze over during the break? Think again…The implication is clear: if you don't want to be persuaded, turn off the message…beware: you won't fully realise that you've been influenced as much as you have!'[14]

And like hypnosis, watching television is also thought to subdue the involvement of the most sophisticated part of our brain – the frontal lobe. This is the brain's executive control system, responsible for planning, organising and sequencing behaviour for self-control, moral judgement and attention. Again, both hypnosis and television reduce our ability to analyse critically what we are being told or what we see. For example, adding single digit numbers uses areas throughout the left and right frontal lobes. Watching a television screen doesn't. Adding single digit numbers is a very mundane task that doesn't sound like it requires much of your brain. So, if television uses even less of your brain than this simple task, then imagine how much less of the brain is being used than during more complex activities such as socially interacting with your peers – that is, living.[15] Most worrying of all is that the frontal lobe, which continues to develop until the age of about 20, may be damaged by watching a lot of television. It is imperative that children and young adults do things which thicken the fibres connecting neurons in this part of the brain, and the more the person is stimulated, the more the fibres will thicken. Doing simple arithmetic or reading out loud, for example, are very effective in activating the frontal lobe.[15] Television may literally idle this brain area and then stunt its development.

The frontal lobe has an important role to play in keeping an individual's behaviour in check. Whenever you use self-control to refrain from lashing out or doing something you should not, the frontal lobe is hard at work. Children often do things they shouldn't because their frontal lobes are under-developed. A study reported in *The World Federation of Neurology* expresses great concern over the way visual electronic media is affecting children by '...halting the process of frontal lobe development and affecting their ability to control potentially antisocial elements of their behaviour...the implications are very serious...children should also be encouraged to play outside with other children, interact and communicate with others as much as possible'. The more work done to thicken the fibres connecting the neurons in this part of the brain, the better the child's ability will be to control their behaviour.[15]

Psychosurgery

Anyone who's heard of a 'frontal lobotomy' or seen the before and after version of Jack Nicholson in *One Flew Over the Cuckoo's Nest* will be left with little doubt that our frontal lobe is central to our autonomy and free will. At one time, I studied patients who had undergone the contemporary version of Mr Nicholson's frontal lobotomy – a bilateral stereotactic sub-caudate tractotomy – to treat their intractable clinical depression. To my surprise, I witnessed patients who had been suicidally depressed readjust to a new and often better life. Far from the film's depiction of psychosurgery as brain butchery rendering its recipients pitiful automatons, in real life the procedure seemed to help, and the patients and their families appeared grateful. Had the patients known of the origins of psychosurgery, however, they would have run for their lives. Psychosurgery was first devised by a Portuguese politician, the Foreign Minister, Egas Moniz. After attending a neurological conference in London, in 1935, Moniz heard how the destruction of the prefrontal brain area of monkeys and chimpanzees produced a number of deficits in problem solving tasks. But what seemed to impress Moniz most was the observation that some of the more excitable members of the lower orders became much calmer following surgery. It was hardly a coincidence that only a few months later he looked further up the evolutionary ladder as he sharpened his scalpel.

Psychosurgery is surgery performed on the normal brain tissue to change or control a person's emotions or behaviour. It has been described as 'therapy by impairment'. I found that neurosurgeons and psychiatrists did not really know why or how some psychosurgery actually worked. However, a common theme in their explanations of the rationale behind the operations was increasing the separation of thought from emotion. Some patients 'think too much' and this leads to emotional distress while the selective reduction in too much of a certain type of thinking 'permits the patient to function in a more effective and less troubled way'. But it was also felt that psychosurgery might reduce the probability of using certain intellectual capacities and persistence in achieving goals in everyday life.[16]

And so again, as with hypnosis research, I've seen some common themes between the effects of watching television and the processes thought to lie behind frontal lobe psychosurgery: the reduction in critical thinking, less motivated and creative problem solving and a lack of perseverence with solving a problem (as in the isolated Canadian community above), and greater separation of thought from emotion. Obviously the act of watching television is not the same as undergoing a bilateral stereotactic sub-caudate tractotomy. However, given the concern that television viewing may literally idle frontal lobe activity and then stunt its development in younger viewers thereby changing their thinking and behaviour, there are some unfortunate similarities. Opponents of psychosurgery saw it as the use of a medical procedure to achieve social goals. Television too is used to achieve social goals.

Media analyst Marshall McLuhan considered television as reducing the separation of thought and action, making human behaviour more conformist. Watching television is associated with increased alpha wave activity, a shift from left to right brain activity and a reduction in frontal lobe activity. As you watch television you are less conscious and less able to understand the reason you are being told or shown something. Now perhaps it's easier to understand why television advertising costs up to $5 million per minute while print media could never demand these sums. These effects are good news for those who want to engage us through television but they don't exactly sound like an exercise in free will. Someone once referred to '...television, with its endless stream of plausible myths'.[17] It is precisely these changes in brain function that make myths seem so very plausible. And there are teams of psychologists working hard to make them entirely plausible.

Immersive Television

Researchers on behalf of the Independent Television Commission in the UK and in the United States and the Netherlands are developing immersive television: a new generation television to give the viewer a sense of literally 'being there' in the depicted scene, making what we see appear more credible and believable than ever. Advances in the medium will drive home the message even more effectively. Research into the 'psychology of presence' has started recently as a result of technical developments in television. Scientists are busy measuring viewers' heart rates, electrodermal activity and postural responses as they watch different types of hi-fidelity television sets in order to refine the ideal 'sensorily rich mediated environment'. And they're finding that 'Strong sensations of presence in users can be evoked by advanced broadcast systems...thereby creating a perceptual illusion.' The academic titles speak for themselves: 'Aroused and Immersed: the psychophysiology of presence', 'Telepresence', or the less technical 'Being part of the fun – Immersive television!' The scientists are now profiling people's attentional characteristics and look forward to answering the question: 'what makes some people more susceptible to presence than others?' This is exactly the same language and question hypnosis researchers worked on for years.[18]

There is nothing inherently wrong about developing a better quality television screen. But it is important to know how powerful television is becoming in order to manage its use and pre-empt our society's further overindulgence.

Reading Versus Watching Television

Those of you who suspect that reading is better for you than watching television are right. It's very useful to compare the effects of television versus reading. It is precisely the flat, impersonal, unentertaining text that produces the neurological and intellectual benefits in reading as opposed to watching television. Reading leads you to actively manage knowledge, to follow a line of thought, which means classifying, making inferences, reasoning, weighing up ideas, connecting one generalisation to another – and more. In reading the printed word, the medium is not in itself the star. You are forced to stand back at a slight distance and analyse and interpret – everything that television bypasses or does for you. As Neil Postman put it in his book *Amusing Ourselves to Death*, 'television's way of knowing is uncompromisingly hostile to typography's way of knowing...'[19]

Perceiving Emotion

The changes in brain function and thought process brought about by the medium of the screen alone allows the content of television to have a far greater impact than it would if you read about it instead. Scientists can now influence complex movements of your facial muscles, your experience of pleasure and mood, your sense of trustworthiness and even your memory simply by exposing you to the occasional subliminal level smiling face when you watch television.[20] Our brains are exceedingly responsive to emotional cues from the television screen. Even cues as small as the size of the whites of someone's eyes can immediately activate the amygdala – a subcortical region of the brain sensitive to emotional signals. A new study in the journal *Science* finds that showing people a subliminal image of eye whites for only 17 milliseconds so they're unaware of it, activates this brain region. Our brain seems to have specialised neural circuits devoted to detecting emotion in characters' faces using only the most minimal information. This alone can change our brain response and our emotions without provoking any conscious awareness in the process.[21]

Telly Belly

Television images affect other parts of our body as well. Two studies involving 400 GPs found that large numbers of people are visiting their surgeries with 'telly belly' – illnesses they believe they share with television characters. One outbreak of telly belly was triggered by a character in the soap opera *EastEnders* being diagnosed with a brain tumour, and another later with kidney cancer. Nine out of ten doctors claim people are reporting symptoms based on what they've seen in soaps.[22]

Further down the body and the age scale, a recent study published in the medical journal *Pediatrics* does what it says on the label: 'Watching Sex on Television Predicts Adolescent Initiation of Sexual Behavior: Exposure to TV that included only talk about sex was associated with the same risks as exposure to TV that depicted sexual behavior.' These scientists identified an 'intercourse effect' among adolescents who either watched shows which only talked about sex or shows which had sex scenes: '...12-year-olds who watched the highest levels of this content among youths their age appeared much like youths 2 to 3 years older...The magnitude of these results are such that a moderate shift in the average sexual content of adolescent TV viewing could have substantial effects on sexual behavior at the population level.'[23] Television is hot-housing young libidos and adolescent intercourse.

The Effects of Television on Relationships

Television doesn't just help initiate underage sexual relationships but virtual platonic ones as well. An education conference in the UK heard that children watch enough television for characters in soap operas to become their surrogate families. 'For some, the television provides the sense of community through soaps and has taken over the personal relationships.' Doctor/patient relationships haven't escaped the influence of the screen. Medical journals are reporting that people who watch a lot of medical drama have false expectations about the success of cardiopulmonary resuscitation (CPR). One study described how viewers ignored rational information 'in favour of vivid, dramatic examples. The message of television fiction is that doctors are not powerless and that treatment does not stop once the heart stops beating. This helps to create what has been called an "illusion of efficacy".'[24]

Parents are often told that they can prevent the negative influences of television by watching and discussing it with their child. The television industry and the academics it funds like this notion because ultimately it says let your children (otherwise known as 'ratings') watch with you ('additional ratings'). Given what you've read above, it should be even more clear that if we as adults are strongly affected by the medium of the television screen, children are even more susceptible to its influence and effects. The study in the *New England Journal of Medicine* mentioned earlier (page 86) found that in the wake of the September 11 attacks, children who viewed more television coverage of the attacks had an increase in substantial stress symptoms. In fact, 35 per cent of children had one or more substantial stress symptoms. And though most parents talked to their children about the attacks shown on television, there was no relationship between the amount of discussion and the degree of stress symptoms suffered by the children. The emotional effects produced by television images could not be rationalised away by civilised parental explanation and reassurance. Again, we must learn that television flies under the radar to achieve its effect. Trying to use conscious, visible means to deal with it after the fact is a very poor alternative to not seeing the material to begin with.

Is Television Relaxing?

But one of the main reasons we watch television is 'to relax'. Yet again, when you actually take a closer look, you find that things aren't what they seem. While watching television does indeed dull your attentional and neurological state, eliciting less electrical brain activity than reading, this is not the same as 'chilling out'. One major study from *Scientific American* involved people watching television at home as normal. Each viewer had a beeper and they were signalled six to eight times a day, at random, over the period of a week; whenever they heard the beep, they wrote down what they were doing and how they were feeling using a standardised scorecard.

People who were watching television when they were beeped reported feeling relaxed and passive. And EEG studies also showed less mental stimulation, as measured by alpha brain wave production, during watching television than during reading. However, in their own words the scientists observed:

> 'What is more surprising is that the sense of relaxation ends when the set is turned off, but the feelings of passivity and lowered alertness continue. Survey participants commonly reflect that television has somehow absorbed or sucked out their energy, leaving them depleted. They say they have more difficulty concentrating after viewing than before. In contrast, they rarely indicate such difficulty after reading. After playing sports or engaging in hobbies, people report improvements in mood. After watching TV, people's moods are about the same or worse than before.'[10]

It seems that within moments of sitting or lying down and pressing the 'ON' button, we report feeling more relaxed. But because the relaxation occurs quickly, we are conditioned to associate viewing with rest and lack of tension. And because we remain relaxed throughout viewing, this deceptive association is positively reinforced.

Why Television is Addictive

In the study, once the screen goes blank again they observed 'stress and dysphoric rumination [feelings of depression and unrest] occurs'. They point out that a similar thing happens when you use habit-forming drugs. You're far more likely to become dependent on a tranquilliser that leaves your body quickly than one that leaves slowly, precisely because you're more conscious that the tranquilliser's effects are wearing off. In the same way, television viewers have subconsciously learned that they will feel less relaxed if they stop watching, and this may be a key factor in determining why they don't turn the television off. 'Viewing begets more viewing...Thus, the irony of TV: people watch a great deal longer than they plan to, even though prolonged viewing is less rewarding.'

Yet, many people like to think of themselves as 'selective viewers'. They typically say they sat down just to watch X, but they're still watching Y and Z three hours later. The attentional inertia accompanied by the alterations in brain function explain why a mediocre television show can have high ratings if it follows a popular one. People wouldn't behave this way with books. The medium of television does not lend itself to being watched in moderation. So it's not surprising that one study identified 'a rarer group who use television selectively. They tend to watch only a few favourite shows'.[25]

Further evidence of the link between television and addictive drugs comes from studies documenting the withdrawal symptoms people experience when they reduce the amount of time they watch. One study conducted by the University of Chicago over 40 years ago examined the behaviour of families whose television sets had broken. The families described the effects: 'The family walked around like a chicken without a head.' 'It was terrible. We did nothing – my husband and I talked.' 'Screamed constantly. Children bothered me, and my nerves were on edge. Tried to interest them in games, but impossible. TV is part of them.'[26]

Further studies in a variety of countries have involved families who have volunteered or been paid to stop watching television, typically for a week or a month. But many simply cannot succeed. Some fight, even physically. The more recent annual 'TV turn-off' week in the United States has produced similar reports from families.

One academic review of these withdrawal studies concluded that 'The first three or four days for most persons were the worst, even in many homes where viewing was minimal and where there were other ongoing activities. In over half of all the households, during these first few days of loss, the regular routines were disrupted, family members had difficulties in dealing with the newly available time, anxiety and aggressions were expressed...People living alone tended to be bored and irritated...By the second week, a move toward adaptation to the situation was common.'

And so the *Scientific American* study (see page 104) describes the term television addiction as 'imprecise and laden with value judgments, but it captures the essence of a very real phenomenon'. The mental health profession considers substance dependence a disorder which involves spending a great deal of time using the substance; using it more often than you intend to; thinking about reducing your use or making repeated unsuccessful attempts to reduce your use; giving up important social, family or work activities to use it; and experiencing withdrawal symptoms when you stop using it. All these symptoms can apply to people who view a lot of television. 'Excessive cravings do not necessarily involve physical substances. Gambling can become compulsive, sex can become obsessive. One activity, however, stands out for its prominence and ubiquity – the world's most popular leisure activity, television.'[10]

If the average person spends the equivalent of more than 12 full years of their life watching television, and after each session of watching television people's moods are about the same or worse than before (see page 105), there must be something about the medium that is more than habit-forming.

The brain's chemical messenger, dopamine, is now being strongly implicated in a range of addictions, from cocaine and nicotine to binge-eating and gambling.[28] Dopamine is also increasingly seen as rewarding us for paying attention, especially to things that are novel and stimulating such as modern television images.[29] Looking at information on a television screen causes our brain to release dopamine.[30] At doses of four hours plus per day, it appears that we're being chemically rewarded for looking at a screen full of changing images and becoming neurochemically dependent. So perhaps that rather nauseatingly comfy expression 'telly addiction' has some substance to it after all.

In the Hands of Big Brother

As a modern Western culture we need to learn to, in the right context, relinquish control, let go, become less rational and overly analytical, to become more 'right brain'. But watching television is neither an effective nor a healthy way to do this. Aside from the issue of television and attentional damage mentioned in Chapter 1, for those whose brains are still developing – including young adults spending many hours per day in front of a screen – this unusual daily alteration in brain function may be causing permanent changes in the way their brain finally develops and functions. For those who find this idea of our brain developing in a user-dependent fashion to be rather far-fetched or abstract, consider this. Even vague concepts such as a child raised without nurturing or love will determine the size and function of that child's brain. Doctors at a conference of the Royal Society of Medicine were shocked to see brain scans showing the frontal-temporal part of the brains of Romanian orphans as underdeveloped and showing little or no activity. The author said 'these children appear to have altered brain growth'. Scans showed that neglected three-year-olds actually had smaller heads than children raised in loving families.[31,32] It shouldn't take new scanning technology to convince us that children's brains and minds are in transition and highly impressionable – physically. For any young person, watching hours of television every day is likely to exact its influence. And television's influence is strong.

As with hypnosis, watching television enhances your capacity for receiving ideas without all the bother of reality-testing. Suspending our disbelief, television slips under our neurological and intellectual radar. The term 'acceptivity' was at one time used to describe this reduction in critical analysis. The French psychoanalyst Charles Baudouin described this perfectly: 'In a word, it is not the conscious but the unconscious which accepts. The idea, instead of being confronted with others and judged from an intellectual and volitional viewpoint, is granted hospitality like a welcome stranger.'[33] This is of course music to any broadcaster's ears.

Watching a television screen is akin to putting yourself in the hands of an unqualified hypnotherapist whose main interest is to keep you coming back to him for longer and longer sessions, a form of ratings-driven professional conduct. When Anton Mesmer first used hypnotic techniques in the 17th century, he was driven out of Vienna and accused of practising magic. Today he'd be employed in the development departments of the great Hollywood studios, adorned in Emmys and Baftas.

This chapter has merely provided a neurological account of what Aldous Huxley foresaw over 80 years ago in *Brave New World*. We in Western liberal democracies have been ever vigilant to those who would infringe our human rights. But in looking for Big Brother, we've failed to see him in ourselves.

In his book *1984*, George Orwell warns that in the classic Hitlerian tradition we will be oppressed by political forces from the outside. But Huxley saw it as being a far simpler affair, taking place much closer to home. In order to erode our autonomy, no enforcer or Big Brother is needed at all. By merely using distraction and the arresting of our attention, as opposed to starting all those unnecessary bonfires and burning all those unwieldy books, we'll come to love our oppression, to adore the technologies that undo our capacities to think critically. A technological determinism will prevail. As Huxley observed in *Brave New World Revisited*, those who are ever on the alert to oppose tyranny failed to consider man's almost infinite appetite for distractions. In *Brave New World*, people are controlled by inflicting pleasure. In the poignantly entitled book *Amusing Ourselves to Death*, Neil Postman concluded 'Orwell feared that what we hate will ruin us. Huxley feared that what we love will ruin us.'[19]

It was either Juvenal or Augustus Caesar (I find attributions to both) who said the way to keep the citizens of Rome from rebelling was to give them 'bread and circuses'. Keep the people well-fed and entertained, and what would they have to rebel against? Perhaps this explains why we haven't had an enormous health debate about the effects of watching 12 years or more of pure television, as we've had on the 'abuse' of drugs. After all, drugs are thought to pose a threat to the established social order. Television, however, is considered helpful in maintaining the social order. Incidently, the UK Government is making sure we'll have plenty of free public television too. The BBC is planning to build more giant outdoor television screens as permanent forms of architecture in city centres throughout Britain. The 300-square-foot screens will be installed in the most prominent locations for maximum 24-hour coverage of sports, quiz shows, news and soap operas. The BBC claims this public television will 'rejuvenate city centres and restore a sense of community. People can watch the latest edition of *EastEnders*. We want it to become a part of the civic infrastructure, as natural as having a theatre or a swimming pool'.[34] These 'Big Screens'...'could become social hubs for city centres just like village greens of the past,' according to John Prescott.[35]

How Much is Too Much?

One of the main obstacles in encouraging people to reduce their consumption of something is the vagueness of the term 'excessive'. We prefer to think of other people as being excessive or watching excessive amounts of television. 'Everything in moderation'…'You can overdo a good thing' may be sound advice which we've adopted to reduce our salt intake, the amount we drink or the degree of suntanning we view as acceptable, but when it refers to television we haven't been told what excessive actually means. Most of the damage linked to television viewing, described previously, seems to occur beyond watching one to one-and-a-half hours per day, irrespective of the content of the programme. Yet the average person watches four hours a day plus many extra hours in front of computer screens or DVDs. Mr Average, along with his wife and two veg, has been watching excessive amounts of television for decades. And because four hours plus is the norm, it's considered 'normal'. The normalcy of watching television is actively supported by everyone from the US president and British prime minister to anti-Establishment icons ranging from Fidel Castro to Osama Bin Laden, merely because we see them appear on the screen. When both the Establishment and the anti-Establishment appear on our screens, the emotional effect is to foster an impression that such a diametrically opposed group of people defer to one universal thing. Their appearance in the medium inadvertently endorses it, lending credibility to its further use and even its inherent goodness.

I've seen many public service broadcasts on television ranging from 'please drink less' to 'please don't smoke' to 'please don't use your mobile telephone while driving'. Despite the mounting medical evidence, I can't possibly imagine seeing a public service broadcast asking us to try and watch less than four hours of television a day – 'Have you been watching for more than 90 minutes? If so, turn this off and leave the room.' Quite the contrary.

In fact, the UK Government has announced that it wants us to 'learn to watch TV' in order to increase our 'media literacy'. The Culture Secretary declared 'media literacy will become as important a skill as maths or science...as important to our lives as citizens as understanding great literature is to our cultural lives...A nation of active and informed consumers who can discriminate between "opinion and fact", who can "question and challenge" the programmes they watch'.[36] And the Government is asking television broadcasters to help 'educate viewers' in this 'media literacy'. The Government doesn't want us to watch less television but to stare at and listen more intensely to the television screen to get at the truth and become better-informed consumers of more television in future. You can see that, like most others, the UK Government focuses almost exclusively on the content transmitted on television, not on the basic influence of the screen as described in this chapter. And for a very good reason.

Peter Bazalgette, Britain's most commercially successful television producer, also curiously avoids the thorny issue of the medium in favour of the content, commenting: 'The media is merely a conduit. The key question is not "what is the technology" but "what is the message?"'[36] While Mr Bazalgette may derive his marketing strategy from Huxley, he obviously prefers Orwell's branding. He is the television producer behind Britain's *Big Brother*.

The academic who truly foresaw what television would bring was Roald Dahl's Professor Willy Wonka, who in 1964 remarked wistfully, 'I don't like television myself. I suppose it's all right in small doses, but children never seem to be able to take it in small doses. They want to sit there all day long staring and staring at the screen...'[37]

FOUR
AMUSING OURSELVES TO DEATH
The Real Story of Television and Violence

I walked into a suburban food shop in the United States that resembled a mini-warehouse with an enormous front picture window and glass front entrance door through which I could see the checkout counter. The rest of the building had no windows, just several rather dimly lit aisles. I grabbed a shopping basket and started perusing the aisles, becoming increasingly aware of a high-pitched tone coming from somewhere, yet no-one was attending to it. I then realised that I was the only customer; in fact I was the only person in the building. There was an eerie peculiarity about the setting, and a strange disquiet came over me as I took each step. But I continued putting things in my basket. Suddenly I heard a horrified scream and spun around to see three women with their hands to their mouths, retracting in horror at something behind the checkout counter. I ran over as they grimly pointed to a man slumped against the wall in a sitting position. He looked as if he'd been knocked out as there was a slight patch of blood on his temple. I then realised the high-pitched noise was coming from the cash till, which was wide open. The women stood back as I went behind the counter to revive him and get help. I patted his shoulder and slapped his face. Then I noticed a larger patch of blood on his chest and realised he'd been shot. He wasn't breathing but his wrist was still warm as I tried to detect a pulse. I tried and I tried but I couldn't find one. I picked up the phone on the floor and called 911, asking for police and an ambulance. I described what I found and the police operator asked 'Is there anyone else in the shop?' It dawned on me that whoever had shot him could still be in the dimly lit shop. I said 'I don't know' and ducked my head below counter level for good measure.

In a few minutes police with rifles and flak jackets arrived and ran to the front of the shop. I raised my hands to make it clear I wasn't the bad guy and beckoned them in to see the victim. The ambulance screamed into the car park and we all tore the entire checkout counter away to enable them to get at him with the defibrillator electrodes. They tore his shirt open and placed the electrodes on his chest, administering shock after shock to no avail.

As they gave him the final shocks, a family car pulled into the car park, a woman jumped out leaving the children behind and ran towards the front of the shop, screaming at the macabre sight through the glass shop front of her blood-soaked husband, his shirt torn open with electrodes on his chest, convulsing in response to the shocks. Her hysterical screams are burned into my memory; the shock on her face and stream of tears still occur in slow motion as I recall this. She had just popped out to pick up the children from school and returned to their family shop to find their life destroyed.

The family were Korean and had recently moved to the United States 'for a better life'. The murderer was later caught. He wasn't a robber; he had killed a number of people in similar circumstances for enjoyment and to 'let off a bit of steam'. He was an educated man with a Masters degree in photography. His final victim survived to describe him. Apparently he would engage his victim in a pleasant chat and then simply pull out a gun and shoot him. The detectives told me the murderer had left about a minute before I arrived and that I was lucky as he probably would have shot me as well.

But what I remember just as clearly is the remark made by the detective at the police station the next day: 'It's getting crazy around here. People are attacking one another for any little thing. Yesterday two guys in their cars had an argument at a traffic light and one guy pulled out a hatchet and attacked the other guy!'

While the availability of guns in the United States makes it far easier to kill someone if you want to, what was it about American culture, I wondered, that made people want to kill so much, whether by gun or hatchet? I've been to plenty of countries with lots of guns and few gun murders. The answer is complex, involving an interaction between the ethos and origins of 'America', the individualism, the win/lose society, the heterogeneous make-up of hyphenated Americans and many other factors. But television has played an enormous part too.

People often point to countries such as Japan, which also has a high level of violent television yet a negligible murder rate as evidence that television isn't to blame for causing violence in the United States. Japan, by the way, does not allow gun ownership. However, anyone who has travelled will have noticed that cultures differ. In fact, that's the main reason I travel. Those who feel that all cultures are the same in terms of how much they are influenced by the same factor have a remarkably naïve view of humanity, or are trying to play devil's advocate for the sake of it or for the sake of the multibillion-dollar television and video games industry that funds them. Some cultures, just like some individuals, are far more susceptible to certain influences, whether political, religious, fashion, dietary or from television. Canada, for example, is in so many cultural, racial and geographical ways markedly different to the United States, and the effects of television on their less violent society are different.

Most importantly, we've been distracted by the simplistic notion of violent television programmes causing violence. Yet the real link between television and violence is far more insidious. Non-violent programmes also lead to violence, and this 'benign' type of television is being neglected by campaigners, who tend to focus on the more sensational examples. The subject of television and violence warrants an entire book but there are key points and new insights that I feel clarify things significantly.

Does Television Cause Violence?

There are stock ripostes to the suggestion that television causes violence. 'There is no evidence that watching television actually causes violent behaviour. Children got into playground fights and arguments, and people murdered one another, long before television existed. People want easy answers to the enormously complex problem of violence while ignoring the real causes of the problem...' Yet no academic study has ever claimed that television is solely responsible for violence in our society.[1]

It's true to say that there is a tradition that blames most new forms of media for society's ills. Every popular art form – the novel, the circus, Punch and Judy shows, comic strips, movies and rock'n' roll – has been singled out for blame upon arrival. 'One generation's trash is the next generation's art form,' says Richard Rhodes, author of *Why They Kill*.[2] But just because those media were held accountable doesn't mean that some of those accusations weren't actually true. In 1950s London, teenagers for the first time tore up the cinema seats when Bill Haley and the Comets performed American rock'n' roll. And certain black-and-white movies may well have caused antisocial behaviour. But that is an issue to do with the content of the medium. Television cannot be compared with any form of media that has come before. The sheer amount of time we watch, the biological effects of the new television technology and the nature of the things we see in such high concentration are unprecedented and incomparable to our previous use of novels, comic books and 78 rpm singles with a photo of Elvis on the sleeve. That is the entire point. Television is qualitatively different to a book, a record or a comic strip.

Just the arrival of television in a country or a community seems to be followed by an enormous surge in the rates of violence. A little-publicised major study published in the *Journal of the American Medical Association* has looked at the prevalence of murder, rape and grievous bodily harm, as they would any other disease such as AIDS or Sars that harm a population. It found that following the introduction of television in both the United States and Canada murder rates doubled, and concluded: 'If, hypothetically, television technology had never been developed, there would today be 10,000 fewer homicides each year in the United States, 70,000 fewer rapes, and 700,000 fewer injurious assaults. Violent crime would be half of what it is.' Across the United States, as different regions got their first television sets, there was a 10- to 15-year delay before violent crime suddenly escalated to double what it had been. The same was true in Canada. And five years on when televisions saturated the households of America's less well-off ethnic minorities, the murder rates doubled there too. England and Wales were not immune either. About 15 years after television sets became the norm, murder rates doubled. This 10- to 15-year incubation period between the time television is introduced and when the rates of violence double is believed to be the period when the first television generation 'comes of age'.[3,4]

What is equally surprising to me is that when the author of the study reported these findings at a press conference of the American Medical Association, referring to this television-related violence as an 'epidemic', there was apparently not a single mention of him in the press the next day. The researcher's prescription was uncompromising: 'Take the TV sets out of children's bedrooms. It's just parental abdication to let them have televisions of their own.' Yet again, this has fallen on deaf ears. While a single copycat video game-related murder makes the news, this much bigger finding is entirely unknown by most well-informed people. When you consider the headlines given to other health issues such as the contraceptive pill, AIDS or MMR, one becomes suspicious as to why this type of study doesn't have similar prominence. Many people and broadcasters simply don't want to hear or don't believe the magnitude of this finding. And many newspapers and magazines are owned by or own the same television corporations who have good reason not to publicise negative studies about television. In fact, one study on this very conflict of interest says that 'although the scientific evidence linking television and violence has grown considerably stronger over the past three decades, recent news reports imply that the scientific evidence is weaker than did earlier reports'.[1]

The introduction of television to other societies has also been studied. Two remote Canadian communities in northern Manitoba were compared after one received television while the other did not. The aggressive behaviour of boys aged between 10 and 12 was observed. Four years after television arrived, the incidence of fist fights and black eyes among the boys increased significantly in the television town. Furthermore, just a few days after an episode of *Happy Days* was broadcast, in which one character joined a gang called the Red Demons, the children created rival gangs called the Red Demons and the Green Demons, and the conflict between the two seriously disrupted the local school. Obviously the arrival of television was merely a coincidence.

And in a completely different study conducted in the mid-1970s by the University of British Columbia, television was introduced to one remote village. Two years later, violent incidents among boys and girls had increased by 160 per cent. Nearby towns with no television used as control groups had no such increase in violence. Obviously the arrival of television was merely a coincidence.[5]

Scientists have also looked at the number of hours people watch per day to see if this is related to violence. Columbia University professor Jeffrey Johnson and his colleagues have found that there is a powerful relationship, and the effect of television is not limited to violent programmes.[6] Just an hour a day of any type of television programming watched by teenagers made a significant difference in how violent they ultimately became as adults. It seems that younger brains and minds in development are not merely influenced by what they do see on television – they are influenced by what they're not doing. For example, unlike reading, television does not provide the cognitive stimulation that produces brain development and the intellectual and emotional benefits that arise from this. It is this seemingly benign factor that has been consistently overlooked.

Johnson tracked 707 families in upstate New York for 17 years, starting in 1975. When the children reached the age of between 22 to 24 years, the researchers correlated the number of hours of television they had viewed at the age of 14 with police and FBI records of violence and interviews. In 2002, Johnson published his findings in *Science*, reporting that children who watched one to three hours of television each day when they were 14 to 16 years old were 60 per cent more likely to be involved in assaults and fights as adults than those who watched less television. And those who watched three hours (less than the national average!) or more a day were five times more likely to behave violently and aggressively as adults. Remember, four hours per day is absolutely normal in most Western countries. In fact this is far less than the average teenager watches, especially if you include videos, DVDs and computer games. The study pre-empted and essentially dismissed the usual criticism that 'These results have nothing to do with television – it has to do with lifestyle. People who watch more than three hours of television are different to those who watch less than an hour.' The effects of parental neglect, poverty, dangerous neigh-bourhoods, a history of psychiatric disorder and other independent risk factors for aggression were statistically eliminated. And the increase in aggression and violence asso-ciated with television viewing held true both for children who had previously displayed violent tendencies and those who had not shown earlier aggression.

In a completely different culture, a study in Turkey conducted by two Faculties of Medicine at Hacettepe and Gaziosmanpasa Universities looked at 800 primary school children. It also found that 'television viewing time is positively associated with social problems, delinquent behaviour, aggressive behaviour...'[7]

Links to Bullying and Fighting in Children

The likelihood of becoming a bully between the ages of six to 11 has been linked to how much television a child watches when he's only four years old. Even taking into account other family and child-rearing factors, the risk associated with the amount of television children watch was 'clinically significant...Maximising cognitive stimulation and limiting television watching in the early years of development might reduce children's subsequent risk of becoming bullies'. Again it seems that it is the lack of brain stimulation that in some way predisposes a child to becoming a bully. The scientists suggest that '...bullying might arise out of cognitive deficits as well as emotional ones'.[8]

Interestingly, in covering this story, the BBC News website had a large boxed statement from a British professor, which in bold letters claimed the findings from this study simply weren't true. The news story finished with the claim of another British academic: 'It is always claimed TV causes aggression, but it is never proved.' And he leaves the reader with this final thought in the form of the predictable soothing balm: 'Parents should have a balanced approach...' However, what the BBC does not tell you is that this 'UK expert' is in fact nothing more than a 'Lecturer in Media, Culture and Communication' who specialises in teaching 'Digital Video Production'.[9]

Another way to look at the influence of television on

violent behaviour is to observe what happens when you remove it from children's lives. The good news is that a more recent study found that violence and verbal aggression can be quickly and dramatically reduced by simply reducing the amount of television children watch. Less television equals less violence. The Stanford University School of Medicine reports a 40 per cent reduction in physical violence and 50 per cent reduction in verbal aggression. Nine-year-old pupils in two similar primary schools were compared, and the households involved had their television sets fitted to a device that could prevent the set from being turned on once the child exceeded an established viewing limit. Youngsters who give up television for 10 days and later watch it for only seven hours per week get into far fewer fights and arguments. The scientists involved say this shows that all types of viewing content, not just violent content, can badly affect early development by preventing children from interacting with each other and improving their social skills. And it is precisely this element that I believe is overlooked in debates about television and violence.[10]

What I find most interesting about both of the studies above and others is that they aren't referring to the effects of violent programmes, but to the effects of all types of television programming.

Loss of Social Skills

This is not a naïve whingeing cry for universal pacifism and state-subsidised emasculation. There will always be violence.

But one of the reasons we are witnessing such high levels of violence-at-the-drop-of-a-hat and gratuitous violence is that we have lost touch with acceptable ways of dealing with everyday conflict, whether in a queue, on the street or in the car. Basic skills such as 'reading' people have been under-developed. A generation has been deprived of learning and implementing the various escalating stages we previously went through before attacking someone, because they've been busy watching television instead. The evidence regarding too much television leading to underdeveloped frontal lobes comes to mind. Researchers have noticed for some time that the family meal-table has begun to disappear from some homes. By the 1990s, even among the middle classes, more than half of meals were taken on a tray in front of the television. Parents knew they were expected to preside over the meal-table, dealing with challenging behaviour ('why should I?'), sanctioning, socialising and interacting with their children. Just as importantly, it also made parents reflect on their responsibilities to give a good example and to keep up their standards in front of their children. And it's not merely that television is usurping the time children would have spent being socialised. Television is actively replacing this void in socialisation with opposing values and behaviours.

This is caused by the medium of television, irrespective of what is watched. But once you add the programme content to this, the recipe for violence improves considerably. It is often what is missing in the content of so many soaps and dramas that has also been overlooked as a cause of violence.

On television the fashion in personal interaction has

shifted to a cool, dispassionate 'I'm unaffected', and the idea of appearing 'caring' is terribly unfashionable – soft, weak and deeply uncontemporary. One can see this reflected in the way a lot of younger people have begun to behave at street level. Many simply don't know how to interact. They increasingly don't know that you say 'thanks' or even 'thank you' to someone who steps aside for you to pass on the pavement. In general, there's a greater roughness and disregard in everyday encounters, which does not lend itself to low rates of grievous bodily harm.

Confrontational Role Models

But what television programmes lack in kindness and consideration, they make up for, not in violent, but in confrontational behaviour among the characters in soaps, police dramas and reality television shows. I come from a medical family. I've also seen a great deal of the inner workings of hospitals and have found – without exception – the staff to always work together closely and amicably, often under dire circumstances. But The Playboy Channel aside, showing nurses being nice to one another makes drab telly. So caring hospital characters sneer and walk off, sneer and snarl, sneer and shout or sneer and sneer. In Britain's cop dramas, camaraderie has taken a back seat to back stabbing and one cop grabbing the other by the lapels and sneering at him (or her) nose to nose, often in the police station in full view of the criminals who must be wondering which side of the law needs the anger management course.

Discord keeps us looking at the screen, while conciliation may compromise those increasingly important ratings. This is not to say that such programmes are not compelling or entertaining. That is an entirely different matter. Crack cocaine could also be described as compelling and entertaining – but that doesn't mean it's good for you. However, there is a social cost for our compelling television entertainment that we must now fully acknowledge because we're paying for it anyway.

The long-standing news journalist and BBC broadcaster John Humphrys hasn't watched television for five years, even though he appears on it regularly – his old set broke and he never replaced it. However, he recently asked each of Britain's 16 channel controllers to send him 10 programmes they were most proud of. 'I was actually quite shocked by what I saw. So much of it seemed…altogether more confrontational than I'd remembered…the violence of the language surprised me. It seems almost impossible to switch on without encountering some sort of aggression…even in the soaps…Characters in *EastEnders* seemed never to walk past each other with a smile and a nod (as they sometimes do in real life even in the East End of London) but with a snarl and a threat.'[11]

And what at first appear to be quality-of-life effects brought about as a result of this type of television – greater general rudeness, indifference, disregard and gratuitous rebellion – become life-and-death effects. I've noticed around the world, too, that as people are exposed to more Western television programmes, their facial expressions and body language change accordingly. One of the main characteristics I've witnessed is a slightly more challenging physical disposition – 'hard' facial expressions and body language to match. This, however, is not merely a cool 'style' in self-presentation. These contrary, bordering on confrontational, physical expressions are more likely to trigger reciprocal reactions in others, which heightens the potential for violence. The new television-derived forms of facial and body language, in effect, play into a low-grade primitive fight or flight reaction and are hardly the ideal influence for achieving greater harmony and a more manageable murder rate. Television plays upon and distorts our evolutionary survival dispositions and the consequences are highly dangerous.

Fortunately, scientists are starting to take this secondary effect of television very seriously. A new generation of studies is looking at the finery of what is referred to as 'hostile attributional bias', in which people come to infer hostile intent from the actions of others, even when intent is ambiguous and might be benign. This mindset in turn 'understandably contributes to the development and maintenance of aggressive behavior', according to a study recently presented to the American Psychological Society. The researchers found that briefly exposing children to media violence early in the school year had longer-term effects, changing their mindset by making the children interpret the benign actions of other children as hostile. It also made the children less sociable and more verbally and physically aggressive: '...these results are surprisingly robust given the short time lag'.[12]

Indirect Aggression

Researchers in Britain have focused on the effects of 'indirect aggression' on screen. They have looked at on-screen manipulation, plotting and scheming, gossiping and spreading rumours in order to hurt others. High levels of indirect aggression have been identified in 92 per cent of programmes popular with British adolescents: more than physical aggression (55 per cent) and verbal aggression (86 per cent). Soap operas such as *EastEnders*, *Coronation Street* and *Hollyoaks* were of particular interest to the researchers. A strong association has been found between girls being indirectly aggressive and the fact that they have watched more indirect aggression on television. Indirect aggressors on television were more likely to be female, attractive, rewarded, justified and realistic. The last four characteristics of aggressors have all been shown to make people more physically aggressive later.

Basically, viewing one form of aggression can lead to a different form of aggression. The author of the study is hardly a puritan and makes several points. 'Obviously I am not advocating that we remove all forms of aggression from television...these forms of aggression occur in real life and should be represented in our media. In fact they clearly make for good TV...what I am suggesting is that the sheer frequency and portrayal of indirect aggression may be giving individuals an unrealistic and counterproductive view of what forms of behaviour are acceptable to use in their own lives.' And she offers some specific advice: '...indirect aggression is also shown frequently on television and influences aggressive behaviour...Parents may wish to regulate the amount of indirect aggression their children are viewing...By showing young attractive females who are often justified and rewarded for their indirectly aggressive actions, the media may be providing inappropriate role models, especially for younger girls...It may even be necessary for programmes with very high levels of indirect aggression to warn viewers...Why not, if viewers are warned of violent content and indirect aggression can have a similar effect on the victim?'[13,14]

Sport on television has largely been overlooked as a cause of violence, but things are changing. In state education, the deputy general secretary of the Secondary Heads Association and in the private sector, the chairman of the Incorporated Association of Preparatory Schools have both blamed the bad behaviour of sporting heroes on television for trouble in schools. 'Every time a player dives in the penalty area, or is seen in close-up on TV mouthing obscenities, our job becomes that much harder.'[15]

The recent trend towards self-expression has also had unintended effects. Television has increasingly promoted unbridled self-expression through myriad role models in reality television, drama and soaps, chat shows and sporting events. Unlike English reserve, this new emotional openness is now considered more genuine, honest and 'real'. But as the public has begun to express their feelings, urges and impulses, they have failed to realise that one man's self-expression is another man's insult or invasion of personal space and tranquillity. People are emotionally trespassing as their desires are stepping on one another's feet.

A further contributory factor to violence is the gulf between television life and real life. This gulf cultivates an underlying resentment, frustration and anger, motives to attach to all that confrontational body language. Beyond the physical expressions subconsciously mimicked from television there increasingly lies the development of an inner sense of entitlement and contempt for those who have more than us, are more successful, funnier and better looking, or hinder our gratification. Television also portrays problems and obstacles as having resolutions, and quick ones at that. Given that we as individuals are now more alienated, interact less with people we don't know and are also more distrustful and wary, our default setting has become having one finger on the trigger.

Violent acts on television may provide us with strategies and techniques to harm or kill, and may encourage us to use violence as a way to express our anger. But it is the television programmes that produce this anger and inner disequilibrium to begin with that, I believe, are far more responsible for increased murder and violence. However, this is a subtler concept, difficult to literally 'prove' and photograph, so the media have ignored it in favour of the much-publicised 'copycat' effects of television violence. I suspect the man I found shot to death in that shop was not the victim of a copycat killing.

How the Media Down-plays the Problem

There are still people who argue that watching lots of television, particularly violent television, does not cause violence, that it merely attracts viewers with pre-existing social or psychological problems. Therefore television is nothing more than a 'marker' for antisocial types who are prone to trouble to begin with. In some cases an early preference for violent television programmes or many hours of television may indeed be indicative that something else is wrong in that child's life. However, this does not in any way discount the evidence that lots of television, particularly violent television, also influences the rest of us to be more violent.

Yet newspapers and magazines like to emphasise the sceptical views of those who claim television does not cause violence. This approach makes more interesting reading and gives us the impression that the journalist is giving a 'balanced view' providing 'both sides of the argument'. This in turn implies that 'the debate' is still ongoing, that the jury's still out – without making it clear that most reputable scientists from a cross section of disciplines are in no doubt whatsoever that violent television causes real-life violence. Many of these scientists are so concerned at this distortion of the truth that they have tried to put the true position more publicly and formally. For example, six of America's most prominent medical groups – The American Medical Association, The American Academy of Pediatrics, The American Academy of Family Physicians, The American Academy of Child & Adolescent Psychiatry, The American Psychiatric Association and The American Psychological Association – are now so concerned that they have made a Joint Statement on the Impact of Entertainment Violence on Children for a US Congressional Public Health Summit. Here are some highlights:

'There are some in the entertainment industry who maintain that
1) violent programming is harmless because no studies exist that prove a connection between violent entertainment and aggressive behavior in children, and
2) young people know that television, movies, and video games are simply fantasy.

'Unfortunately, they are wrong on both counts.

'At this time, well over 1000 studies – including reports from the Surgeon General's office, the National Institute of Mental Health, and numerous studies conducted by leading figures within our medical and public health organizations – our own members – point overwhelmingly to a causal connection between media violence and aggressive behavior in some children. The conclusion of the public health community, based on over 30 years of research, is that viewing entertainment violence can lead to increases in aggressive attitudes, values and behavior, particularly in children. Its effects are measurable and long-lasting.

'Children exposed to violent programming at a young age have a higher tendency for violent and aggressive behavior later in life...It can decrease the likelihood that one will take action on behalf of a victim when violence occurs.'

And in considering violent computer and video games they added 'the negative impact may be significantly more severe than that wrought by television...'[16]

The American Psychological Society was so concerned at the way the link between television and violence was being massaged in media reports that they selected and commissioned eight scientists to analyse the influence of media violence on youth as 'an important issue of national interest'. They concluded unequivocally '...the scientific debate over whether media violence increases aggression and violence is essentially over...' They voiced concern over 'the disparity between on one side, the actual research findings and, on the other side, the intransigent assertions made by a number of vocal critics. That is, although research shows the adverse effects of media violence, and there is increasing consensus among researchers in this area about these effects, the critics continue to pronounce that media violence cannot be affecting youth'.[1]

One of the more colourful examples of the way in which television influences violent behaviour was recently played out in a British courtroom. The television viewer and defendant, 19-year-old Adrian Brooksbanks, was sentenced by a British court to seven years for violent robbery and assault against elderly women. What seemed most ironic was that the court accepted that Mr Brooksbanks was literally inspired by the BBC's flagship crime-prevention programme *Crimewatch*. After watching a couple of episodes re-enacting attacks on older women, he realised 'just how easy it was to mug old ladies', and after mugging one 79-year-old

woman twice in three weeks, he began specialising in octo-
genarians, finally moving on to 90-year-old Louisa Wood,
whom he held hostage in her own home. He punched her in
the face, held her in a bear hug and placed his hand over her
mouth while pinching her nose as he implemented the plans
he borrowed from the crime-prevention show: 'I will kill you
if I don't get £30.' The show's catchphrase is 'Don't have
nightmares.'

Another way the influence of television violence is played
down is to claim that because the statistical effects reported
in a study are small, the everyday practical or public health
effects are small. Not true. Statistically, small effects can have
very large practical consequences. In the case of television, its
effects on violence can be enormous for at least three different reasons. First, almost everyone is exposed to this risk
factor. Second, the effects are likely to accumulate within the
individual with repeated exposure. And third, 'even the
short-lived effects of a single exposure can add significant
amounts of aggression and violence to society because at any
given waking hour a large proportion of the population
either is currently being exposed to violent media or has been
exposed to such violence in the last 20 minutes'.[1] The fact
that estimates of the size of the effect of media violence are
typically in the small-to-moderate range should not mislead
people into thinking that the overall impact of media violence
on aggressive and violent behaviour is small to moderate.
Because of the large numbers of youths exposed to many
hours of media violence, even a small effect can have
extremely large consequences. In Britain, a major review

published in *The Lancet* calls for television violence to be considered a 'public health' issue. The report identifies 'an effect size that has a substantial effect on public health'. The researchers consider the failure of parents to monitor their children's choice of television programmes as a form of 'child maltreatment' and abuse.[17]

Most of us don't realise that the size of the media-violence effect is equal to or larger than the size of many medical effects. A paper in *Science* describes it as 'larger than the effect of wearing a condom has on decreasing the risk of HIV. It's larger than the correlation between exposure to lead and decreased IQ levels in kids. It's larger than the effects of exposure to asbestos. It's larger than the effect of second hand smoke on cancer'.[18]

Britain recently achieved its highest murder rate since records began over 100 years ago. Rates of attempted murder and violent assault are also at record levels. Police say random killings are rising, and the proportion of murders in which the victim is not known to the killer has nearly doubled in the past decade. But body counts don't reveal the increased potential for GBH or murder that many people sense. Some people stay indoors at night because they're scared to go out. Ironically, this gives a false statistical impression of the crime rate because they're safely locked indoors. A group of scientists suggests that in trying to reduce violence in a given society, reducing the amount of violent media in the home 'may be the least expensive risk factor to modify – it costs little to choose non-violent forms of entertainment for oneself or one's children'.[1]

In the way the media have dealt with news of television causing health risks to children, they have been a 'co-factor' in massaging or under-reporting the link between television and violence. Next time you read an article by a journalist who 'examines the evidence' or hear an actor, television presenter or 'celebrity' say 'I watched lots of violent telly and I didn't turn out to be a mass murderer,' or a politician advocating more 'media literacy' as an answer, and every time you hear a further 'debate' on whether television causes violence, ask yourself a very straightforward question: who would you rather trust with our society's health and well-being and with your child's life – a writer striking an interesting journalistic pose because it looks open-minded and provocative? Or perhaps an actor, television presenter or highly qualified 'celebrity'? What about a representative from the BBC or ABC? Or an all-things-to-all-people politician who always has to consider re-election without criticising the electorate's favourite waking activity? (And remember that more people voted for 'Will and Gareth' in the television final of *Pop Idol* than for the entire Labour Party in the last two general elections.) Or perhaps a media-friendly professor involved in 'learning how children as individuals and as differentiated viewers interact with developing forms of media' who when confronted with evidence of television causing violence counsels 'caution in interpreting these one-dimensional results' and considers the issue as being stoked up by polemics, and whose research is often indirectly funded in some interesting way by the television, computer or video games industry.

Or would you rather trust groups of eminent professors of

public health, child medicine, psychiatry, family medicine and psychology, whose life's work is to protect our children and our society from disease and damage? What could these health care professionals possibly gain from claiming that television causes violence? Money? There's no 'industry' to fund or corrupt researchers into finding that television causes violence. There's no benefactor to finance a move to watch less television or less violent television. Glory? Hardly. Telling people that their favourite pastime is bad for society doesn't win a scientist many friends or research dollars.

Future Research into Television and Violence

The direction of future research will be in looking at the changes that take place in our brain as we watch violent television, and asking whether there are any lasting changes in brain function. Two studies have recently found disturbing evidence that violent television, films and video games affect children's and teenagers' brains in a way that may make them violent in future. One study used functional magnetic resonance imaging to monitor brain activity and see whether different areas of young people's brains reacted to bloody boxing scenes provided by Sylvester Stallone in *Rocky IV* as opposed to calm films of baby animals playing or blank screens. The researchers were surprised to find that in all children, watching *Rocky IV* activated a section of the brain that is also believed to hold long-term memories of traumatic events. That is where rape victims store memories of being attacked, for example, and where war veterans with post-traumatic stress disorder store their experiences in battle. The study's author, Professor John Murray, recently testified before the US Senate that the brain 'treats entertainment violence as something real...[and] stores this violence as long-term memory'. He also commented that 'People dismiss entertainment violence as something passing or not very important but that's not true. The brain is treating it as serious stuff.'[19] Perhaps neurological changes which leave the child unable to distinguish between fictional and actual violence are why 'media literacy interventions' to counteract the effects of watching television violence simply do not work, and why parents should not assume they can minimise the effects of what their child is seeing by discussing it with them (see page 103).[1]

Another approach has been to look at the brains of non-aggressive adolescents versus those who have been diagnosed as having disruptive behavioural disorders (DBD) as they watch moderately violent scenes on a screen. Unlike the non-aggressive adolescents, the adolescents with DBD showed less brain activity in their frontal lobe, which is responsible for decision-making, behaviour and impulse control, attention and a variety of other executive functions. What was even more interesting was that the way the 'normal' adolescents' brains reacted to this new televised material was related to the amount of violent media they had watched in the past years.[20] A new follow-up study has found that screen violence changes the frontal lobe brain function of 'normal adolescents' who were previously well-behaved, to the brain patterns of aggressive children with DBD.[21]

The more I travel and the more research I read, the more

I'm convinced that television does indeed cause at least 'half of all murders in the industrialised world'. I've found that where television arrives, violence, murder and rape follow. And I agree with professor Joanne Cantor who was invited to report to the US Subcommittee on Science, Technology and Space 2003: 'Our children's heavy immersion in today's media culture is a large-scale societal experiment with potentially horrifying results (and with hardly a child left behind to serve in the control condition).'[22]

So, why haven't we acted before? After all, a huge body of evidence going back decades has found a strong connection between television viewing and aggression. One of the reasons lies with the profit motive. Few television shows will break even in the domestic market. This means that programme-makers sell their shows abroad – from which more than half of their money comes – if they wish to make a profit. But selling shows abroad requires a proven story formula that travels well. The most common formulas are sex and violence. Sex travels well. An Albanian or a Bolivian can understand Pamela Anderson in her bikini on *Baywatch* as well as a New Yorker can – hence *Baywatch* was until recently the most watched show in the world. Violence travels well. When Bruce Willis rains bullets on the bad guys, a viewer in Beijing can understand what is going on as well as a viewer in Bognor Regis. That's why Saddam Hussein's favourite video is *The Godfather*, not *Lost in Translation*.[23]

Violence is a natural televisual genre: it's image-driven. There's an overwhelming global marketing imperative in favour of the simple, the naked and the bloody. Cheap to produce, easy to distribute – violence is the surest road to profit. And programme schedulers are also bound by the bottom line and are obliged to buy. Slapstick also travels well. Norman Wisdom, I discovered, is an icon in Iran.

After reading about the worst aspects of human behaviour there are, however, some life-affirming insights that have also come from brain imaging. Scientists at Emory University Medical School wanted to look at human altruism and asked: what makes most of us trust, befriend and help one another? Why is violence, even towards strangers, the exception rather than the rule? What motivates a Good Samaritan? They took functional MRI brain scans of 17 subjects playing a video version of The Prisoner's Dilemma, a game that gives players high rewards for betraying a colleague who trusts them. Players receive a lesser reward if they remain true to each other, and no reward at all if they trust and are betrayed. Yet, despite the known benefits of letting someone down, the most common outcome in The Prisoner's Dilemma is mutual trust and co-operation. Why? The researchers believe that social co-operation intrinsically pleases us, switching on a neural 'reward circuit' that is hardwired in to our brains. 'Our study shows, for the first time, that social cooperation is intrinsically rewarding to the human brain, even in the face of pressures to the contrary,' said Gregory S. Berns, professor of psychiatry. 'It suggests that the altruistic drive to cooperate is biologically embedded – either genetically programmed or acquired through socialization during childhood and adolescence.'[24] However, it's important to remember that the subjects were all female. But it's a start.

FIVE
MEET THE
TELLY TUBBIES
How Television Makes Us Fat

'You're nuthin but a lazy fat-assed disgrace...Just look at you...you disgust me...you're still fat...it just ain't good enough!' The television fat-club drill sergeant is so disappointed and angry at the rather substantial woman before him that his nostrils are flaring. It's clear he's not a chubby-chaser. The camera cuts to our camp, perma-tanned host who asks the fat teams to sit on the scales of justice: a giant fat-measuring see-saw with several seats on each side. Once the participants are (widely) seated, the scale teeters back and forth, finally resting in a tilted position. It's clear that team A is fatter than team B. Perma-tan man then gives us the raw scores: 'Team A 678 pounds, team B 589 pounds.' The drill sergeant shakes his head in dismay at the slovenly state of his charges. Television is remarkably resourceful. The world's medical authorities now say unequivocally that watching television makes us fat. So what do the television networks do? They make a meal out of obesity.

In the same way that the British used to poke fun at Americans' overflowing emotions, they also marvelled at the Yanks' ever-expanding appetites and waistlines. But this has now come back to haunt them as they too are letting it all hang out. Britain is now Europe's fattest country, where overweight and clinical obesity affect two-thirds of the adult male and more than half of the adult female population. And childhood obesity is rising twice as quickly as for adults. The Government's Chief Medical Officer and the Food Standards Agency have warned that due to this epidemic of obesity, children 'may die before their parents'.[1] The authors of a study in the *New England Journal of Medicine* say 'the tsunami of childhood obesity has not yet hit the shore...the consequences to public health are potentially disastrous. Imagine a heart attack or kidney failure becoming a relatively common condition of young adulthood'. The study warns of a cut in US life expectancy and predicts 'A nine-month fall in life span would be greater than the negative effect of all deaths from accidents, murder and suicide.'[2] And television is now being identified as a direct, independent cause of obesity. The European Union's Statistical Office has just found that when it comes to watching television, British men are Europe's second biggest couch potatoes, spending half of their free time glued to the screen. Hungarian men are the 'winners'.[3] Another global study concludes that 'Britons watch more TV but read less than any other country in Europe.'[4]

Television's Effects on Metabolism and Appetite

The act of watching television is unique in its ability to fatten us up. Obviously television displaces a tremendous amount of physical activity but it is also thought to actually reduce a child's resting metabolism more than if they were to lie there and do absolutely nothing. In the study 'Effects of television on metabolic rate: potential implications for childhood obesity', children's and adolescents' metabolic rates were 'significantly lower' while they watched television than when they merely rested. On average, they burned the equivalent of 211 kilocalories less per day than if they did absolutely nothing. The authors concluded that 'television viewing has a fairly profound lowering effect of metabolic rate and may be a mechanism for the relationship between obesity and amount of television viewing'.[5]

Watching television also makes both children and adults eat more, even if they are not physically hungry. The title of a new study about to be published speaks for itself: 'Television Viewing Nearly Adds an Additional Meal to Daily Intake.'[6]

Television also has subliminal effects on your appetite which may literally cause you to take more bites per minute (BPM), to take larger mouthfuls and to eat more food than you would otherwise. Just the effect of the television soundtrack can make you eat more. Background music is known to make people eat faster or slower and to eat more or less. For example, one experiment used three different musical backgrounds while people ate a meal.

- ❑ The subjects in the no-music background took four bites per minute, finished their meal in 40 minutes, and 33 per cent of them asked for second helpings.
- ❑ The lively music group averaged five bites per minute and finished eating in 31 minutes. Half the group asked for second helpings.
- ❑ The subjects who ate their meal to calming flute music took nearly an hour to finish, averaged 3.2 bites per minute, took smaller bites and not even one asked for second helpings. Not only that, most of them left a quarter of their food on their plates.

The study implies that if you want to eat less, make sure the soundtrack while you eat is relaxing music. Mealtimes are probably not the right time to play the latest dance tracks.

If you add a bright changing light pattern to faster music, the effect can be intensified.

In one experiment set in a restaurant, people who were led to tables with bright lighting and upbeat music ate more and ate faster than the people who were led to tables with dim lighting and soft music. Now you know why fast-food establishments have bright lighting, vibrant-coloured decor and energising music.[7]

One of the mechanisms by which television makes us eat more is through disrupting our brain's ability to respond to 'food cues', in other words to tell us when we are full. Television tampers with our attentional resources, causing our brain to monitor external 'non-food cues'– the television screen – as opposed to internal body cues telling us that we have stuffed ourselves and should stop eating. Experiments reveal that when we're distracted in this way we even continue to salivate unnaturally in response to more and more food when normally we wouldn't.[8]

All of these effects are taking place at a time in our history when at least half of dinners are taken in front of the television.

Even on non-commercial television networks we're constantly exposed to images of food. And recent physiological evidence suggests that just seeing tempting food can enhance our actual hunger by increasing the release of dopamine, the neurotransmitter associated with pleasure and reward. The impact of this effect on eating can be quite powerful. You may remember that dopamine is also central to attention (see pages 27 and 108).[9]

How Programme Content Affects How Much We Eat

Most people, perhaps unknowingly, watch television to feel different in some way, to relax, to be stimulated, to feel more cheerful, to be frightened, to be moved in some way from the emotional position you were in before you turned the television on. While the effects on appetite and metabolism mentioned so far are in reaction to the medium of television, the content of the programme can also influence how much you eat. For example, one study found that watching a frightening or highly charged film on television made women more likely to raid the fridge.

Your physiological and emotional reactions to what you see on television can cause significant shifts in the neurotransmitters which regulate appetite and mood.

The increase in the number of television channels has made competition for ratings cut-throat. Just the invention of the remote control has enabled viewers to surf and audition each channel briefly until something grabs them. That something is a more highly spiced, arresting type of programming. I recently saw an example of *Oprah*. As I turned the television on, I saw a still photograph on-screen of a real bullet-riddled car window. And I heard the actual voice recording of a young mother really being shot to death as she called the emergency services for help. She had already been shot and was bleeding to death, pleading for help. The scene cut back to the studio, where Oprah talked live to the victim's mother about her feelings and thoughts on the matter. On another random occasion, I turned on the television, and the BBC1 news reporter Ben Brown was on a beach destroyed by the Asian tsunami. He approached a grandmother gazing upon her missing family, missing village, her entire missing life, trying to make sense of it. She sobbed, cried out and clung to Mr Brown in desperation, who hugged her somewhat awkwardly in front of the camera.

In both cases, it's hard not to stare and be moved. My neurotransmitters are moving right along with me. Any stress, fear, anxiety or anger can, for example, increase the level of a transmitter called neuropeptide Y, which in turn can vastly increase my cravings for refined sugars and carbohydrates.

The brain doesn't want to feel stressed, anxious, depressed or guilty. It immediately seeks equilibrium and pleasure from the things you've trained it to seek when these emotions surface. Refined carbohydrates and fats make you feel calm, temporarily numbing the unpleasant feelings by releasing powerful mood-altering neurotransmitters. For women there's the additional dimension of the menstrual cycle. When oestrogen levels drop and progesterone levels increase (as is the case during PMS), serotonin levels can drop. This can increase cravings for sweets, chocolates, pastries, biscuits and other sugary carbohydrates, which increases the brain's concentrations of tryptophan, the building block for serotonin. So the impact on the appetite of a premenstrual woman watching emotive television is only accentuated during this time.

Lack of exposure to daylight can also depress serotonin levels and may cause increased feelings of depression and craving for carbohydrates. I'm writing this chapter in Helsinki in early January – I'm living the theory. It's dark most of the time. There's little inducement to go outside. And television is a further four-hour-a-day inducement to keep you indoors away from scarce daylight, which could be slightly cheering. And as you eat more instant-gratification processed carbohydrates in front of the emotive television, you are also physically passive.

The Consummate Immobiliser

Television's special draw – 'strategic attentional inertia' (see page 24) – along with its ability to neurologically subdue, marks it out as the consummate immobiliser. And the route from pressing the ON button to developing a more substantial bottom has now been mapped out. The Scottish Executive funded scientists to look specifically at the effect of 'an imposed sedentary routine' like watching television, on food intake, appetite and energy balance in lean men. Energy balance (EB) means how many calories you've eaten versus how many you've burned. A positive EB means you have a calorie surplus ultimately appearing as body fat, while a negative EB means you have a calorie deficit, causing your waistline to go into a recession. As you sit watching television, your body should ideally realise that you don't need as many calories because you are immobile, and it should compensate by decreasing your appetite to ensure you eat fewer calories. But this does not happen. Instead, the scientists found that this 'sedentary routine does not induce a compensatory reduction of energy intake and leads to a significantly positive EB, most of which is stored as fat'.[10]

And to pile on the misery, an Australian study of 8,300 adults involving six medical institutions found 'a deleterious effect of TV time on the risk of abnormal glucose metabolism in adults'. This applied to people who watch 50 per cent less television than the average Briton or American and 'was also associated with an increased risk of new type 2 diabetes... Population strategies to reduce risk of abnormal glucose metabolism should focus on reducing sedentary behaviours, such as TV time'.[11]

Type 2 diabetes is also linked with obesity. The *Journal of the American Medical Association* reports that for every two hours a day spent watching television, there is a 23 per cent increase in obesity and a 14 per cent increase in the risk of Type 2 diabetes.[12] Yet the Australian research also found that only two-and-a-half hours of physical activity a week had a 'protective effect...on the risk of abnormal glucose metabolism'.

In *The Lancet* the first study to assess how much physical activity children do at ages three and five revealed that most youngsters do not move at all for 80 per cent of the day. Many are active for only 20 minutes a day. The activity patterns of the children were then shown to a separate group of scientists who were asked to identify the people involved. The study's leader, Dr John Reilly, explains 'They wrongly guessed these children aged three and five years were desk-bound office workers. It was a truly shocking finding. They have the lifestyle of middle-aged adults, they are old before their time. They are more likely to suffer from heart disease, diabetes, osteoporosis and other health problems.'[13]

As an exhausted father of four I can say one thing with certainty: children both in my sitting room and around the world are naturally unstoppable, perhaps unfairly endowed with the energy and vitality that I'd like to have. Or as my grandmother used to say, youth is wasted on the young. I am not using journalistic or dramatic licence when I tell you honestly that as I write this very paragraph my wife rings to inform me, not for the first time, that: 'I just can't do anything – because anything I do is instantly undone by them! They just won't stop running around, doing naughty things!' It takes a tranquilliser as powerful as Valium to keep a child inactive for 80 per cent of the day. So what on earth could compel a child to sit still for such long periods? The authors of the study in *The Lancet* mention television.

And the links with television continue. A study of girls aged five and nine in the medical journal *Obesity Research* found that even 'In families where neither parent was over-weight, television was the only significant predictor of girls' increase in Body Mass Index.'[14] Another study of 12–13-year-old boys and girls again finds 'Significant associations between Body Mass Index and hours of television watched per evening...'[15]

Again, this obesity occurs when children watch even less television than the national average. Remember it isn't merely television displacing children's physical activity. Television does more to fatten you up than reading or listening to the radio. It contains special ingredients. And television viewing begets more television viewing.

Television, Sleep Deprivation and Obesity

A completely unexpected link between television and both child and adult levels of body fat is just coming to light. The popular image of fat people spending more time sleeping the day away may be completely the opposite of the truth. New research is finding a link between obesity and a lack of sleep. And it may be no coincidence that as we now get less sleep we've grown fatter. Three studies, including one involving 1.1 million people, found that getting less sleep is associated with having a higher body mass index (BMI). One study found a completely inverse relationship – the less sleep the person got, the fatter they were.[16] What is emerging is the discovery that sleep directly influences two vital appetite-controlling, fat-producing/fat-burning hormones.[17] People who sleep less have lower levels of leptin, a hormone that acts to suppress your appetite and stimulates calorie burning. At the same time, less sleep causes an increase in ghrelin, another hormone that has the opposite effect – stimulating your appetite as well as your fat production and body growth. Scientists have concluded, 'The changes in hunger are proportional to the changes in these hormones. If you are sleep-deprived, you will crave high-carb foods and will need an iron will to resist.' Biscuits, sweets and cakes are favourites.[18] Remember the study at Oxford University, which found that children who have televisions in their bedroom are being deprived of up to a month's sleep a year (see page 35). And there's the study at Columbia University finding that young adolescents who watch three or more hours of television a day end up 'at a significantly elevated risk for frequent sleep problems' as adults (see page 35). Imagine what this may be doing to their leptin and ghrelin levels.

Obesity, Sex and Fertility

The implications of television causing girls to be overweight go further than we may think. Overweight girls are now thought to reach puberty earlier. Furthermore, the earlier a girl reaches puberty, the earlier she is likely to have sex. And British girls are having more of it than ever, at even younger ages. The UK has the highest rate of underage pregnancy in Western Europe, twice that of Germany, three times higher than France and six times that of the Netherlands. A quarter of sexually active 13-year-olds have had four or more sexual partners.

While television has played a significant role in causing British children under 13 to have more sex and possibly the highest rate of pregnancy in the Western world, adult couples who want to have children are finding it more difficult to conceive. Television is helping to make us less fertile and the birth rate is dropping significantly, down to 1.7 children per couple. One of the reasons for reduced fertility lies in the fact that television is now considered a direct independent cause of obesity. Obesity reduces fertility. In short, people who watch less television are more physically active, have more sex and are more fertile.

Obesity and Health

So, television is highly fattening and a great way to develop Type 2 diabetes. And all this can be achieved by watching as little as two hours a day, 50 per cent less than the average person. The scientists in the various studies I've cited use the term 'excessive viewing' to describe this. But how do you then describe the 'average' person who watches four or five hours per day?

Another way to look at this is to consider that if the average viewer allocated just one of their four hours of television per day to any kind of physical activity, even housework or walking the dog, they could make a big impact on their weight and reduce their risk of having a heart attack. What many people don't realise is that exercise also seems to activate the body's immune system and is believed to play a significant role in staving off the onset, or worsening, of many types of cancer.

An editorial in the *British Medical Journal* explored the relationship between physical activity and cancer. It noted that exercise has significant effects on several functions of the human body that may influence cancer risk. These effects include changes in cardiovascular capacity, energy balance, pulmonary capacity, immune function, bowel motility, antioxidant defence, hormone levels and DNA repair.

The *BMJ* also points out that in the past decade alone, over 200 population-based studies have linked physical activity to a reduced cancer risk. The cancers that have been researched most extensively are: bowel, breast, endometrium, prostate, testicular and lung. They concluded in light of the fact that we are becoming more physically inactive '...doctors should advocate moderate endurance-type activity, such as walking and cycling. As well as reducing the risk of chronic diseases such as coronary heart disease and non-insulin dependent diabetes, such physical activity does seem to protect against some cancers.'[19]

Steven N. Blair, an epidemiologist with the Cooper Institute for Aerobics Research in Dallas, Texas, is studying the effects of exercise on lung cancer. His results suggest that higher fitness levels are associated with a lower risk of developing the disease. In his study, unfit men were about twice as likely to die of lung cancer as fit men. His research found that moderately fit men had a 20 per cent lower risk of dying from lung cancer compared with men who were not fit. And men who were highly fit had a 60 per cent lower risk than men who were not fit. This appeared true even after allowing for smoking habits.[20]

Teenage girls who sacrifice a small amount of their television watching time and do some exercise can reduce the risk of developing breast cancer by an average of 20 per cent, according to research published in the *European Journal of Cancer Prevention*. The scientists announced 'Each 1-hour increase of recreational physical activity/week during adolescence was associated with a 3% risk reduction.'[21] A second study, which appeared in the *International Journal of Cancer*, reported that women who exercised for more than four hours a week, for 12 or more years, were 24 per cent less likely to develop breast cancer than were more sedentary women.[22]

Cutting back on television is healthier than joining a slimming club. But if you use a small amount of this new spare time to go for a 30-minute walk, you will lose weight while also gaining tremendous protection from an array of other diseases.

Scientists from as far apart as China and Mexico are becoming increasingly concerned that television is in itself a specific, independent cause of obesity, linked to a wide variety of fatal diseases. Mexico's health ministry was recently shocked to discover that its population's rate of obesity had risen by 170 per cent in a single decade, nearing levels witnessed in the United States: 'Odds ratios of obesity were 12% higher for each hour of television program viewing per day.'[23] While in China, a study of 10,000 people found that 'Each hourly increment of television viewing is associated with a significant increase in the prevalence of obesity. CONCLUSION: Time spent watching television is directly related to an increase in obesity, television viewing is an independent factor for obesity.'[24]

The Stanford University Center for Research in Disease Prevention in the United States has issued a statement that 'Television viewing is a cause of increased body fatness and reducing television viewing is a promising strategy for preventing childhood obesity.'[25] And at the US Government's Centers for Disease Control, Dr William Dietz, Director of Division of Nutrition and Physical Activity, finds that six out of ten children have a risk factor for heart disease by the time they are 10 years old. His message is unequivocal:

'The more TV children view, the more likely they are to be overweight. Reduction in TV viewing constitutes the single most effective way for children to lose weight.'[26]

Some scientists now propose that the link between television and obesity shares the same mechanism as the link between television and Attention Deficit Hyperactivity Disorder. They see television as providing an 'oversupply of information' which leads to 'environmental oversampling syndrome' – in other words too much stimulation.[27]

Despite the insurmountable evidence of television causing obesity, it's unlikely to have escaped your notice that very few overweight people are used in television programmes. Despite countless scenes featuring whippet-like characters such as Monica in *Friends* eating chocolate chip ice cream, many of the actors are permarexic – always clinically underweight – and often suffer serious eating disorders. As a result, both children and adults are repeatedly given the message that what we eat, how much we eat or when we eat has no impact on our weight or health.

And in the way television creates and drives clothing and hairstyles, it also inadvertently creates food fashions. For example, a study by a British supermarket has discovered that customers' appetites are influenced by the American television shows they watch. The sudden increase in sales of fattening foods such as doughnuts to eat for breakfast, blueberry muffins, cookies, maple syrup and beefburgers was found to be directly related to the American television programmes customers recently watched. It seems the British television viewer has subconsciously fallen prey to aspirational eating. The supermarket was quick to capitalise on this by slapping promotional stickers on various foods which read 'As Eaten In...'[28]

Television and Alcohol

While food is a major prop on American television the major prop in British programmes is the pub bar. The portrayal of alcohol in British programmes influences alcoholism and obesity, and death by liver damage, heart disease and murder. In fact, binge-drinking is costing Britain £10 billion a year. A report in 2005 found that of all patients at hospital A & E departments, 40 per cent are drunk. After midnight, this rises to 70 per cent: 'All of this means that people with non-alcohol-related problems who need emergency attention are at a disadvantage.'[29] A study at Leicester University has pointed out that while you hardly ever see smoking on screen now (0.9 cigarettes per hour in British soaps) as it's not PC, boozing is the constant lazy recourse of the British scriptwriter. The proportion of drinking scenes has doubled in the last 20 years (seven boozing scenes per hour).[30] The Institute of Alcohol Studies is convinced that soap operas, where the pub is portrayed as the centre of the community, actually cause many youngsters to go on binge-drinking sessions. As television has been remarkably successful in changing drinking and driving behaviour, binge-drinking could be another successful televisual social project.

It seems readily accepted that young people like pubs and clubs; it's part of British cultural life. This is quite different to America, where young people's exposure to alcohol is a far more serious matter. Despite folksy notions to the contrary, the earlier young people are exposed to alcohol, the more likely they are to become heavy drinkers or alcoholics.[31] Delaying a young person's exposure to drinking is more likely to prevent this. By the way, there are scientists and alcohol 'education and awareness' bodies who will speak in forked tongue, telling you differently. They are funded by the billion-pound alcohol industry, while those who believe teenagers shouldn't drink have no such financial backing. But it isn't just a case of the pub appearing too often and as a positive role model on our television screens. As fictional pubs appear on our screens to attract viewers, real pubs are installing wide-screen televisions to attract and retain drinking customers.

Alcohol and behaviour is an enormous topic. Most people don't understand why alcohol is particularly fattening, sending our energy balance (see page 150) into high surplus figures. A single gram of alcohol has nearly twice the calories of a gram of pure sugar. While a gram of fat has nine calories, alcohol has seven. So on a nutritional basis alone, alcohol is fattening. However, there is some evidence that the hidden effect of drinking is to slow down your metabolism– the rate at which you burn calories – by a third, making you store fat. And it is this unbeatable combination that isn't fully appreciated.[32]

Beyond the notion of the passive 'couch potato', television actually makes us fat and more drunk. But if television does this to the flesh, what does it do to the spirit?

SIX
SEXUAL
STEALING
How Television is Lowering our Libidos

Architecture is thought in some way to reflect culture. And so I was intrigued by the architect and writer James Howard Kunstler's thoughts on the design of the typical house. American houses have what builders call a 'family room'; in Britain it's the 'living room'. Kunstler, however, exposes this as a euphemism of the trade. 'Family rooms are really television rooms. People don't want to admit that all the family does together is watch television. But it is the family's chief connection with the real world. The physical envelope of the house itself no longer connects their lives to the outside.'[1] And television causes a loss of connection between the family members living in the house.

But there is a new trend seen as a backlash against this central 'family room' with its television-centred, enforced camaraderie. After decades of the family room or open floor plan where domestic life revolved around a big central space, major builders and top architects are walling people off. At the recent International Builders Show in Las Vegas, the showcase 'Ultimate Family Home' hardly had a family room. It was broken up into a 'media centre' and separate 'home management centre', which itself was divided by a counter-top. The boy's personal playroom had its own 42-inch plasma television, and the girl's bedroom had a secret mirrored door leading to a 'hideaway karaoke room'. There was even a separate room under the stairs for the family dog. The designer refers to it as 'the ultimate home for families who don't want anything to do with one another' and the director of research for the National Association of Home Builders sees the new generation of designs which incorporate 'Internet alcoves' as 'good for the dysfunctional family'.[2]

The rise of this new antisocial architecture has been made possible partly by the light weight and small size of new televisions, DVDs and computers. In 1953, Admiral colour television sets were the first to go on sale in the United States at $1,175, the same price as a Chevrolet – a quarter of the average income. Today a much better set costs only one five-hundredth of the average annual income at around $60. While in Britain, people can still remember 'taking delivery of the colour telly' – it took two strong men and a lot of money. And if you didn't have your own set you would visit others for the evening who did. Today you can put one in your shopping trolley at your local supermarket for only £59.

In remembering his culinary coming of age during the summer spent in France in 1966, the writer and chef Anthony

Bourdain writes 'Television was a Big Event. At seven o'clock, when the two national stations would come on air, my Oncle Gustav would solemnly emerge from his room with a key chained to his hip and ceremoniously unlock the cabinet doors that covered the screen.'[3] From 2004 to 2005, prices of televisions have dropped considerably, especially for small plasma flat-screen televisions. Now every member of the family can have their own set, so there's no need to share and negotiate over what the family will watch this evening. William Sherman, chairman of the department of architecture and landscape architecture at the University of Virginia, sees the new architectural trend as making families more isolated and lonelier than ever. 'People don't even gather in the same spot to watch TV anymore. It's sad.'[2]

To think that television has changed the structure of houses invites the question: how has television influenced the structure and dynamics of the family? If television has neurological and metabolic effects and is a powerful influence on behaviours ranging from appetite to murder, how does it influence our everyday relationships at home, particularly between men and women?

Television Time Versus Family Time

Our divorce rate has risen along with greater television ownership. And as the number of hours we watch increases, the duration of our relationships decreases. Obviously television isn't entirely responsible for society's marital and family breakdowns. However, both the medium and the content have conspired to separate people in the home geographically, emotionally and sexually. More than anything else, couples spend the majority of their time together watching television. And they spend even more time watching television alone. The British Government now refers to 'The main shared activity – watching television.' Parents now have more eye contact with characters on the television screen than with one another as the television set coaxes marriage into an unholy *ménage à trois* but without the additional sex. And a new study in the journal *Science* indicates that they may prefer it that way. Professor Daniel Kahneman, a Nobel prize-winner at Princeton University, and an interdisciplinary team of psychologists and economists developed a more accurate evaluation of 'national well-being' to enable government and medical authorities to gauge and plan policy according to the requirements of individuals and society. Nine hundred and nine employed women were assessed and asked to rate their favourite activities in terms of time spent and how much they enjoyed each activity. Many observers were surprised that watching television was rated higher by women than was spending time with their own husbands.[4]

Many people now talk of the benefits of 'interactive' television and the Internet because it is used for communication. But even that has damaged family relationships. A detailed classic two-year study of 73 households examined 'the effects of the Internet on social involvement and psychological well-being'. The families used the Internet extensively for communication. Yet the researchers concluded 'Nonetheless, greater use of the Internet was associated with declines in participants' communication with family members in the household, declines in the size of their social circle, and increases in their depression and loneliness.' They also considered that 'watching TV causes both social disengagement and worsening of mood...and limited face-to-face social interaction'. Both the Internet and television were found to cause 'poor quality of life and diminished physical and psychological health. When people have more social contact, they are happier and healthier, both physically and mentally'.[5]

Television's Family Role Models

But television time doesn't merely detract from the interaction that could take place between men and women. The content of the programmes also goes some way in undermining the very basis of a relationship in a number of ways.

Distorting Relationships

If the 1950s and 60s bathed society in idealised images of the television family – 'Honey, I'm home!' – times have changed. Unhappy relationships, along with the scenery of changing partners, now dominate programming. Who would prefer to watch a wife kiss her husband on the cheek and ask: 'How was your day at the office?' when you can watch her kick him in the balls and scream 'Get out you bastard!!'? Broadcasters explain that their shows are 'merely reflecting the changing nature of relationships in society'. They're lying. They are actually reflecting the fact that discord makes for more compelling television and therefore higher ratings. Obviously, there are many unhappy relationships, but there are also many contented relationships. Believe it or not, I actually know of at least four contented couples within 10 paces of my front door. Would this make compelling television? Of course not. Contentment isn't photogenic so television enlarges a small snapshot of reality, making the prevalence of bitter marital discord seem larger than life. But of course we know it's only make-believe and take it all with a pinch of salt...don't we?

Enter the Supermum

And if the television in the 50s and 60s projected the accommodating, apron-clad, biscuit-baking contented housewife, the past 15 years have wiped that smile off her face. In an oblique take on the modern empowered woman, the status of the television housewife or full-time mother has taken a dive. Full-time mothers are now often portrayed as unfulfilled, killing time until they can get back to work and do something really worthwhile. A 'successful' woman, as seen on television, is a slender young professional woman or just a slender young woman. But the image of a woman whose success is defined by being a wonderful mother is conspicuous by its absence. Like the contented couple, the full-time mother who derives a subtle, more enduring form of reward and satisfaction and a deeper contentment lacks televisual excitement and an immediacy. Contentment is hard to capture on camera. It lasts considerably longer than 24.6 minutes, so it never even makes it to the casting couch.

There is, however, a variation on this: the 'supermum'.

The high-achieving, full-time professional woman who has children at home. The print media often use this term when describing celebrities with young children or, for example, cabinet minister, Ruth Kelly, Secretary of State for Education and Skills. Ruth Kelly is married with four young children and a nanny. Upon her appointment Ms Kelly appeared on television screens and in newspapers with her children, accompanied by the caption 'Supermum'.

It isn't clear why a mother with a glamorous, highly demanding, full-time job who is away from her young children for most of the day is portrayed as a 'supermum' – while a full-time mother who is with her children is neither portrayed nor described as being in any way 'super'. Wouldn't it seem more accurate to describe a female cabinet minister with four young children as a 'super Secretary of State'? Or the very slim actress with a nanny who flits from Barcelona to LA, as a 'super-slender celeb'?

And wouldn't it therefore seem more accurate to describe a full-time mother who never had a career, or who put her career aside intentionally to bring up her children, as a 'supermum'?

By pointing out this media phenomenon, one runs the risk of being accused of wanting women to remain in the kitchen, tied to the sink, barefoot and pregnant. But the point is rather the reverse. Television has discriminated against the vast majority of mothers. And by eroding the status of the full-time mother, television is underplaying the importance of children in our society. Bringing up young children well is, in the scheme of things, rather important. This is also not intended to 'make working mothers feel guilty'. If anything, it is intended to make television producers feel guilty for devaluing the standing of the full-time mother on screen. But of course we know television is only make-believe and take it all with a pinch of salt...don't we?

And when full-time mothers do make a rare appearance on television they are not portrayed as sexy, just mumsy. In real life, many women often feel less attractive as full-time mothers, and this is reinforced by their portrayal on television.

On television, in the transition from woman to mother, a woman apparently loses her sensuality and identity as a sexual being. Men, on the other hand, are having none of it. Unlike television producers, men find full-time mothers attractive and sexually appealing, more so than the particularly slender actresses and newsreaders that are offered up each night. The evidence may come in a crude form but it clarifies matters immensely. There is a burgeoning area in wayward websites visited by millions of men each day, classed as MILFs (Mothers I'd Like to Fuck). Type the word MILFs in to your Google search engine and there are over two million web listings. Men around the world are at this very moment typing in their credit card details, paying to look at pictures of naked mothers or films of 'Hot Moms Having Sex – Now!!' Television casting directors would be horrified to find that many of these 'hot moms' actually have real hips and thighs, and many are actually over 30 years old.

And in a curious twist of redressing past inequities between men and women in society, television has portrayed women as behaving more in the way men have traditionally behaved. Apparently, once women are freed from the social and economic restraints suffered before, they naturally behave in a more masculine way. They 'have balls' and 'kick ass'. As women's bodies have become leaner and harder on television, so has their behaviour. It's as if a sense of physical, emotional and behavioural otherness is being played down. For example, it's now less fashionable to portray women as caring and nurturing towards a man. Perhaps media culture considers these images as akin to showing a woman being servile, deferential and weak, or in some way compromising her independence. Or perhaps it's simply uncool to be caring. Yet it's precisely these caring, nurturing qualities that make the world a bearable place. In a publication of the American Psychological Association, Professor D.C. Geary concluded that females are more sensitive to nonverbal communication than males. He argued that 'in comparison to men, the greater emotional reactivity of women might then complement a greater sensitivity to the social cues and the nuances of social relationships. In combination, these competencies will provide women with a relative advantage in managing social relationships'.[6] Many other female scientists, such as S.E. Taylor, have identified characteristics that make women good parents and close friends – characteristics such as becoming anxious when hearing about the problems of friends and acquaintances, and heightened sensitivity (compared to men) to emotional facial cues. In one study 'Tend and Befriend', she and her colleagues pointed out that, under conditions of stress, 'the desire to affiliate with others is substantially more marked among females than among males' and that this is 'one of the most robust gender differences in adult human behavior'.[7] One of the best-kept secrets in all areas of the media is that simple caring and kindness are an enormous subliminal sexual attractant to men. These are the female qualities that make a man fall in love.

Taking a Position on Sex

To drive home further the image of the single, slender young woman being in charge of her own life and sexuality, sexual positions on television have been quite literally turned upside down. Sex scenes routinely show the woman on top, riding the man who is rarely active or dominant, while the vision of a woman being held by the back of the neck while being taken from behind doggy-style would be broadcasting the symbolic act of a man being dominant, and is televisually non-U. The unlikely bedfellows of Genghis Khan and the *American Journal of Human Genetics* would be interested in the BBC's position on positions. In their documentary *Genghis Khan*, the BBC mentions tactfully that Mr Khan was the world's most prolific fertiliser cum mass-rapist. It is thought that a full half per cent of the entire world's male population carry his genes today. A study in the *American Journal of Human Genetics* reports that his genes were 'spread by a novel form of social selection resulting from [his] behavior'.[8] This novel form of spreading his DNA followed the wholesale slaughter of the vanquished – it is the fact that Genghis Khan ('supreme conqueror') ritually and methodically got first pick of the beautiful women. Khan told his autobiographer how much he relished this aspect of his empire building. His grandson, Kubilai Khan, added only 30 virgins to his harem each year. Yet from his bedroom conduct as portrayed by the BBC, one could be mistaken for thinking Genghis Khan was a Mills & Boon-style lover. To be specific, you see him kissing his inexperienced virgin wife on their wedding night who then wrestles with him and rolls on top.

Interestingly, across cultures and over time, the world's favourite positions among men and women are the missionary and doggy-style. This isn't at all surprising, as they are the positions which allow for deep penetration and provide the sperm with better access to the cervix. The woman-on-top position, however, is not popular with women, and is considered the world's worst position for trying to conceive since it causes the semen to leak and may result in fewer sperm making their way to the egg. The organisation ParentsPlace.com includes this in their 'Positions to Avoid', while BabyCenter.com publishes advice in 'What are the worst sexual positions for conception?' A journalist providing 'sex advice and guidance', Ann Andriani, explains 'But those are not the only reasons women like the rear-entry position...besides the physical, there's the mental stimulation women get off on. Some women feel like they're being taken by their lover. There's an animalistic, I'm going to grab you and do you sort of excitement to it. A feeling of helplessness, that I can't get away.'[9] So who exactly are the television directors appealing to, or who do they think they might offend politically by showing women in the sex positions the majority of them prefer?

Portraying Female Sexuality

Irrespective of the sexual position the slender young female settles into in front of the camera, she is likely to be enjoying the 'zipless fuck' – an expendable recreational sexual encounter without those old-fashioned wimpish afterthoughts, the inconvenient emotional consequences that bedevil real one-night stands. Again the modern woman is portrayed as being in some way 'strong' because she is seen as easily able to separate her sexual enjoyment from her emotions, like men.

In surveying television's contemporary sexual pose, journalist Amanda Platell writes 'Women on top? No thanks! Is such nonsense really what we all fought for? I don't know whether to laugh or to weep. If women really think lasting happiness comes through a sexually submissive male, they are in for a rude awakening. That's not a partner, that's a slave. A door mat is a door mat in any gender.'[10]

In the 1990s I met the originator of the television series *Sex and the City*, Candace Bushnell. Ms Bushnell was on a current affairs programme adamantly promoting the 'truth' about modern women as portrayed in her book and on the television series which was allegedly based on friends, acquaintances and her way of life in New York. I pointed out that I had two single brothers in New York and knew of other men living there who should be coming into contact with the type of women she described but who told me that women in New York aren't at all like that. She said that I must be ill-informed and that the city was awash with modern, promiscuous, independent women as seen on television. And so I was rather surprised to see that when she left the studio and re-entered civilian life, Ms Bushnell fell immediately into the arms of a tall, successful, authoritative man and clung to him in, what I thought, was a dependent, girly manner quite unrelated to anything that resembled Kim Cattrall's character or the 'zipless fuck'. I was later told that *Sex and the City* was actually produced by gay men. The creator and executive producer of *Desperate Housewives*, Marc Cherry, is also gay. This explains a lot about the sexual behaviour and attitude of the female characters on screen. This is not to say that programmes such as these are not highly entertaining or compelling, only that claims that television behaviour is merely reflecting real life often need a forced reality check.

Something closer to the truth about the relationship between sex and emotions in women can be found in the publishing world where a Mills & Boon/Harlequin romantic fiction novel is sold every two seconds, and in the incarnation of Bridget Jones, both in print and on film. What has struck me as most duplicitous is the physical appearance of the role models that television producers use to convey this image of the modern, empowered woman. From pretty, slender, wrinkle- and cellulite-free young actresses to permarexic, Botoxed news presenters, these examples ultimately have effects which are disempowering to the female viewers, effects which damage their health.

Sex on Television – Too Much Information?

Irrespective of what appears on the screen, there are now televisions in more couples' bedrooms than ever before. Furthermore, since the rise of sexually explicit television, a strange thing has happened – as we watch other people having passionate sex, we are actually having less sex and less satisfying sex ourselves. When you pull away the bed sheets, the real scandal lurking in an increasing number of British and American bedrooms is that it's not our trousers that are dropping, but rather our libidos. Television is now also being cited as a major cause of insomnia and sleep deprivation – the national sleep deficit experienced by a large section of the population since the arrival of television with its seductive power to draw viewers into staying up unnaturally late. Too tired to fornicate, they seem to be achieving multiple snorgasms instead.

And more couples are simply becoming celibate. The counselling organisation Relate (formerly known as the Marriage Guidance Council) confirms that couples are having less sex and many are now celibate, while a survey carried out by a well-known women's magazine surprisingly reported that married women had more sex in the 1950s – half a century before *Sex and the City* or the appearance of Oprah's sexperts, who supposedly enlighten us.[11] Lending credibility to *No Sex Please: We're British*, research at Reading University, 'The National Enjoyment Report', found that the British prefer to stay at home and watch television than go out with their friends or have sex.[12] Perhaps if she were alive today, Mary Whitehouse would be surprised to find that television has proved to be both a remarkably effective contraceptive and a broadcast bromide.

This trend can be traced back to the 1960s, a time which marked an increase in our sexual literacy. In the way that child-rearing became the province of informed authorities on the subject, so too people came to believe that there were professionals whose greater understanding of sex could be imparted. Psychologists and therapists encouraged people to talk about sex, making it a more cerebral affair. The logic of this was that translating something primordial into a rational form of communication should enable us to share our feelings about sex, understand, refine, manage and ultimately enjoy it more. This was encapsulated in the postcoital, post-mortem catchphrase of the day: 'How was it for you?' Being better informed about sexual issues and techniques should lead to greater fulfilment. Books, magazine articles, television programmes and video guides followed to help us 'understand' the nature of sex. Openness and transparency were good for the national orgasm.

Yet when I first lived in both Britain and France in the 1970s, I was amazed to discover that while Americans back home were busying themselves writing and talking about the practice of sex, the British and French were busy actually doing it with far less fuss, deliberation and self-consciousness. In many Western industrialised countries, sex has now become increasingly demystified and dissected, most obviously on television. But I've come to believe that there is a myth surrounding the benefits of our openness about sex, whether in drama or reality television. While pornography may indeed arouse us in an immediate sense, the growing pervasive openness about sex on mainstream television has actually had the opposite effect. Shining such a bright light into dark corners seems to erode the intuitive, instinctive, nonverbal language of sex, replacing it with a conscious awareness that detracts from it. The power and charge of sex is maintained when there is less of it on television.

Catholic sexuality has often been described as a procession between the bedroom and the confessional. Talking about one's sexual behaviour was something done in the confessional box. A divine combination of guilt and a lack of openness was thought to prevent the unfortunate 'victims' of this authoritarian religion enjoying sex the way that the more liberal sects do, or to experience the ultimate – secular sex. But a closer look at Catholic sexuality provides an insight that should cause many to reconsider these liberal assumptions.

In a study of 5,700 people entitled 'Sex: The Catholic Experience', a Catholic priest and senior director of the National Opinion Research Center at the University of Chicago actually concluded that Catholics have sex more often, approach sex more playfully and are more likely to enjoy sex than Protestants or Jews. In fact, the lowest rates of sexual intercourse occurred among Protestants with Jewish spouses. The findings hold true for both married and single Catholics, and the effects appear rather enduring. Among older people, half of Catholics aged 55 and older reported having sex at least once a week compared to

40 per cent of others. The data suggested that those people looking to spend more time having sex than falling asleep in front of the television on the sofa, should consider Catholic spouses.[13]

I was also surprised to find that in Muslim countries such as Iran or Mali, men and women seemed genuinely more romantic and sexually charged in a way I haven't seen in our liberal all-talking-about-sex West. Even in the remote village of Songo in the Dogon Valley in West Africa, where there is ritualistic male and female circumcision (and no television), I found this to be true. Yet many people arrogantly think of these 'unfortunate less enlightened, less advanced and less sophisticated' developing countries as needing to 'develop' their understanding of proper male/female relationships. I'm convinced the key factor in enabling the sexes to retain a degree of otherness and frisson, nature's unspoken language, is that it remains unspoken. The lack of television has been a significant factor in this.

This is not a call for greater sexual repression and guilt. Rather I'm drawing attention to a glaring oversight. We're led to believe that the more we see of life and the more information we have, the better. After all, we're told 'knowledge is power' so this can only be a good thing. Yet by putting every aspect of the human condition under the spotlight to reveal and illuminate 'real' experiences, we often diminish our own experiences in the process.

An editor at *Playboy* magazine and author of *Playboy's History of the Sexual Revolution*, Jim Petersen, cites the arrival of television as almost 'killing sex in its tracks'.

Television has affected sex through 'omission rather than commission. It displaces other romantic opportunities. Like brushing up against your wife's backside in the kitchen…the old fashioned challenge of having to entertain each other. Those are sexual things'.[14]

The Contrast Effect

Yet another component of the anti-aphrodisiac effect of television is now referred to as the contrast effect, a principle of perception whereby the differences between two things are exaggerated, depending on the order in which you see them. For example, if you lift a light object and then a heavy object, you will judge the second object as being heavier than if you had lifted it first or by itself without the previous point of comparison.

The contrast effect also applies to the way we judge the sexual attractiveness of other people. A succession of studies over the past 20 years has demonstrated that the way we make judgements about ourselves and others is strongly influenced by whom we can be compared with. A woman of average sexual attractiveness seems considerably less attractive than she actually is if you have first seen a highly attractive woman. If a man is talking to a beautiful female at a party and is then approached by a less attractive one, this second woman will seem relatively unattractive to him.

The contrast principle also works the other way around. A woman of average attractiveness will look more attractive than she really is if she walks into a room of unattractive women. This is described as 'A theory of sexual relativity where points of comparison determine our judgements about the appeal of others.'[15]

But it doesn't require 'real' people to create this contrast effect, and television does it even better. In an early experiment, for example, men were asked to judge the sexual attractiveness of the photograph of a potential blind date. The photos had already been judged by other men as being of average attractiveness. The scientists observed, however, that if the men were watching an episode of *Charlie's Angels* when they saw the photo, they judged the blind date as less desirable than she was by similar men watching a different type of show. Their judgements of these women in the photos – women who were actually available and likely to be interested in them – were so badly influenced that the men didn't even want to bother meeting them.

The contrast effect doesn't just cause us to find strangers less (or more) attractive, it also affects our views of our own sexual partners and of ourselves. For example, women who are surrounded by other attractive women – whether in the flesh, in films or in photographs – judge themselves as being less satisfied with their degree of attractiveness and less desirable as a marriage partner. The researchers concluded, 'If there are a large number of desirable members of one's own sex available, one may regard one's own market value as lower.' These women have good reason to be concerned. A man's feelings about his current partner are influenced by the media. Seeing photos of attractive women weakens his commitment to his partner. Men report themselves as being less in love with their partner after viewing *Playboy* pin-ups than they did before seeing these photos.

This result is surprising, as making someone sexually aroused normally increases their attraction to their mate. However, viewing beautiful models negated whatever benefit the men might have experienced from being sexually aroused.

Apparently, this media effect isn't due to us perceiving our partners as less attractive. It acts by altering our perception of the pool of potential mates available to us. Television images seduce us into believing that there's an enormous field of choices out there, altering our estimate of the number of potential mates available. The subconscious effect is an underlying feeling that we could always do better. The researchers explain, 'The perception of the comparison pool is changed. In this context our partner doesn't look so great. You think, "Yes, my partner's fine – but why do I have to settle for fine when there are just so many great people out there?"'[16]

Primitive man and woman had to estimate the possible pool of sexual options against an estimation of their own sexual mating value to arrive at a vague marketing strategy. But in primitive times, people didn't actually see many people, and certainly not many highly attractive people. Most people lived in a little village of perhaps 30. By the time they died, they might have seen only 450 other people. And among those 450, some were old, some were young, but few were particularly attractive. On the other hand, in the 21st century you can view magazines or the television and easily see 450 people in a single day. And the visual voodoo of television leads our brains to count these fake faces into our pool of sexual possibilities, subtly and insidiously contributing to a low-grade dissatisfaction with our lot.

Our minds have not evolved to differentiate between reality and television's sea of beautiful people. We process these images as real possibilities, even though we know rationally they are electronic images. Even when the television is off, our brain is reviewing all the beautiful virtual possibilities. We have a bias towards recalling the beautiful, which contributes further to us overestimating our pool of possibilities out there.

Television's Beautiful People

In the early 1960s, mathematicians looked at matching men and women up as a large-scale statistical enterprise whereby most people arrive with a mate with whom they are more or less content. More recently, however, they have added what they refer to as the 'Vogue factor' – the influence of high-concentration media exposure to the beautiful people – and have discovered that people become dissatisfied with their own partners. It isn't merely the prominence of highly attractive people that has bred dissatisfaction; it is the fact that attractiveness itself has become far more standardised because of the relatively small pool of beautiful people appearing in the media for everyone to desire.

Television has misappropriated another evolutionary mechanism, delivering to our screens what we are instinctively interested in. Even newborn babies appear to enter this world with a built-in preference for attractive faces. A study at Exeter University tested around 100 babies with an average

age of only two-and-a-half days. The babies were held 12 inches from pictures of two adult human faces that were equal in every respect except for their attractiveness as judged by adults. Researchers watched the babies' gaze and found they had a consistent tendency to stare more at the attractive face.[17]

In an essay 'Why I Hate Beauty', the marketing author, Michael Levine, who works as a publicist in Hollywood, describes himself as 'a confirmed case of the contrast effect...I live in what is likely the beauty capital of the world and have the enviable fortune to work with some of the most beautiful women in it...Women don't look like this anywhere else in the country, and certainly not in the quantity they do here...these are the women whose images are broadcast all over the globe. While most people do not live in LA, they visit it every day when they turn on the TV or go to the movies. It is safe to say that, to one degree or another, we all live in the shadow of the Hollywood sign'.[16]

The contrast effect holds up even in the more mundane environment of the provincial classroom. And it causes divorce. A study published in the journal *Evolution and Human Behavior* entitled 'Teaching May Be Hazardous to Your Marriage' put the contrast effect to the test in an everyday environment.

The researchers predicted that male high school and college teachers would be most vulnerable to the effect as they are constantly surrounded by young women.

Generally speaking, teachers are especially unlikely to be separated or divorced. However, being a male teacher or professor negates this effect. While male kindergarten and

primary school teachers had monogamous stable relationships, the researchers observed that 'There appears to be
something about male teachers who come in daily contact
with teenage women that increases the likelihood of being
currently divorced or separated.' Further, these teachers then
stay unmarried because any women older than college age
they might approach after their divorce would seem less
desirable than the pool of pretty young things which
surround them every day. The senior researcher commented,
'Most real-life divorces happen because one or the other
spouse is dissatisfied with their mate. The contrast effect can
explain why men might unconsciously become dissatisfied.
They don't know why they suddenly find their middle-aged
wives not appealing anymore; their exposure to young
women might be a reason.'[18]

While most of the discussion above describes the contrast
effect as it relates to the attractiveness of women, this is
because it is easier to study. Males are more responsive to
visual images of the opposite sex, and judge potential mates
using physical criteria. Men, however, have not escaped the
contrast effect. There has been an increase in eating disorders,
body-building and steroid-taking in men, partially in response
to idealised male images on television and in films and video
games. Both women and men have suddenly been surrounded
by virtual 'gorgeous guys' with interesting jobs sporting a six-
pack, a suntan and perfect white teeth, who have the perfect
funny one-liner always at hand. Although women seem to
respond to a far greater range of attraction factors in men,
particularly a man's 'charm' and social influence, they are also

influenced by a high concentration of distorted media images of ideal men.

So, the plethora of glamorous, successful, young, beautiful people – sometimes in dazzlingly uncompromising positions – is actually being found to lower both our sexual self-confidence and the degree to which we're attracted to others, including our own spouses or partners. It is negatively affecting our ability to be, as the Old Testament puts it, 'satisfied with the breasts of the wife of thy youth'. The response to this is, 'Of course television characters are younger and better looking. Viewers prefer to watch better-looking people kissing than unattractive people kissing or even embracing – the ratings prove that. Why would anyone want to watch an average-looking 45-year-old kiss and cuddle with a 43-year-old when they could watch a couple of 24-year-olds instead?' This is absolutely true, but I feel it's necessary to state the obvious.

Just because television is entertaining doesn't mean it has no unfortunate effects which are less than entertaining. Most importantly, just because ratings are higher for programmes featuring slimmer, younger, better-looking people, it doesn't prove that they are good for us. The 'ratings' in terms of consumption of chocolate, hamburgers and soft drinks are infinitely higher than for watercress, but that does not prove that chocolate, hamburgers or soft drinks are good for you.

In the way that we all compute our own risk/benefit or pleasure/pain analysis about other things we enjoy, we have to acknowledge that there are costs associated with the pleasure we get from watching the amount and type of television we do. Ultimately the costs involve children affected by divorce: the collateral damage of social disengagement and the contrast effect. And real break-ups are quite unlike television divorces where, by the next episode, the kids bounce back after Mummy and Daddy split up. Overconsumption of television and of the beautiful people has become a public health issue.

Perhaps we more readily acknowledge the risks of other pleasures such as taking drugs, eating saturated fat or rollerblading because these involve physical, tangible entities that either enter our bodies or we put our bodies through. And we often choose to ignore the advice and accept the risks. But television and lashings of beauty seem intangible, not possibly substantial enough to cause the kinds of problems discussed above. If we were told that something in the food, air or water supply was adversely affecting our family relationships and sexual behaviour, perhaps we'd take it more seriously.

SEVEN
SHINY HAPPY PEOPLE
Television's Effects on our Happiness and Mental Health

At this moment depression is – across the world – at the highest levels ever witnessed, and increasing. Rates of depression have risen along with both television ownership and the amount of television we watch. A recent study from the World Health Organization found that depression is a deepening global health crisis affecting 150 million people and spreading fast. They predict it will overtake diarrhoeal diseases and perinatal conditions in 'disease burden' – moving into second place, behind heart disease, by 2020. Depression is afflicting poor countries as well as rich. Ten per cent of the population in Germany, the United States and other countries are depressed.[1] A major Europe-wide study reported in the *British Journal of Psychiatry* found that Britons are the most depressed people in Europe. 'Depressive disorder is a highly prevalent condition in Europe. The major finding is the wide difference in the prevalence of depressive disorders found across the study sites.' Urban Spain, for example, has a prevalence of 2.6 per cent while the urban UK has almost seven times this rate of depression.[2]

The impact on people's lives can be devastating. Between 15 and 20 per cent of sufferers commit suicide. The tide of depression is seen as the result of social changes, particularly in 'developing countries' – the fragmenting communities, eroding moral certainties, exposure to increasingly global media. And this last cause actually adds to the first two.

The escalating incidence of depression is particularly true for children. Those children who are watching a lot of television are more likely to have a host of different psychiatric symptoms – depression, anxiety and aggression.[3] And a study of 22,079 American adults for the pharmaceutical industry quantified the link between television viewing and rates of depression, concluding 'The incidence of depression is a monotonic increasing function of television viewing.'[4]

It seems that a television nation becomes a Prozac nation, and a Prozac nation turns on the television to feel better. Which only makes the depression worse. If someone were to design an instrument specifically to work against the things that sustain and improve our society's happiness, nothing could be more effective than the television set. Britons are richer than at any time in history yet there are many who ask: so why are so many people so unhappy? The British have more and better food, clothes, holidays and cars, warmer houses and better jobs. They also have more and better televisions. Despite all the efforts of psychologists, doctors, teachers and the Government, our level of happiness has not improved – it has declined.

What's gone so very wrong? Happiness is now a science studied by academics ranging from neuroscientists to economists. The most important factor found to influence your happiness is the quality of your personal relationships, followed by your friends and your community life. The average Briton watches television for more time over his lifetime than he spends doing paid work. This time comes mainly out of our social life. And looking at the screen for four hours a day fails to nourish family relationships too. Furthermore, the content of television cultivates greater individualism and an entitlement to self-fulfilment, which causes further erosion of relationships and community.

Television Breeds Dissatisfaction

As television has taken on the role of displaying solutions to our emotional problems, it has created further problems in the process. One of the benefits television is said to afford us is to show us a greater vista of possibilities that life could hold for us, new ideas that inspire and widen our horizons. Television can be a catalyst for change or at least create a feeling that you need a change: 'Move on', 'Go for it!' or at the very least 'Get over it'. Infinite choices dancing before our eyes become aspirations, which in turn become expectations. Ignorance may be bliss but knowledge (endless information) is, we're led to believe, power. Day in and day out, television provides us with examples of the exceptional.

Should we be surprised that we're left feeling rather unexceptional?

A short time ago, the way we would see these points of comparison was to actually see them. Our dissatisfaction that may have triggered a revolution was more often the result of having some physical, geographical connection with the people or objects that made you feel relatively deprived. But now television brings points of comparison in abundance right into our sitting room. The physical contrast effect discussed in Chapter 6 has its counterpart in 'social comparison'. Moreover, television provides the viewer with the out-of-the-ordinary and the exceptional in an unnaturally rich concentration that does not occur in the real world. So do all of these new insights actually inspire us and lift our spirits?

Research in Britain is finding that these televisual points of comparison translate well into depression. 'There is more pressure on people to live up to some sort of image today than there was in the past. The problem is that people try to model themselves on something external' is a conclusion from an ongoing 16-year study by clinical psychologists at the University of York. This study involving 2,000 subjects has documented the rise in 'perfectionism', which is defined not simply as having high standards, but having expectations that are unrealistic, and becoming anxious and frustrated when they are not met. Perfectionism often causes depression. Nearly one in five people was found to have developed extreme 'perfectionist' traits, which the researchers concluded 'can lead to ill-health'.[5]

Television seems to intensify a sense of relative deprivation and distorts our sense of where we stand in various
pecking orders and hierarchies, such as age, appearance and
social influence. Britain's class system provides an interesting
model of how hierarchy influences mental health, and sheds
some light on the psychiatric effect of your sense of place
within the scheme of things. In his book *The Origins of
Unhappiness*, psychologist David Smail refers to the concept
of 'class injury' as being greatly responsible for psychiatric
disorders and depression in Britain. In fact, he holds psychology accountable for ignoring class as an enormous factor in
determining our mental health. 'Therapeutic psychology has
been remarkably silent about the actual experience of relative
social insignificance – the awareness of being among the
"little people".'[6]

And there's no escaping the finding that it isn't only a
'better' class of person who enjoys better mental and physical health. There is also a 'better' class of baboon – and the
low-ranking baboon is prone to various diseases which are
believed to be stress related. The same is true amongst British
civil servants.

'Class injury' is a lesson in how our sense of our social and
material significance in comparison to others encompasses
more than psychic pain. Inequality in social esteem has been
linked to ill-health and other general measures of 'wellness'.
The effects are not due to material poverty but rather a sense
of relative deprivation by some groups of low status in relation
to other groups. For example, women who merely perceive
themselves as being lower on the social ladder, even if it is

untrue, suffer real physical injury. Their feelings actually cause hormone changes – raised cortisol levels – which make them accumulate more dangerous abdominal fat, their bodies truly function differently and they even take longer to fall asleep at night.[7] It is thought that a perceived inequality of opportunity rather than money is central to a society's class-related woes. Television seems to rub salt in the wound and exaggerate this by alluding to infinite possibilities and opportunities.

In his study 'The Psychology of Social Class', professor Michael Argyle at Oxford University observed: 'Heavy TV watchers are less happy than those who watch less.' He also concluded that 'Happiness is affected by social class, especially at the lower end of the scale...The most likely explanation is that higher-class individuals enjoy their leisure more, belong to more clubs and leisure groups, engage in more sport and have more friends, while working class people just watch more TV.'[8] Argyle later wrote that television is inherently dissatisfying: 'The bad thing about TV is it means you are not doing something else like talking to your friends.'[9] His conclusions were supported by the study where both the Internet and television were found to cause 'social disengagement...associated with poor quality of life and diminished physical and psychological health. When people have more social contact, they are happier and healthier, both physically and mentally'.[10] Social contact and social support are linked with better immune system function, lower rates of disease and lower rates of death.[11]

Most of the influence of television on depression is cumulative and insidious. Our society's growing melancholy comes from the increasing gap between reality and expectations raised by vague, ambient, emotive images over time. As the electronic delivery system of distorted points of comparison, television acts as a false reflection of the outside world. In more straightforward cases, we are bathed in images of beautiful, dynamic, influential people. When compared subconsciously with our self-image, these make us feel bad and set us up for bouts of depression.

According to Dr The-Wei Hu, an economist at the University of California, depression costs countries three to four times more than it does to treat the problem. And it would be interesting to see what would happen to rates of depression if a nation watched far less television or no television for a decade. I personally believe it would actually result in a decrease in the prevalence of depression.

Those who defend television justifiably claim that people who are depressed may watch more television as a result of their depression. However, this does not by any stretch of the imagination nullify the observation that television can also make people feel dissatisfied, frustrated, worried and depressed in both the long and short term. In fact, one British study has found that watching negative news clips on television doesn't make worried people feel less anxious – it increases their negative mood. Therefore, watching a troubling news broadcast, which is the norm, leads to greater worry and a sadder mood. Bad news is bad news.[12]

And if television leaves us feeling more anxious, helpless or merely with a mild sense of failure, this in turn makes us more easily influenced by attractive people on the screen.

A study found that when people were made anxious by experiencing a sense of failure, they were more noticeably persuaded by the attractiveness of the person portrayed in adverts instead of the integrity of the message. When you feel this way, you are more likely to rely on superficial aspects of an argument, rather than use logic and rational thinking to process what you're being shown or told. You can see this creates an interesting cycle of despair and belief.[13]

How We Become Desensitised by Television

Television sets us up for depression by eroding our psychological coping mechanisms through training us in non-reaction. Psychologists such as Dr Erik Peper point out that viewing such a high volume of international and domestic tragedy and despair cultivates a passive do-nothing attitude when confronted with needs and problems. We develop a form of learned helplessness, which undermines our capacity to deal with our own needs and problems. Even watching the news day after day tends to induce a non-reactive attitude, as a protective mechanism. When you view starving children in Somalia, you cannot go to the television set and give them some food. When you see war-ravaged lands, you cannot lend a helping hand. The more we see tragedies that we cannot respond to, the less we tend to react: we are learning to be non-reactive. We become desensitised. And while we may donate heavily while the tragedy continues to appear on the nightly news, when the pictures dry up so do our donations.

The Effects of Too Much Novelty

Even with more uplifting types of broadcasting, television by necessity has to employ novelty to engage our attention. There is an insatiable need for new stories, developments, people, fashions and scenes. And while all of this engaging novelty may attract our gaze, it also makes our world appear to spin faster. We experience an exaggerated sense of perpetual change. And a change is certainly not as good as a rest. When communities, the job market, relationships, social norms and the world economy are changing more rapidly, most people actually need a greater sense of continuity and stability. We as individuals and as societies are not designed to cope well with a sense of rapid change. Change damages health by producing increases in stress hormones and blood pressure and decreases in optimism and contentment.

The historian Arthur Schlesinger Jr. once said: 'Television has spread the habit of instant reaction and stimulated the hope of instant results.' Research is now focusing on the way television portrays life as having quick resolutions to all kinds of issues. Like the full stop at the end of a chapter, television life offers closure. Some scientists now believe that this time-lapse view of the world is causing us to subconsciously expect resolutions to our own problems, and faster resolutions at that. These images and expectations are then literally translated into biochemical changes, which lead to widespread clinical depression. Even documentary programmes purporting to improve our mental health can fall into this trap. On two separate occasions I have been approached by

BBC1 and BBC2 television executives to discuss how I could participate in documentary series by helping to make people appear happier and more confident, raising their self-esteem within only a few weeks. This quick-resolution approach would, they felt, make good, inspiring self-improvement television. Needless to say, they found my reservations about such a quick-fix feel-good approach rather depressing.

Other Ways Television Causes Depression

Some other reasons why television contributes to depression can easily be addressed. For example, watching television displaces time we need to spend in our 'inner landscape'. We need time to carry out some basic emotional housekeeping: processing, integrating and filing feelings, perceptions and thoughts, with or without our awareness. Yet by absorbing ourselves in someone else's world on a screen, we avoid and fail to connect with the truly relevant and important people, issues and feelings in our own life. And this lack of attention to our own inner life can ultimately cause depression.

Inactivity and Depression

The sedentary nature of watching television leads to depression through other means. We need the neurochemicals that come from being physically active or we feel less happy. Yet television is the antithesis of physical movement. And findings within the new field of ecopsychology also show that we need exposure to the outdoors for our psychiatric well-being.

Nature produces biochemical changes that improve our mood and sense of happiness in both the long and short term. Watching the Discovery Channel is not the same as going for a walk in the park. Is it therefore surprising that people whose working day involves physical effort are less likely to suffer from depression?

And one of the consequences of parents who are depressed is that their children end up watching more television, causing later health problems. A study presented to the North American Association for the Study of Obesity reported that 'Decreasing television viewing time may improve child health and well-being. These viewing patterns are shaped during the preschool years. Because mothers play an important role in determining how much TV their preschool children watch, a better understanding is needed of the maternal factors that influence children's TV viewing.' More time staring at the screen translates into less time outdoors say the study's authors. As you can guess, this starts off a cycle of inactivity and a greater chance of depression in the children. This is an unusual route through which both depression and obesity can be 'passed on' from parent to child.[14]

Depression and Suicide

Depression precedes suicide, which is now the second biggest killer of young men after road accidents. I was involved in an initiative by the Department of Health, which attempted to reduce the male suicide rate in Britain. One of the themes that came up again and again with young people was how the idealised images and lifestyles they saw on television made them feel so very helpless. There are a growing number of studies showing that television portrayal of suicidal behaviour actually causes copycat suicides. Even the fictional portrayal of specific methods of suicide in television drama causes a considerable increase in viewers killing themselves using those exact methods – the macabre face of product placement.[15,16] And a study on suicidal behaviour and 'self-harm' conducted at the Warneford Hospital, Oxford recently found that children learn about the act of suicide and form concepts surrounding it following exposure to television. They found that those stories presented visually through television programmes or films have more influence than those in magazines and newspapers.[17]

Body Image, Eating Disorders and Depression

Perhaps the most widely talked about influence of television on mental health is on 'body image', dieting and eating disorders. In a new study entitled 'Body satisfaction in college women after brief exposure to magazine images', the scientists found that you don't even need moving images to lower your self-esteem over your body shape, and the effect occurs in only a few minutes: 'It appears women who are dissatisfied with their bodies may be at risk for a further decrease in body satisfaction after even a 15-minute exposure to fitness and health magazines.'[18] Another study found that only five minutes' exposure to photographes of thin women's bodies 'can have a negative short-term effect on body image'. The scientists found 'Substantial changes in what looked normal were accompanied by changes in what looked attractive.'

They think it is the corruption of what we gauge as 'normal' that underlies body dissatisfaction.[19] And in a 'meta-analysis' of 25 studies published in the *International Journal of Eating Disorders* on how viewing slender images makes a woman feel worse about herself, the results speak for themselves: 'Body image was significantly more negative after viewing thin media images than after viewing images of either average size models, plus size models, or inanimate objects.'[20]

There may be a new neurological explanation as to why women are particularly sensitive both to comments about their body shape and to media images of slender women. It also sheds some light as to why women, more than men, may go on to develop eating disorders. A study at Hiroshima University in Japan entitled 'Gender differences in brain activity generated by unpleasant word stimuli concerning body image' found that women's brains responded very differently to men's. In women, certain words such as 'obesity', 'corpulence' or 'heavy' caused the part of the brain associated with being under threat (the amygdala) to become very active, while the part which deals with rational thought processing (the left medial prefrontal cortex) became inactive. In men the response was the reverse. Naoko Shirao and colleagues now believe 'Our data suggest that the prefrontal region is responsible for the gender differences in the processing of words concerning body image, and may also be responsible for gender differences in susceptibility to eating disorders.' A British psychiatrist commented that 'men have a much more rational response to language about body shape than women – and they get angry about different things than women. The part of the brain in men which reacts to unpleasant words is also the area which interprets railway timetables'.[21]

Men and women may indeed differ in the way they respond to words about their big bottom or thighs, but men are affected in other ways. The difference in the way television influences men's and women's body image is now also taking on a striking form. There is a significant increase in the proportion of men who are dissatisfied with their muscularity, now referred to as muscle dysmorphia. A snapshot of what men and women want was recently published. Both sexes completed four measures of body image that were meant to evaluate two distinct attitudes about their appearance: muscularity and body fat. Women and men had little in common in terms of how muscular they wanted to be. But they both wanted less body fat. The most prominent finding was that men scored highly on the 'Drive for Muscularity Body Image' scale – they wanted bigger muscles soon and this was linked to 'behaviors used to increase muscularity'.[22]

Television is being directly implicated in this increasing dissatisfaction experienced by men. They're now experiencing poor self-images due to the muscular, handsome men seen particularly in razor and aftershave adverts. In one study, men were required to view television ads awash with toned, muscle-defined men, often without their shirts. Results of the study showed that the men watching these commercials felt more unhappiness and depression compared to those watching the 'neutral' commercials. The study also suggested that the 'ideal male body' portrayed in the media is linked to men feeling negatively about their bodies.[23]

The Biological Psychiatry Laboratory at Harvard Medical School has taken an international snapshot – in Austria, France and the United States – of what men think about their bodies and what women think about those men's bodies. They noticed that 'modern Western young men are constantly exposed – through television, movies, magazines, and other sources – to an idealized male body image that is far more muscular than an average man...the most masculine male stars of the 1940s and 1950s were clearly less muscular than many of the modern action heroes of today's films...Therefore, we hypothesized that in both the United States and Europe, men would desire to have a body much leaner'. The researchers tested the hypothesis that men in modern Western societies would desire to have a much leaner and more muscular body than the body they actually had or perceived themselves to have. They found that men weren't bothered by their level of body fat: 'Modest differences were found between the men's measured fat and the fat of the images chosen. However, measures of muscularity produced large and highly significant differences.'

And these differences were startling: 'In all three countries, men chose an ideal body that was a mean of about 28 lb (13 kg) more muscular than themselves and estimated that women preferred a male body about 30 lb (14 kg) more muscular than themselves.' Yet in a pilot study the authors found that 'actual women preferred an ordinary male body *without* added muscle. CONCLUSIONS: The wide discrepancy between men's actual muscularity and their body ideals may help explain the apparent rise in disorders such as muscle dysmorphia and anabolic steroid abuse'. The scientists were concerned that their findings 'may warn of a widening gulf between the average Western man's body and the more muscular ideal to which he aspires. As body ideal moves steadily away from body reality, some vulnerable men may be more likely to develop muscle dysmorphia, anabolic steroid abuse or dependence, or other psychiatric disorders'.[24] And anabolic steroid use is becoming commonplace; it's dangerous not only to the user but also to the rest of society as it makes people not only more powerful, but more aggressive and violent as well.[25]

Early exposure to television images of slim role models is being increasingly linked with the development of eating disorders. It's now estimated by the Eating Disorders Association that the number of people with an eating disorder in the UK 'is an astounding 1.15 million'.[26] While the US Department of Health and Human Services reports 'the number of American women affected by these illnesses has doubled to at least five million in the past three decades... Approximately 1 in 10 women afflicted with anorexia will die of starvation, cardiac arrest, or other medical complication, making its death rate among the highest for a psychiatric disease'.[27]

It's thought that only 10 per cent of those with anorexia nervosa or bulimia ever seek treatment. I have always been advised not to try to calculate a minimum number of deaths from anorexia because it is an unclear area. Unfortunately, however, I feel that many of us don't fully comprehend the scale of this problem unless we see it in black and white and can compare it to more immediate causes of death that the news prefers to cover.

In Britain, the death rate from anorexia is estimated to run at around 13–20 per cent of sufferers per year. If you calculate the number of deaths using the lowest conservative mortality rate of 10 per cent this comes to at least 41,000 dead females per year.[28] As a point of comparison, the Government reports that the number of women murdered each year through domestic violence is around 100.[29] And in 2004, the number of women in the UK who contracted HIV infections through heterosexual sex with a heterosexually-infected partner presumed infected within Europe was approximately 33, and they are presumably still alive.[30]

In their recent report 'Eating Disorders, Body Image and the Media', the conservative British Medical Association states quite categorically that 'Eating disorders are a significant cause of mortality and morbidity', and they identify television for the first time as a major factor. Studies by Leeds University Medical School and the British Psychological Society are now finding that girls as young as six hate their weight and body shape; some are dieting already and others are anorexic. In one experiment, when asked which picture they preferred – one of a fat child or one of a child with missing limbs – the girls chose the latter. The scientists cite 'Exposure to visual imagery, much of it depicting stereotypical body shapes' as the cause.[31,32]

Television is not the sole cause of deaths from anorexia nervosa but it is certainly a direct cause of much body dissatisfaction. This leads in some cases to extreme dieting, and in the vulnerable, to anorexia and bulimia. Television is a significant co-factor. Even if you believe that 95 per cent of anorexia cases are caused by sexual abuse, overbearing parents or other emotional reasons, and that only 5 per cent of cases are triggered by too many slim images seen on television during a girl's developmental years, you still arrive at an annual figure of 2,070 females who die in the UK alone because of television changing their psychology and physiology.[28] While we can quibble over the number of women who die from anorexia and to what extent television contributed to the development and progression of their disease, there are many women who would be alive today had they not been exposed to the high concentration of slim, beautiful, successful, Western television images during their formative years. And there are girls who will die in future because their self-image is profoundly influenced by the role models they see time and time again on television today.

All of this contrasts so sharply with what I see in countries that do not have television or the amount or type of television to which we are accustomed. In Burma and Bhutan, one of the most endearing sights is simply the way women walk. There is a palpable lack of self-consciousness. As they sway, their gait and cadence is endowed with grace. And when I spoke to the doctors and health officials, they confirmed that dieting, body hatred and eating disorders are not prevalent yet. While in other countries I see that with the arrival of Western television, dieting and body dissatisfaction have appeared.

Those who prefer to dilute the culpability of television in

causing eating disorders should explain what has happened
to the girls of Fiji. Just to remind you, in 1995 the proportion
of girls who made themselves vomit to control their weight
was zero. But three years after the introduction of television,
this soared to 11 per cent of the young female population.
Within three years, dieting increased dramatically among
healthy Fijian teenagers who started to watch television. The
study showed that girls living in houses with a television set
were three times more likely to show symptoms of eating
disorders. And the effects of television were 'dose-dependent'. The Harvard researchers said: 'The impact of television
appears especially profound...'[33]

The amount of television our society consumes serves as
an inadvertent frame of reference. For many it is the main
frame of reference. The screen is often the window through
which we observe the world and make comparisons, absorb
values and make judgements. The outside world has become
an abstraction filtered by television, just as the weather has
become an abstraction filtered through air-conditioning. It's
time we replaced the filter.

EIGHT
LIVING IN A TELLYTOCRACY
Television as our Social Engineer

In the early 1990s I wrote and presented a medical/political documentary for one of the main television networks in Britain that was also aired in the United States. I had noticed new academic research suggesting that modest dieting as practised by people in most Western industrialised countries was bad for people's health, and that the claims made by the big dieting organisations were dishonest and misleading. The film crew and I went to Harvard Medical School where I interviewed a scientist who had just completed ground-breaking research. It showed that, contrary to the received wisdom at the time, dieting may actually shorten your life span.

Upon my return to London I was asked to attend a meeting with the big television network executive to watch the 'rushes' of some of my interviews with various scientists. I was very excited and pleased that we managed to compile such a prestigious collection of academics on film who explained their studies clearly and concisely, exposing dieting for what it really was and the harm it was doing. However, when the Harvard scientist appeared on screen, the executive stared intently, taking notes, and then turned excitedly to the director and me exclaiming 'Great! – a member of an ethnic minority and a female! That's two boxes ticked!' (The scientist looked Oriental.)

It was this incident more than any other that opened my eyes to a side of television that I hadn't thought much about until that point. I have thought a great deal about this since.

I'd had a behind-the-scenes glimpse of the light, tokenistic end of a deeper influence television is having on our society. The previous chapters addressed the effects that television has on shaping our physical and mental health. But television also influences our social and political health as a society. These effects are far more difficult to identify and quantify. They don't appear in medical journals. And so much of what I point to is borne of my own observations, along with things I've been told by reliable sources.

While some of the examples I provide may seem controversial or politically incorrect, my emphasis is not on the examples per se but on the underlying process they reveal. I'm sure you will be able to identify your own examples and look out for many more in the coming years.

News Management

There has already been a great deal of discussion about the way in which the ownership of television networks has increasingly been concentrated in a very few hands. And how this 'oligopoly' is by nature politically conservative and capitalist. The influence on the content of programming is perhaps most apparent in 'news management'. For example, there was a great deal of controversy (not broadcast on television of course) about the way in which American television networks covered the build-up and execution of the war on Iraq. Many news programmes had a constant banner on the bottom of the screen saying 'War on Terror', while supposed links between Osama Bin Laden, al-Qaida and Saddam Hussein were left to the imagination of the millions of viewers. The pursuit of answers to key questions about the existence of so-called 'weapons of mass destruction' lacked any journalistic vigour. Many people wanted to know whether those who owned the television networks or advertised their products (oil perhaps?) on the networks had any financial, political or ideological links to the Republican administration which was seeking re-election – and got it.

Selling Social Values

However, the conservative right does not have a monopoly on using television to influence opinion. More recently, television has been a conduit for what is often loosely referred to as 'political correctness', trying to change our impressions within the softer end of politics. Advertising techniques are being used not only during commercial breaks and not only to sell you products – they are also employed to change the way we think and feel about issues in our society. Television provides the best means of persuading you to buy into the right values.

Today, we are enlightened by the most effective vehicle for social engineering ever envisaged. Our views and attitudes towards everything from domestic violence, drug abuse, divorce and single motherhood to immigration and racial groups are carefully manipulated by decisions taken behind the screen. Even the social class and regional accent of presenters, newsreaders and continuity announcers are carefully selected to create an effect. It's as if you, the viewer, can't be trusted to think about or form opinions – these issues are far too important. Nowadays television executives talk of 'raising public awareness of...' This used to be simply called propaganda.

At times, the obvious nature of the social message we're supposed to absorb is insulting to our intelligence, a blatant product placement. But more often the broadcaster wants to create a different feeling about something, a form of ambient advertising. One communications agency specialising in changing our feelings about social issues through public service broadcasting puts it beautifully: 'Long after people forget what they hear, they remember how they feel. So Bonneville creates those unforgettable feelings...'[1]

Interest groups are all desperate to influence 'what is shown' as if all that matters is how issues and people are 'represented'. And now, the way that social themes ('pro-social values') are integrated into television dramas and soap operas has even been turned into a fine science. Many writers and producers are using these techniques quite intuitively.

One man, Miguel Sabido, has put these principles into words, creating a formula – the methodology – used to implant social messages into serial dramas. The methodology involves using a 'values grid' to decide which 'pro-social' values are to be emphasised.

Sabido applied the principle of selling washing powder on television to the process of selling social values on television. As television viewing is now the main recreation for most of the Western world, Sabido observed that viewers often end up talking with their peers about the social issues raised on screen. This is because the characters provide us viewers with a model of how to discuss issues that are sensitive, or even taboo, and discussions between characters indicate a certain social acceptance of these issues.[2]

Sabido began his career as a theatre director, carefully observing the effects of his actors on the audience. However, he lacked a theoretical explanation for what he was observing until he came across a chapter entitled 'A Triune Concept of the Brain and Behavior' in a Canadian mental health textbook. Why a Mexican theatre director would be reading such a book at bedtime is unclear, but Sabido finally had a structure to hang his observations on. He was particularly attracted to the idea of the brain being divided into three hierarchical zones:

❏ The first zone was considered the reptilian zone. Most basic, its function is that of self-preservation through satisfying impulses and instincts. Rather reminiscent of Freud's id.

❑ The second zone was seen as the palaeo-
mammalian brain. Common to all mammals, this
is the source of most memory, the seat of emotions
and the primary residence of human values.

❑ The third zone was the neo-mammalian brain,
considered the centre of thinking and exclusive
to humans.

This view of the brain and behaviour provided Sabido with
the rationale of focusing his social engineering on the
emotional (second zone) and human instinctive/impulse (first
zone) as the basis for his serial dramas, with the third zone of
the brain being used primarily to reinforce the first and
second zones' messages in the drama. You can see again that
it is not our thought but our feeling that programme makers,
advertisers, politicians and social engineers want to appropri-
ate. Joseph Goebbels would agree.

At the 1934 Nuremberg Rally, the consummate spin meis-
ter gave a speech presenting Nazi propaganda as the model
for the rest of the world, calling it the 'background music' to
policy making: 'The genuine propagandist must be a true
artist. He must be a master of the popular soul…It is not only
a matter of doing the right thing; the people must understand
that the right thing is the right thing. Propaganda includes
everything that helps the people to realise this.'[3]

Goebbels would do well in television today. He was
visionary in understanding the need for 'dumbing down' to
enable your audience to feel their way to the 'right thing':
'[Propaganda] is aimed at the broad masses. It speaks the

language of the people because it wants to be understood by the people. Its task is the highest creative art of putting some-times complicated events and facts in a way simple enough to be understood by the man on the street.'[3] And like Sabido, Goebbels recognised the power of people chatting about the right thing the next day at the pub. In January 1928, during one of his regular 'training talks', Knowledge and Propaganda, he noted: 'Where an idea finds entry, it enters, and soon that person is influencing others.'[4]

Yet Goebbels would be horrified to discover that his approach to changing people's feelings about ethnic minority groups in the Germany of the 1930s through the big screen is being used to change people's feelings about ethnic minority groups in the other direction today through the small screen. Yesterday's negative role models are today's positive ones. And even if the issues are presented as rather black and white, at least the film is now in colour.

Representing Ethnic Minorities on Television

The representation of 'ethnic minorities' on television has become a very important issue. In particular, the frequency with which the actors or interviewees appear, the roles they are cast in and the way they are portrayed are often subjects of great concern and analysis. Studies involving 'ethnic monitoring' are conducted to measure which minority group is appearing in which type of programme, and how their appearance may influence our feelings about that minority group. In the United States the television networks are literally issued with a 'report card' each year where they are given grades on their achievements and commitment to 'representing diversity'. The National Latino Media Council[5] uses the following grading system:

A+ = Exceptional results

A = Outstanding effort **and** results (e.g. several 'regular' roles)

B = Very good effort **and/or** results (e.g. some 'regular' roles)

C = Good effort **and/or** results (e.g. some 'regular' and 'recurring' roles)

D = Inadequate effort **and/or** results (e.g. few or no 'regular' roles, few 'recurring' roles)

F = Poor effort **and** results (e.g. no 'regular' roles or loss of prior 'regular' roles, sporadic 'recurring' roles or loss of prior 'recurring' roles)

At times, the measurements become very specific. In Britain, even the precise 'skin tones from lighter to "dark ebony"'as well as length and slenderness of nose, and nostril circumference of ethnic minorities on screen are 'judged', 'coded' and 'categorised' by the Commission for Racial Equality (CRE).[6] While nowadays these physical characteristics are measured to ensure inclusion, in Goebbels' day the same physical characteristics of ethnic minorities were being measured for very different reasons.

Whichever country you look at and whatever form of

ethnic monitoring is used, some interesting findings emerge. For example, if you ask the average Briton, Australian or German to name Hispanic-American television stars they can usually think of only one or two, such as Jennifer Lopez. Yet Hispanic people are the largest 'ethnic minority' group in the United States, accounting for 15 per cent of the total population (including Puerto Rico). Mysteriously, they get only 4.8 per cent of television roles.[7] As a point of comparison, black people account for around 13 per cent of the US population yet 'African-Americans represented a larger share in television roles (15%)'. Latino/Hispanic-American people continue to be drastically under-represented on television, so much so that the Screen Actors Guild commissioned a report, 'Missing In Action: Latinos In and Out of Hollywood'.[8]

The National Latino Media Council is a coalition of all the major Latino organisations in the United States. Their most recent report still finds 'limited progress on Network Television', revealing a curious slowness of progress.[5] And even the way viewing figures (the Nielsen rating system) are gathered has been shown to be biased against Hispanic/Latino viewership and programmes. Esteban Torres, former Congressman and Chair of the National Latino Media Council, concludes, 'Nielsen's systematic exclusion of Latinos is shameful; the company has been slow in remedying this despite the significant economic losses to both the industry and our community.'[9]

I've heard a variety of interesting explanations as to why the largest minority group in the United States is so profoundly under-represented on television but none of them is entirely convincing.

British Asians – the Missing Majority

And there is a British counterpart to this story. 'TV for millions misses the minorities', a study on behalf of the Commission for Racial Equality, reported: 'Researchers found that people of Asian, Chinese and other ethnic minority backgrounds are pitifully sparse in British TV programmes and serials. Black people fared better and appeared on television more than their actual numbers in the population.' The CRE itemised the racial casting results as follows:

'Black people occurred more frequently in UK programmes (3.7% of all participants) than in the real world (2.1%).

'Asian people (including Indian, Pakistani, Bangladeshi and "other Asian") were the most under represented. Compared with the real world, where they account for 3.7% of the population, they were almost invisible on television at just 0.9% of UK TV programme participants.'[6]

And a more recent study by the Broadcasting Standards Commission and Independent Television Commission also found Asian people missing in action on television: '...the analysis also shows that this increase was, certainly in 2001, almost totally confined to roles played by Black characters.'[10]

There have been considerable changes in the language that Britain uses to describe itself: a multicultural society, multiracial society. And even the bluest of blue-chip companies now speaks fluent 'diversity'. All of the major British television networks, from the BBC to ITV, have formed the Cultural Diversity Network (CDN). The outgoing chairman is the BBC's Director of Sport, Peter Salmon, whose formal job title is: 'the BBC's Race Champion and Chair of the CDN' ('Race Champion' does not relate to winning at Ascot), and their mission statement is 'promoting cultural diversity in the television industry. We do this by encouraging member companies to take action to address employment and on screen portrayal issues'.

At their last Annual General Meeting, the BBC's Director of Sport and Race Champion called for 'an even stronger commitment to promoting cultural diversity within broadcasting'. The report then highlighted 'the diversity achievements of the CDN during 2004'. These included:

❑ BBC Drama introduced a 10 per cent target for all ethnic minority characters across drama.
❑ At Channel 4 each commissioning genre now has a Diversity Representative to promote multicultural content and contributors in programmes.
❑ Channel 4 broadcast multicultural series such as...*God is Black*.

'Models of good practice' included:

❑ Setting targets for minority ethnic employment.

- ❑ Modernising the casting and portrayal of ethnic minorities in mainstream programming.
- ❑ Sensitising broadcasters to support greater diversity in content and employment.[11]

The BBC has issued a public statement declaring 'It's not about targets, it's about reflecting real life...We are proud there is a fair representation of modern society across the BBC.'[12]

But in pursuit of 'modernising the casting and portrayal of ethnic minorities' the BBC and others have excluded Indian, Pakistani and Bangladeshi actors from playing the very roles they occupy in real life. This group constitutes by far the largest 'ethnic minority' in the UK. For example, most of us in Britain are at least subconsciously aware that there are a disproportionately high number of 'Asian' and Middle Eastern doctors and scientists. The NHS would have collapsed a long time ago without them. In addition, Indians are considered by many to be the best software writers in the world; Silicon Valley in California is utterly dependent on them. Yet Asian people are rarely cast as such in television dramas or film. In fact, in the very dramas the BBC has boasted 'about reflecting real life', Asian surgeons and doctors are conspicuous by their absence. The same occurs in scientific roles and in forensic investigation dramas.

At the same time, however, there are numerous examples of black surgeons (Hugh Quarshie in *Holby City*) and doctors ('Anthony' in *EastEnders*). And in the enormously expensive primetime BBC1 docu-drama *Space Odyssey: Voyage to the Planets*, 'Science Officer Nina Sulman'

(Michelle Joseph), the first to land and walk on Mars, is black while there isn't an Indian or Pakistani person in sight. In fact, there isn't an Indian, Pakistani or Bangladeshi listed in the production credits either. Why?

In the BBC primetime docu-drama *If*, about the first British prime minister from an 'ethnic minority', the minority chosen is not an Indian, Pakistani or Bangladeshi person, he is black ('Andrew Kirk' a.k.a. Colin McFarlane). While on Channel 4's urban yet Asian-less hospital sitcom, *Green Wing*, the IT medical expert ('Lyndon' played by Patterson Joseph) is neither Indian, Pakistani nor Bangladeshi – he is black. And in the more incidental roles portraying QCs, barristers and forensic scientists, as well as in most ethnic minority roles in advertisements, Asian people are again missing in action while black people are heavily represented. What is far more subtle is the subliminal impression left by cutaway and out-of-focus background shots in offices, of courtroom audiences and juries and in CID offices, where I've noticed the same patterns of ethnic representation continuing. Why?

The state of British television casting seems even more extraordinary when you consider the real life facts put forward by Dr Tony Sewell, the Director of the Learning Trust, who is black: 'Teenagers from African and Caribbean backgrounds have worse examination results than any other ethnic group...young black males in Britain have a better chance of ending up in prison than at university.'[13] And there's a radical suggestion from the Chairman of the Commission for Racial Equality – segregating black boys into separate classes should be employed to deal with their academic underperformance. 'None of us, least of all the next generation of black children, can afford a repeat of the past 40 years.'[14]

Given that Asians are the largest ethnic minority and that Chinese and Indian pupils have the highest academic achievements in British schools and excel at medicine and sciences, and given the BBC's claim that 'it's about reflecting real life...there is a fair representation of modern society' and the Cultural Diversity Network's code of 'modernising the casting and portrayal of ethnic minorities in mainstream programming', surely one would expect the achievements of Asians to be at least marginally portrayed in the dramatic arts.

Young children are given the same impression regarding Asian people. While the casting director for *Bob the Builder* has been careful to ensure that fish ('Fin' the goldfish), birds ('Hamish' and 'Squawk') and even a potato-headed scarecrow ('Spud') are represented along with black single-fathers and daughters ('JJ' the building merchant and Molly), I can find no Asian characters. In another key programme, *Balamory*, an excellent BBC2 rural series for young children, a quarter of the main characters are black. An Indian family is briefly glimpsed during the opening credits only but is never seen again and you never hear them speak.

One of the basic intentions of ensuring that 'there is a fair representation' of ethnic minorities on television is to create a greater sense of familiarity so that white Anglo-Saxon/Celtic British people feel more comfortable and accepting of 'ethnic diversity'. Television is used as a form of social medicine where familiarity is intended to lead to reduced racism. So in terms of social health priorities, those in charge of television casting should be aware that Asians suffer a far higher rate of racially motivated assaults every year than any other ethnic minority. In a report by the Office for National Statistics entitled 'Victims of Racial Crime: Highest risk for Pakistanis/Bangladeshis', Pakistani and Bangladeshi people have *twice the risk* of being a victim of a racially motivated incident than black people, while Indian people have a 65 per cent higher risk than black people.[15]

Distorting National Identity

Now, one of the ironic outcomes of the recent drive to portray ethnic diversity on British television is that according to a report by the Commission for Racial Equality, 'People of all ethnicities massively over-estimate how many people in Britain are from an ethnic minority – most think one in five is, compared to only one person in twelve in reality. The proportion of the British population who are immigrants to this country is also hugely over-estimated.'[16] And a new report by MORI found that the average British woman when surveyed thinks that 28 per cent of the UK population are immigrants. The actual figure is 4.8 per cent.[17]

The United Kingdom is overwhelmingly (93 per cent) white, Anglo-Saxon or Celtic, and Christian. So how can British people, as the CRE says, 'massively over-estimate how many people in Britain are from an ethnic minority' and how can British women believe there are almost six times more immigrants here than there actually are? Television has been remarkably successful in raising awareness of the existence and relevance of ethnic minorities in the UK. There has been an obvious zeal among some people to acknowledge the UK as a 'multicultural society'. Yet by exaggerating this image of a highly 'diverse' society, there has been a distortion of Britain's – and in particular England's – sense of national identity. In the way it has already tampered with individuals' self-identity and body shape (see Chapter 2), television has helped to distort the nation's demographic shape and cultural identity. There was a clear example of this on both of Britain's main news programmes during the 2005 general election. BBC's *Ten O'Clock News* carried a nightly series called 'My Britain', which 'gives people across Britain the opportunity to share the views that matter to them'. And to represent Britain, each film begins with five 'representative' faces: a black man with dreadlocks, a young Asian woman and three Caucasian people. The main ITV News had a similar series, 'The Ballot Box Jury', where there were many more photos on the screen – a mosaic reflecting Britain's ethnic make-up – but again the proportion of photos of ethnic minorities had little to do with the true racial make-up of Britain. There appeared to be no Asian people, while 15 per cent of the photos were of black people, and there was one man of Middle Eastern appearance. As is the case with the casting policy in television dramas, this type of subtle misrepresentation over a period of time contributes to a false consciousness about Britain. This carefully designed misrepresentation is now refined for children to absorb. *Balamory*, for example, takes place in a tiny rural Scottish village filmed on the Isle of Mull. Curiously, at least 60 per cent of the children in this remote Scottish village nursery are from darker-skinned ethnic minorities.

The advent of the terms 'multiculturalism' and 'diversity' no doubt came with the best of intentions. It formally acknowledged that British society included members who were not white, Christian and British, and that they should not be discriminated against. However, the current climate of reflecting diversity on television has taken on a different connotation. In the past three decades, the ethnic make-up of Britain has changed remarkably little. Ninety-three per cent of people in Britain are white Anglo-Saxon/Celtic and Christian; the largest ethnic minority is from the Indian subcontinent while black people constitute about two per cent of the population. However, I have noticed that when some white middle-class English people, often working in the media, are presented with these statistics, they seem surprised; some react as if they in some way wished it weren't true. Others question the motives behind providing them with this information as if it were an attempt to minimise the importance of ethnic minorities: in a sense, racist.

I recently turned on the television to hear a local councillor boasting that her borough was the 'most multicultural', having more ethnic groups than any other in Britain. Her pious tone was one I increasingly recognise in many white middle-class Anglo-Saxon/Celtic Christian people who talk in terms of 'multi-ethnicity' being in some way a superior way of life. They seem to have an attitude of 'the more, the merrier' to ethnic groups as if diversity is better and, more to the point, in some way 'right'. This is distinctly different from accepting ethnic minorities in a genuine, uncontrived way, and I often wonder if their ebullience is really a comment on their own self-worth as white middle-class people. I frequently sense an element of self-loathing among the English middle classes in particular. It's as if there's something inherently less acceptable about a society of people who are predominantly white, something less acceptable about themselves. This is neither healthy nor productive, yet in indulging these feelings, television has become their co-enabler.

Downplaying the Dominant Culture

And while the terms Scottish, Welsh and Irish are common-place on television nowadays, the term English is decidedly not. Presenters and reporters are discouraged or actively prohibited from using it. In the way that the middle-class guilty are drawn to the idea of classlessness, so, too, denying their cultural and national identity holds similar appeal. These feelings are accompanied by an underlying belief that if Britain does have a dominant host culture (white, Anglo-Saxon and Protestant), it is in some way disrespectful to or ignores the relevance of ethnic minorities, denying them a place in British society. A dominant host culture is seen as excluding, so it shouldn't be shown on television.

However, all countries have a dominant host culture, even those whose hosts are not actually dominant in number. In China, it is the Han Chinese. In France, it is the French, who unashamedly have a cultural protection ministry, which attempts to retain the traditional dominant culture. Nor do the Italians or Portuguese feel uneasy about their dominant cultures. In South Korea, the Koreans consider themselves to be of divine origin; in Bhutan the Sharchops and Ngalong dominate; and in Laos it is the Lao Loum. In the United States, which is often described as a melting pot of cultures, the choice of presidential candidates clearly reflects a visible Anglo-Saxon, all-American cultural identity. If countries did not have dominant host cultures, world tourism and social anthropology would be thrown into chaos, with most destinations being indescribable melting pots lacking particular traditional indigenous identities. Ironically, most visitors to Britain come here with the desire and expectation of experiencing the very culture Britain and its television producers now seem to be so busy playing down. And when I visit foreign countries and witness the locals imitating what they believe is an Englishman, as they still consider the British to be, they do it with extraordinary unanimity, a clear stereotype.

Is television being used as a means to vent a collective guilt for Britain or the United States' past treatment of ethnic minorities? If so, there is a growing body of academic research on 'collective guilt' or 'white guilt' indicating that 'a guilt-based approach can backfire'.

A key finding is that dealing effectively with racism, colonialism and social exclusion of the past 'should not represent a threat to people's social identity...collective guilt threatens social identity [of the majority] by calling in to question the group's morality'.[18] Therefore, venting guilt by carefully managing the casting of ethnic minorities on television can be counterproductive. The social identity of most of the population of the UK should not be intentionally played down by leading people to feel as if being white and English – the 'dominant culture' – carries a sense of original sin or unfair privilege. More worrying is the fact that racist groups are benefiting from the television-induced perception that there are three times more ethnic minorities or six times more immigrants than actually exist. This has handed such groups just the ammunition they need to gain credibility, to heighten concern over race and immigration issues and to win greater support and votes.

The Anointed and the Benighted

The black American economist and political theorist, Thomas Sowell, grew up in Harlem, left home early and did not finish high school yet ended up graduating from Harvard and Columbia. Yet in *The Vision of the Anointed* Sowell refers to those in the television and film industry who present this distorted picture of the way society should look as 'the anointed'. While we, the television viewers who are being enlightened by their new vision of diversity, are the 'benighted'. As Sowell puts it, 'The benighted are to be made "aware", to have their "consciousness raised", and the wistful hope is held out that they will "grow".'[19] And in a chapter entitled 'Optional Reality: Visions, Politics and the Media', Sowell writes 'Deceptive appearances have been with us long before the rise of the modern mass media. But never before have those appearances been able to reach so many people, with so much immediacy and so much seeming reality. The dangerous dramatizing of half-truths is the fatal talent of the television or movie camera. The ease with which the media can choose what images to contrive and spread across the land feeds the dangerous illusion that reality is optional... [these images] have great leverage in determining the course taken by a whole society.'[19]

I'd like to think that the television executive I described at the beginning of this chapter (see page 207) wasn't one of Sowell's 'anointed'. They had a sense of humour, and I suspect realised they simply had to be seen to tick the boxes. But there are other, far more prominent, members of television's anointed who have revealed themselves publicly since then. Gavyn Davies, the former Chairman of the BBC, denounced the influence of the 'white, middle-class, middle-aged and well-educated people' on the content of television.[20] Although he later tried to apologise, it is thought that his remarks accurately reflected the feelings of those in power – the anointed – at the BBC.

And many more people may remember the statement by the former Director General of the BBC, Greg Dyke: 'I think the BBC is hideously white. I think the BBC is a predominantly white organisation.' As I'm writing this, it has just been reported that Mr Dyke has, during a speech, boasted that in remedying the 'hideously white' condition of the BBC by boosting the number of ethnic minorities, 'much of what we did was illegal'.[21,22]

Curiously, both Mr Davies and Mr Dyke are themselves white, middle-aged and well-educated. And very rich. Davies is a former Goldman Sachs economist and millionaire, while Dyke was the Chairman of Pearson TV, one the largest production companies in the world.

As a psychologist, I am intrigued by the unspoken motives behind this type of self-recriminating posture. But what is most interesting are the motives that underlie why the anointed working in television casting overlook Asians in Britain and Hispanic people in the United States so profoundly. Why are Asians, as the CRE states, so '...pitifully sparse in British TV programmes...the most under represented...almost invisible on television'? Why are Hispanics described in terms of 'exacerbating the invisibility of Latinos on television...Missing in Action'? And why do those who influence the casting and portrayal of television characters display such a distinct preference for other ethnic minority groups? In both the UK and United States, 'Black people fared better and appeared on television more than their actual numbers in the population.' There is certainly not a shortage of Asian and Hispanic talent available.[6]

Is there a self-serving aspect to the casting of ethnic minorities? Could it be that those white middle-class people who do the casting and write the parts gravitate towards an ethnic minority that makes them feel better? Do they prefer ethnic minorities who are seen as more enfeebled and therefore dependent on them? Do those in television in some way pity black people more than Asian or Hispanic people? Is the overt preference for casting prominent black characters over Asian or Hispanic ones fetishising a particular race for selfish reasons? As the black American journalist and broadcaster

Ken Hamblin once told me, 'It's the same behaviour that I see people display when they look through the window of a pet shop and ask "how much is that doggy in the window?" in response to the more playful, dependent breeds of puppy that wag their tails and roll their eyes.' While this explanation may appear crass and uncomfortable, it is intended to prompt a degree of badly needed introspection. For if television is to be inadvertently used to democratise society by raising awareness and being inclusive, greater awareness should be raised concerning the true motives of those running this tellytocracy.

Another ironic consequence of the current casting policies on television has been the hijacking of ethnic images by conservative global capitalist organisations to make these institutions and their messages appear more caring and enlightened. They know that the public have already been primed by television. The Mexican artist and writer Guillermo Gomez-Pena believes '…the propagandists of this "new" capitalist multiculturalism have outsmarted us'.[23] And the psychologist, Professor Dion Dennis, observes this use of 'the diversity of deeply aestheticized and idealized racial, ethnic and class images' as a form of 'Post-Ethnic, Post-Racial Fascism'.[24] All this globalised ethnic inclusiveness will surely have Greg Dyke and Gavyn Davies wringing their hands. Or buying their shares.

How Television Portrays Families

Hispanic or Asian characters aren't the only group marginalised or misrepresented on our television screens. Anyone who has children may be continually surprised by the variety presented on television. In most sitcoms, the small child is little more than an accessory to the plot or merely a prop. Babies are born to main characters and then go missing in action – they're never seen again. Anyone with children composed of flesh and blood knows that the opposite is true. Like trying to get anything done around the house with children around, the same is true of trying to run a television programme with children in the script. It is an understandable artistic necessity to keep the kiddies incommunicado and unseen if you want to get on with the plot.

What interests me is how the children in divorced families are portrayed, because this is having profound consequences for children in real life. One box that television executives don't have to tick on their sheet of 'groups to represent' on screen is children-made-miserable-by-divorce. Unlike the casting of ethnic minorities, the reactions of children of divorced families in television dramas don't warrant the same scrutiny and measurement. And, unlike the concern that accompanies the portrayal of ethnic minorities to prevent 'negative stereotyping', I see the opposite problems in the way children of divorce are portrayed. Children in divorced or separated families suffer from unremitting positive stereotyping in their television portrayal. American programmes are the most nauseating, often involving a little boy – 'Jimmy' – with a Hollywood (pudding) Bowl haircut and his pretty, slim, well-rested Mom. And Mom invariably brings home her love interest who addresses Jimmy as 'Hey big guy', throws him a football, and they bond and are soul mates before the end of the episode. In other programmes the love interest actually picks one of the children up in his arms, and the child takes to it without batting an eyelid. The children of television divorce welcome the kindness of strangers.

People who've been through a real divorce know differently. And studies on the long-term effects of divorce on children paint a very different picture. For example, children of broken families are twice as likely to become depressed as adults. And a new study, 'The long reach of divorce', shows how the effects are passed on to grandchildren – even those who haven't yet been born.[25] Their portrayal on television can again be seen merely as artistic expediency in trying to make a tidy telly programme. But television produces ambient effects that ultimately influence what we feel is acceptable. After repeated exposure to social themes, we come to be more accepting of those themes. This principle applies to the treatment of phobias. The technique of a 'graded exposure' – showing the sufferer the subject of their phobia on a television screen increasingly – is one approach to desensitising them to the thing causing their upset, reducing their degree of negativity towards it. In another approach, 'flooding', the sufferer is simply flooded with the subject of their fear (frogs, marshmallows, magenta trousers) until a process called habituation sets in, the sufferer accommodates the fear and the negative feelings subside. Televisual familiarity breeds complacency.

On television, there's often little difference between the ease with which childless unmarried couples and married couples with children separate: 'Right, I'm off then!' or alternatively,

'I want you out, you bastard!' One random example I watched last night was a row between a 15-year-old girl and her mother who suddenly announced that, after a relatively recent separation and divorce, she was going to marry her boyfriend – a man the daughter loathed. Any protests by the admittedly obnoxious daughter were met with 'I have a right to my own life you know!' Repeated exposure to this type of television scene yet again gives the id carte blanche to seek gratification.

Parents who become 'fed up' and 'split up' on television in order to seek self-fulfilment may provide compelling drama, but the children are left out of the equation. The parents' self-gratification is central to the action on camera, while the quiet nonverbal despair of their children may take years to become visible. And by then it's a wrap anyway; the show's over. Besides, viewing quiet despair makes watching paint dry seem positively shocking. Divorce is portrayed as a lifestyle option; there simply isn't enough time to portray it in any other way. And television changes our perception of every aspect of life from loo fresheners to political parties. Why should our perception of the gravity of divorce remain impervious to the screen?

This is not a call to turn television dramas into public service announcements or earnest educational films reeking of social integrity. Rather, it is to point out an inadvertent subtle effect, which contributes to a large social cost. In addition to the contribution made to divorce by 'social disengagement' in families through the sheer time spent watching television, there is the disenchantment couples have with one another fostered by the so-called 'contrast effect' (see pages 178–85). And now we can add to this the small matter of the collateral damage of divorce, which is misrepresented, or more often doesn't appear on screen.

As a society with the highest divorce rate in Europe, we in Britain can be forgiven for preferring to believe or to see on television that 'kids bounce back' after a divorce. It's uncomfortable to have the truth dramatised in our face. We prefer the media to reinforce, or to at least not contradict, our 'lifestyle'.

There is a desire for television portrayal to be seen to support our lifestyle or circumstances so that we are left feeling good. So, instead of facing up to the fact that divorce is a necessary evil, a burden and, perhaps, a sense of failure that we must carry, we prefer to watch programmes or acknowledge studies that show that divorce doesn't affect children as much as we thought. This is particularly important because it involves our society's children. Like a developing flower, a child needs the right type and amount of nurturing or he will wilt. This is more important than our gratification or our guilt. Those in television understandably don't want their plot lines straying off at less-exciting tangents, or contradicting their own highly divorced lifestyles. I was interested to read the views of a well-known television dramatist and novelist, Deborah Moggach, who fell in love with a cartoonist she met at a party and left her husband of 15 years.

'It was as if my soul had left my body and gone to live elsewhere…Breaking up a family is a terrible and murderous thing to do – the children were only six and eight at the time – but people recover and they were eventually fine.'[26]

Yet despite the views of rich, successful television writers, across time and across cultures, family disruption has been regarded as an event that threatens a child's well-being and even survival. And no matter how you write the script or cast the parts on television, social engineering will not change this. By portraying a reduced-pain version of divorce accompanied by cut-and-paste family units, television gives permission to the id to go forth and express itself, without revealing the true cost.

Viewer Feedback: Our Role in Television

The process of social engineering through television shouldn't be considered a case of 'them' doing this to 'us'. We have played a significant role in engineering the type of television we're exposed to. Part of the new tellytocracy involves ratings. Even the public service networks such as BBC and PBS have become hysterical about ratings. Increasingly, 'focus groups' are asked to decide the ending and even to shape the story, not only in films but in television programmes too. Even the popular *Desperate Housewives* has viewers' paws all over the rudder. On the surface this makes modern television appear all the more democratic thanks to 'viewer participation'. Unlike the oppressive 1950s when we were merely broadcast to by those in the know, we can now help the master chef to bake our own cake.

At a time when we're told that true 'people power' means

giving the people what they want, we have to ask ourselves some very uncomfortable and perhaps politically incorrect questions. Do we really know what is good for us to see on the screen? Given the extraordinary effects and power of television, do people in editorial positions of responsibility have a duty of care not to give us what we want, but what they believe is truly important or artistically good? Should we engage in more self-censorship or let someone else impose restrictions on us for our own good?

More to the point, do the 'majority' actually have good taste? Don't recoil at the prospect of answering this question with your true feelings. And why do we recoil at the suggestion that sometimes there are people who simply know better than us? Why is it that programming which does not pander to the majority is considered either elitist or a commercial failure?

Ratings drive the television market and favour popular majoritarian culture. This may sound very people powerish, but remember that as producers compete to imitate successful mainstream programmes, this will squeeze out anything too innovative or different. These points may require us to face some crude realities about people power à la *Animal Farm* – but these issues must be confronted.

And once the programme is on air, we're now encouraged to interact with it in real time. We can email or text our immediate responses and even 'vote' on certain matters. In Britain we're invited to 'press the red button now' to follow the yellow brick road and involve ourselves more in the programme. There is also the chance to engage in a live 'web chat' with the stars or programme-makers as soon as the show finishes. And then there is the opportunity to give the network our 'viewer feedback'. Again we can deliver our opinions – even complaints – by email, telephone or letter. So much choice.

I should point out that I have actually seen producers at the BBC and other networks laugh at the viewers who bother to respond with their so-called 'viewer feedback'. I was told by one executive producer at the BBC that when he sifted through the viewer feedback and passed it on to the staff, they all sniggered. So he stopped after the first day. While on an ITV show, a producer was very straightforward: 'We completely and utterly despise anyone who bothers to give us their "feedback". They are sad fuckers, that's how they will always be regarded by people in the media who think they are so much better than any sad fucker of a viewer. They are absolutely never taken seriously, and any colleague who does wouldn't be taken seriously and would be despised themselves.'

While networks are indeed interested in the feedback they receive from organised focus groups, and take feedback in the form of ratings very, very seriously, spontaneous feedback is merely seen as the musings of a rather unfortunate soul... with nothing better to do than watch television.

The belief that we can all interact with television programmes both before, during and after the show, thereby supposedly influencing events, has been the ultimate act in social engineering. Every time I hear a television presenter say 'and you can email or text us now with your views' or 'you can learn more by pressing the red button now' I think of a classic psychology experiment involving 'executive monkeys'.

The 1950s experiment involved two identical monkeys, each one sitting in a restraining chair like an enforced spell as a couch potato or at a desk. A simultaneous electric shock was delivered to both monkeys at various intervals. One of the monkeys (the 'executive monkey') had a lever he could pull to influence events by turning off or even preventing the shock for the two of them. The 'helpless' monkey had no lever and no control over events. Yet it was the executive monkey with the choice who developed the duodenal ulcers. Having the opportunity to influence things by 'pressing the red button now' – sorry, I mean pulling the lever – was more of a poisoned chalice. And the media are now making monkeys out of us.[27]

The new approach of being part of your television may in years to come merely be considered a time when a new social control was imposed by offering us a false sense of influence. It reminds me of the 'sugar pills' my grandfather, a surgeon, sometimes used to prescribe patients as a placebo to satisfy their expectations that something was being done by a powerful medicine. Time and effort spent watching and then responding to your programme-makers may also be seen as having siphoned off much of the political energy of our young. 'They thought they were changing the world. But instead they just changed the channel.'

Drowning in a Sea of Channels

Another feature of our tellytocracy is not only the choice provided by 'pressing the red button now', but also the increasing choice among the growing multiplicity of channels. Our belief in the inherent goodness of choice has now become deeply ingrained in our culture. Choice is the bedrock of our society's liberal democratic assumptions and romantic belief in being masters of our own destiny. I've even heard a growing number of news reports end with the obligatory '...and so the new regulations will allow the public more choice. And that can only be a good thing'. You may have noticed that British people have recently come to consider themselves not as subjects but as citizens. I'm convinced that this psychological transition has occurred not through political changes but through how they have redefined themselves as consumers with rights and, most importantly, choices.

In the retail sphere, greater consumer choice is seen as offering greater control. And with the growing choice among so many new products including television channels, today's consumer or viewer should in theory be more empowered and happier than his predecessor. But as he peruses the new shopping aisle or television channels, today's consumer feels the burden of a tyranny of options brought upon him, drowning in a sea of alternatives. Choice has become our new oppressor. It keeps us preoccupied with pressing not only the red button but plenty of others too on our remote controls. And the television reciprocates by pressing our buttons. From my experiences of foreign countries, I am convinced that when it comes to unbridled freedom of programme choice on the screen, ignorance is bliss. Unlimited screen choice is often disadvantageous, and within restrictions and limitations lies liberation, even salvation.

These questions may seem political yet they also stand apart as issues of our psychological and social well-being.

Dumb and Dumber

When John Logie Baird transmitted an image for the first time he wasn't merely inventing the television; he was also hiring the world's first presenter. The first grainy 30-line image appearing on the screen was a ventriloquist's dummy sitting only a few feet away. In his memoirs, Baird enthused 'The image of the dummy's head formed itself on the screen with what appeared to me almost unbelievable clarity. I had got it! I could scarcely believe my eyes and felt myself shaking with excitement. I ran down the little flight of stairs to Mr Cross's office and seized by the arm his office boy, William Taynton, hauled him upstairs and put him in front of the transmitter. I then went to the receiver only to find the screen a blank. William did not like the lights and the whirring discs and had withdrawn out of range. I gave him 2/6 and pushed his head into position. This time he came through on the screen. I saw the flickering, but clearly recognisable, image of William's face – the first face seen on television – and he had to be bribed with 2/6 for the privilege of achieving this distinction.'[28]

What Baird would think of the transition from ventriloquist's dummy to the ubiquitous ebullient television presenters of today can be left only to speculation. Perhaps he would be relieved to find that nowadays he wouldn't need to pay someone for the privilege of showing their face – and much more – on television.

The last tool of engineering is the face on screen. We're biologically predisposed to look at faces and are engaged by those that appear to be looking straight at us. At one time television presenters appeared on our screen because they knew something about the subject matter under discussion, or they were journalists who had switched mediums, or had a genuine passion for explaining things to an audience and were good at it, or were terribly amusing. In most countries there were few television channels, so only the better class of presenter made it to the screen. However, a combination of an overwhelming desire by a large number of people to be validated by being on television and an explosion in the number of channels on air has conspired to breed a lower echelon of presenter.

When the Department of Health was launching a particular health education campaign in the UK, I was asked to give a brief talk to journalists about the subject. As soon as I finished, a very pretty celebrity presenter started talking about how important the campaign was and how she hoped it would succeed, and then she left the stage as well. She immediately approached me, and with the most genuine sense of curiosity asked 'How do you talk to people without an Autocue?' She was very serious and appeared to believe I had a trick or technique I used to talk about something I already knew a lot about. I hadn't realised that she'd had an invisible glass Autocue in front of her when she spoke so that she could read a speech, which I suspect had been written for her. I have come across a growing number of television presenters who, when I ask why they want to present television programmes, are lost for words and then reply: 'Because I want to be on television.'

There have been social consequences as a result of this attitude. Research by Britain's South West Learning and Skills Council found that teenagers increasingly believe there is no actual link between their achievements in school and their potential to succeed. The reason: their intense exposure to reality television celebrities and wannabe presenters. The researchers found that 40 per cent of the teenagers were 'realism deficient. These young people are convinced that life will present them with a lucky break and that they simply have to sit tight and wait for their moment. The biggest group did not see the link between education and success. It could be seen as *Fame Academy* or *Pop Idol* syndrome because there was an expectation that you could become a winner overnight, the idea that you would be walking along the street and someone would decide that you should be a model'.[29] And the Commons education select committee has taken evidence that 'It is worse than pupils leaving without qualifications at 16. A lot are dropping out of education at 13 or 14. They may physically be in the classes but they are not really there because they are uninterested.'[30]

Television will continue to be used to guide us towards some sort of greater enlightenment through social engineering. Yet our society can suffer an overdose of even the most well-intentioned social medicine.

NINE
FADE TO GREY
Why Television is Responsible for Ageism

Can you think yourself into an early grave? Research from Yale University Medical School indicates you can. The scientists conducted a 'survival analysis' on people aged 50 and older to identify what factors were associated with living longer – or shorter. They included current age, gender, socio-economic status, degree of loneliness, and functional health as obvious candidates.

Yet even when all of these factors were taken into consideration, the findings were remarkable: 'This research found that older individuals with more positive self-perceptions of aging, lived 7.5 years longer than those with less positive self-perceptions of aging.'[1]

So, the way we are made to feel about ageing translates into changes that have a powerful effect on our life span. As one British academic who reviewed the study wrote: 'This is far greater than the additional four years or less associated with low blood pressure and cholesterol, and the one to three year gains in life expectancy of people who have not smoked and exercised regularly. The message is simple: Think that growing old is good, and you'll live longer!'[2] If pharmaceutical companies could bottle this life-extending social elixir, it would overtake sales of Viagra, Prozac and all vitamins combined.

In another study, the Yale authors show that the way we view ageing actually affects how healthy we are for years *before* we die.[3] And in the first of its kind, new research finds that if in middle age and beyond we view ageing as an especially negative thing, we are more likely simply to give up trying to be healthy through a balanced diet, exercising and even taking the medicines our doctor has prescribed. These are things that would make us live longer and with much better health.[4] The conclusions of these epidemiologists have placed television under great suspicion.

Obviously no-one wants to get old. They never have. However, compared to many other cultures we have developed what often amounts to a revulsion or phobia to ageing that is relatively new. How could this have happened?

The answer, I believe, is reflected in a little-known statement made by the then Entertainment Chief of CBS Television in the United States:

'How this country thinks of older people and relates to older people, and how older people think of themselves…is directly affected by what is put on television.'[5]

Ageing Disgracefully

In the way television is helping women to dislike their body shape, thereby contributing to deaths through eating disorders (see page 202), it is now contributing to a gradual euthanasia by assisting the majority of the population to revile itself – to age in disgrace.

The message from television is hardly subtle and it targets you before you even hit middle age. A programme on prime-time British television, *Ten Years Younger*, chooses 'ordinary members of the public', often in their 30s, and 'helps' them to look 10 years younger. Predictably the process involves fashion advice along with a change in hairstyle and make-up. But what differentiates this new genre from the makeover shows that came before is actually showing the 'old'-looking candidate undergoing brutal cosmetic surgery as part of the transformation. And any seriousness about surgery is entirely absent as it is treated merely as an extension of the makeover. A jolly narrator's voice accompanied by a 'muzak' sound-track eases the gravity of the scene showing the 32-year-old mother's bloody head being rocked violently as the surgeon hammers away at her nose while she is unconscious. The woman's name is Jane but she's referred to as 'plain Jane'. One of the criticisms made of Jane is that 'she looks like a mother'. Apparently television values consider maternal appearances to be ugly.[6]

In a documentary about the history of soap operas in Britain, a former executive producer of the longest-running soap, *Coronation Street*, boasted about his major contribution to character development in the programme on his first day in the job. He explains how, after making himself comfortable at his new desk, he picked up the telephone and ordered the personnel department to give him the age of every actor on the programme. He couldn't contain his amusement as he then explained how he immediately rid the programme of some of the older members of the cast in a mass cull. He spoke about them as if they were in some way sullied.[7]

Can you imagine a programme entitled *Ten Shades Lighter* in which members of ethnic minorities are helped, through medical procedures, to look more white and Anglo-Saxon? Or *Straight Eye for the Queer Guy* which helps gay men return to the closet? When you consider that British and American broadcasting networks are bending over backwards to 'carry out our duty to reflect all aspects of the UK's diverse society', grey is apparently not one of the shades that appear on their colour chart of 'diversity'. This is despite the fact that we live in a rapidly greying society. For the first time in history, most British people are over 50. Older people are the only 'minority' who are actually the 'majority'. Age is *the* allowable -ism. And generous sprinkling of fairy-dust euphemisms such as 'reflecting diversity' fails to conceal the basic sophistry at work. Curiously, the former Director General of the BBC never referred to the corporation as being 'hideously young'.

In 2005's BBC Statements of Programme Policy the corporation has a section entitled 'Reflecting the diversity of the UK' but there is scant mention of age. The only mention occurs in a pathological sense much further down the report where the term 'ageism' is found nestled between 'terrorism' and 'disability', just before 'mental health'.

Yet at the same time the BBC's 'grey police' have been busy removing middle-aged reporters, presenters and actors from its screens. And according to a study by Age Concern, the BBC was less 'ageist' than the other networks.[8] Those ever-vigilant to the 'negative stereotyping' of ethnic minorities on prime-time television may consider their sympathies somewhat misplaced when they read an article published in 1988 in the science journal *The Gerontologist*. Even then it was found that older populations suffer from so-called 'negative stereotyping' more than any other identifiable social group, and that in American culture, increasing age seems to portend decreasing value as a human being.[9] In Britain wartime tea rationing continued until 1952. Each person was allowed two ounces per week. But from 1944, the over-70s received an extra ounce. Would we see the same benevolence and respect towards older people today?

Now we can begin to understand how what we see constantly on television relates to the research conclusions 'that the self-perceptions of stigmatized groups can influence longevity'.[1] This is similar to the way that perceived inequality in your social standing is linked to poor physical and mental health through hormone changes and raised cortisol levels (see page 192). The medical effects of feeling our culture's increasing aversion to the look of older people are similar to those of so-called 'class injury'. They are both different aspects of the same principle: a sense of relative deprivation by some groups of low status (older people = not preferred) in relation to other groups (younger = much preferred). It is this sense of relative deprivation of being older while society doesn't like the look of you that is highly accentuated by television. And these feelings are then translated into the physiological changes that lead to poorer health and shorter life in people who have poorer self-perceptions about ageing.

The Grey Police

I was interested to discover exactly how middle-aged people are removed from our television screens. Are they actually told 'You're old, you're fired'? Is there a discussion behind closed doors where one exec says 'Have you noticed Peter's looking a bit rough round the gills?' or 'Do you think Anna still has the "F-Factor"?' and the other execs then vote 'in' or 'out'?

I put this question to one of Britain's main agents representing news anchors and other presenters. He revealed how the end is achieved without a smoking pistol being found. 'The networks are very careful to ensure that it doesn't look as if the ageing presenter is simply "taken out". Usually the presenter is on a relatively short-term contract so when it comes up for renewal, the network simply doesn't elect to renew it. They don't need to provide a reason and they certainly aren't going to write to the news anchor and say "Sorry, but you've got bags under your eyes, perhaps you have a younger sister we could employ instead?" Botox and face-lifts are standard issue for women on television nowadays.'

And as television role models resort to cosmetic surgery as *de rigueur*, so too does the British public. There have never been so many face-lifts, tummy tucks and other forms of new 'elective' surgery, not to mention facial injections to prolong youthful appearance. How ageing is represented on television is a big health issue.

Some presenters are issued with a diplomatic *fait accompli,* handed a pistol and urged to go quietly to the study and do the right thing or the trigger will be pulled for them. Others see the writing on the wall and jump first to other low-key roles. Their routes may differ but ultimately the network manages to put them out to pasture.

As someone who is keen on good weather forecasts, I've noticed the disappearance of proper meteorologists from our screens enthusing about gusts of up to 50 miles an hour in places. I'm also aware of the appearance of an increasing number of 'attractive' women in their place. I find it hard to believe that most of this young, attractive set actually started off with a genuine interest in weather and then ended up on television talking about the thing they've always loved: rain and drizzle with brisk easterly winds over Lancashire. The agent confirmed my worst fears. 'The young women and some young men are sent on what we call "The Little Course", which is really just a three-month crash course on the weather and how to talk about it.' At one point, pretty women were chosen to be 'weatherpersons' from a promotion by BBC Talent, which asked ordinary members of the public 'Is weather your thing?'

I also spoke to an executive at one of the three main

American networks about their preferred method of euthanasia for ageing actors. The executive told me that on one of their main soap operas they were trying to get rid of an actress who'd turned 40. But every time they reached for the pistol, she threatened to sue for age discrimination. The network decided to leave the hit to be carried out by the scriptwriters, who would simply kill her off in the story line. Drama can always use the ultimate weapon – the script – to remove ageing actors. It's all part of the creative process.

Year after year in every area of television it is clear that women receive particularly bad treatment as they venture over 30. And the following decade for them is even worse.

In Britain, Age Concern reports that older men outnumber older women on television by 70 per cent to 30 per cent, even though 57 per cent of the UK population is female. While in the US, more than twice as many roles were cast with actors who were under the age of 40 than actors who were 40 or over.[10]

These statistics are not merely stylistic considerations that affect the acting profession. They affect our health. In the way that images of slimness are being linked to eating disorders, long-term daily exposure to television's unrepresentative, ever-present youthful points of comparison in such an unnaturally high concentration is damaging people. This is precisely how the 'self-perceptions of ageing', which are linked to health and life expectancy in the Yale studies, are distorted.

While it may be true that viewers prefer younger people in some television positions, there is no reason to assume this applies to all areas of the medium. Nigel Ryan, the former editor at ITN in Britain and former vice-president of NBC in the United States, has pointed to a strange anomaly between the two nations. Unlike the United States, in the drive to ensure that everyone on television is easy on the eye, seasoned male newsreaders in their 50s have started to disappear from British screens. And female newsreaders are vanishing at a far younger age.

When the veteran BBC news anchor Peter Sissons disappeared, Ryan was compelled to write 'Peter Sissons is out and everyone knows why – he's in his sixties. It's all part of the trend to be "modern"; Sissons follows Kate Adie and a line of star professionals who are deemed past it. Being modern – a.k.a. youthful – is part of the drive to attract younger viewers...it is surprising and sad to see how lightly the BBC and ITV let the old pros go...[But] do younger viewers really want to hear the Iraqi crisis analysed by someone their own age who was probably at school during the Gulf War, or by an experienced figure who reported on it?' Ryan's essay is entitled 'Age before beauty – the Americans teach us a lesson', and he concludes '...all the evidence is that seasoned veterans command reverence: familiar faces for older viewers but authoritative faces for the whole nation to turn to in a crisis'.[11]

It may be comforting for actors and actresses to know that some of their assassins have been getting a taste of the same rough justice. Emmy award-winning Hollywood writers who'd written for legendary shows like *M*A*S*H* and *All in the Family* have experienced something akin to the Hollywood 'blacklist' of the 1950s. They have been facing an entertainment industry phobic about grey hair. Twenty-eight television writers over the age of 40 even filed a class-action lawsuit against the major television networks and most of the big movie studios and talent agencies. Things have not improved. If the ideas behind the screen only come from the young then our non-visual perceptions of our age are being influenced as well.

Television Stereotypes of Older People

But there is another side to this. When middle-aged and older people do appear on television they often seem to have 'earned' their place to the extent that they can emulate the behaviours of younger people. At times the older person on screen trying to ape the young is simply undignified. In particular, the over-sexualising of older people is both factually incorrect and denies one of the great reliefs of growing older – less performance anxiety. Yet morning chat shows would have you believe that one's frequency of sexual intercourse is simply down to your 'state of mind'…'you're as young as you feel'. Apparently it's cool to know that old people are at it like rabbits too, without having to watch them prove it.

In mainstream programmes, older people are often afforded a part provided they are parodied as figures of fun. Another highly insidious part of television's new devotional position towards youth culture lies in the way the various generations interact, particularly the power relationship between older and younger people in both drama and factual programming. In drama, older characters are spoken to as equals and at times subordinates by the more knowing younger characters. And when children speak out it has been the fashion for them to hold court while parents take note or even 'obey' the child's edicts. This affects the way young people treat older people in real life. Is it therefore surprising that older people on television today are generally not appreciated as experienced elders or possessors of wisdom? In America and Britain where the birth rate is falling and society is greying, the silver-haired sage is obsolescent on the screen. Instead we are encouraged to revere the ideas and importance of the young as never before. The growing lack of respect for older people, reinforced and driven by television, has eroded the social value of more than half of the population. Furthermore, it has weakened a long-established foundation of a civilised society. The effects on family and classroom discipline and law and order are incalculable. With youth culture, everyone's equal so the older person has to 'earn your respect'. In other cultures I've visited, he is afforded respect naturally.

Negative Effects on the Young

But the veneration of youth culture through television also betrays and damages the young. Young people crave and need figures of authority, if only as a frame of reference to rebel against. This is a necessary part of their development. But when their elders end up trying to emulate them it is actually unsettling and confusing for them and the rest of society. After all, someone has to be older and unfunky on television and in real life to enable the young to feel...young. And in a world which changes more quickly in every aspect, older people serve as a form of continuity and quiet reassurance. Given the detrimental health effects of our high rate of divorce and our increasingly mobile society, this is particularly so for children. To deprive the young of these things is selfish and short-sighted. It also denies the majority of the population permission to simply grow old.

Approaches to Ageing in Other Cultures

When I was in China I was told they would be celebrating The Year of the Old Person, something I couldn't imagine ever happening in Britain. And I found the same invisible hierarchy appearing in completely different cultures, such as in Iran, Korea and in the villages of Mali where there was a council of elders who made decisions. In other countries some tribes eat their elders (*after* they die naturally) to gain wisdom. The Wari' tribe in Brazil and the Fore tribe in New Guinea are thought to have practised 'funerary cannibalism'. In most cultures, however, the wisdom of elders isn't something that requires any conscious recognition; older people are naturally respected. Those who seem unconcerned must remember that age is the great leveller, and in the West it is the one form of discrimination that will come to us all.

When seniority and privilege are conferred incrementally with the accumulation of years, *everyone* feels they have an opportunity to gain increasing respect and influence as they

grow older. This is itself highly therapeutic to the ageing individual by taking some of the sting out of growing old. It is
exactly the opposite of the damaging medical effects
described in the Yale study. This system also provides good
social medicine – a second form of government which has a
most powerfully civilising influence.

With so much emphasis on 'bringing democracy' to non-
Western countries by 'regime change', people fail to realise
that Western 'youth television' is already overthrowing a
more naturally evolved long-standing *social* democracy based
on age. As the result of globalised youth television disman-
tling this hierarchy of ageing, more countries are beginning to
experience the social and health consequences. Ironically this
was inadvertently revealed *on* television. In the BBC series
Tribe, the presenter was the first white man in living memory
to visit the Adi people in the Arunachal Pradesh region of
India. He interviewed an elder Adi woman who also acted as
the tribal medicine woman. But when she was asked about
her matriarchal status she pointed out forlornly, 'The young
people go to the other villages and see television. Now, they
don't respect me anymore.'

And this feeling is both a cultural and a health issue
affecting a growing part of our society. It seems it happens
rather invisibly, and those enveloped by it accept it with a
sense of inevitable resignation. One of the defining aspects of
ageing is that you are simply not as militant. Perhaps this
explains why the majority are treated as a minority in the
Western world.

However, not all ageing people have laid down their

weapons. The British broadcaster Joan Bakewell, now 71, has a marvellous riposte to youth-obsessed television functionaries: 'I hate TV channels chasing a young audience. Teenagers shouldn't be watching TV: they should be out taking drugs and getting pregnant.'[12]

PART 2
UNTELEVISED

TEN
CONTROLLING THE REMOTE
A Recommended Daily Allowance for Television

Perhaps because television isn't a substance or a visibly risky activity, it has eluded the value judgements that have befallen other health issues. We can more easily accept the idea of others knowing better than us about more obvious health and safety issues, even though we may choose to ignore their advice. But television involves the communication of ideas, which we feel we can take or leave. To suggest that we take many of the ideas without fully realising it, and that this is bad for our health, has a patronising ring to it. In a culture that reveres freedom of information, thought and expression, pointing to any short-comings in these freedoms is taken as disbelieving of our capacity for free will, quite an undemocratic sentiment.

The evidence presented in this book makes it abundantly clear: there's nothing to be lost by watching less television but much to be lost by continuing to watch as we do.

And the good news is that many of the ills and consequences attributed to television can be dramatically reduced or eliminated immediately by simply controlling how much and what type of television programmes we watch.

While we all need mindless distractions, the issue here is whether television is the right one and, if so, how dominant that distraction is. How much of our lives is being spent on television, and what is this type of distraction doing to us in the process? Even if we ignore the content of television, we now need to conceptualise all time spent watching television as a health issue and to think in terms analogous to dose versus overdose. Most of the negative effects of television reported in the medical literature are associated with watching as little as one-and-a-half hours a day. Yet we watch on average four hours a day, and that doesn't even include DVDs, videos, cinema and time spent on computers. So, when you hear a report in the press refer to the adverse effects of watching television 'excessively', stop and think that 'excessively' often means only two hours a day. And of those media-friendly academics who stroke public concern with popular phrases such as 'moderation is the key', we need to ask what exactly is this comfortable term 'moderation' as it applies to my child's health and well-being?

Exactly How Much Television is Safe?

It's time to define publicly what 'moderate' and 'excessive' amounts of television are in terms of hours and minutes per day. Chapter 4 cited the body of scientists commissioned by the American Psychological Society to review the influence of television on youth as an 'important issue of national interest'. They had some rather clear final thoughts: 'Media use is often described in nutritional terms: people talk about "media consumption" and "a steady diet of"...nourishing children's minds through media is like nourishing their bodies...from a public health perspective, today's consumption patterns are far from optimal. And for many youths they are clearly harmful.'[1]

In the way that we have quantified and provided guidelines on health issues ranging from units of alcohol to hours of sunbathing, we need an equivalent recommended daily allowance (RDA) concept for watching television, especially for children. This is hardly nannying, scaremongering or polemic. It is a firm, considered position adopted by many scientists including the lead researcher of *The Lancet* study cited in Chapter 1, 'Association Between Child and Adolescent Television Viewing and Adult Health'. Dr Robert Hancox commented, 'We believe that reducing television viewing should become a population health priority.' And he goes on to recommend an absolute maximum of less than an hour of television a day for children over five years old.

The American Academy of Pediatrics has issued guidelines clearly recommending that children under the age of two watch no television or any screen entertainment at all, and that no young child should ever have a television in their bedroom because television 'can negatively affect early brain development'. And new evidence published in their journal means this age should now be raised to three. Remember the essay entitled 'Say "No" to Teletubbies', in which the Harvard Medical School academics write: 'Television viewing is exactly the opposite of what toddlers need for their development...young children's television viewing should be postponed as long as possible, and other activities provided and encouraged' (see page 39).

And the author of a seminal study published in the *Journal of the American Medical Association* is unequivocal: 'Take the TV sets out of children's bedrooms. It's just parental abdication to let them have televisions of their own.'

Television is a major health issue and getting around this by offering reassuring incantations like 'everything in moderation' is highly irresponsible.

An RDA for Television

Until we know more about the effects of television on children's neurological circuitry, neurotransmitter regulation and their brain's attention systems, we should listen to this advice:

❑ Children under three should see no screen entertainment.
❑ After this age, television viewing of good quality programmes should be limited to *an hour a day*.
❑ Teenagers should be limited to one-and-a-half hours a day.
❑ And for adults, two hours a day.

This should include any time spent watching DVDs, videos

or video/computer games. Time spent using computers and surfing the Internet should also be taken into consideration as it's all screen time.

Controlling Children's Viewing

In addition to how much screen time should be 'consumed', there's a more basic issue of who's controlling the screen in your home.

- ❏ Children should not have a television set in their bedroom until at least the age of 15 and even then they should watch no more than one-and-a-half hours a day until they're old enough to move out and pay their own rent, buy their own television and pay their own licence fee.

- ❏ Don't surf the channels looking for something for your child. Plan your child's viewing using the listings guide and reviews so you and your child can decide what to watch. Turn the screen on so they can watch the programme, and turn it off when the show's over.

- ❏ Don't let your child watch television while they do their homework. This will reduce their ability to learn and the quality of the homework they produce. The amount and type of television your child watches will influence their desire and ability to read. If the desire to read diminishes, so does their ability to read, and the ability to read well is directly related to ability to learn. This determines school performance and future career opportunities.

❏ When children over the age of three do watch television, make sure that you choose the programmes they watch. It's better that they see videos and DVDs, which you choose, as children generally don't care where the images on the screen come from as long as they enjoy them.

❏ Channels that are specifically for children's cartoons are generally bad for children, as cartoons have higher rates of editing, and event changes, and are less likely to have as much continuity in narrative or the narrator's voice. In this respect, classic cartoons, a classic Disney film like *Jungle Book* or *Mary Poppins* and even a *Carry On* film are infinitely better than a modern cartoon.

❏ It's better for children not to have their programmes interspersed with advertisements, as this conditions their developing attentional systems not to fully invest their attention in a story because it will inevitably be interrupted. The speed of editing and event changes in advertising is very high and may be ideally suited to causing damage to their attentional circuits.

❏ Allowing your child to watch things you're not happy with and then hoping to offset the influence of the programme by talking with them about it is *bad*. It smacks of a damage-limitation approach. Don't let them see it in the first place. After all, you're the parent.

❑ It's best if you can watch the programmes you approve of with your child and help to interpret what they see by talking about it. That way you'll know exactly what they're being exposed to as it happens. If you can't do this because you're busy, record the programmes so you can both watch them later.

❑ Set a good example. What you do strongly influences what your child will do or want to do. By limiting your own television viewing and actively choosing carefully what you want to watch, your child is more likely to do the same.

❑ Watching a screen can become a habit for your child. Help them find other things to do with their time. Obvious candidates are reading; playing; activities with family, friends or neighbours; learning a hobby, sport, an instrument or an art.

Addicted Adults

For many people, simply being aware of the main issues in this book will result in them effortlessly halving their time in front of the television. Others may need to think in a more deliberate way. The following may seem an asinine example of stating the obvious but it's necessary:

- ❏ Simply decide on what you want to watch by circling it at the beginning of the week, or recording it, so you control how and when it's watched and aren't sucked in to watching the following programme and then the following programme...

- ❏ Furthermore, research has shown that many of us record a programme but then never bother to watch it. This is an inadvertent way of reducing the amount of television you watch.

- ❏ There's also the possibility of having a monitor that can't receive television signals, so you can watch only DVDs and videos. Many computers enable you to do this already. That way you actually have to think about what and when you watch, and you actively have to buy, borrow or rent it. You also won't need a television licence.

The emphasis should be on how you can harness television for your own benefit. These, along with *conscious*, *selective* viewing, are clear examples of what the term 'remote control' should mean – the dog wagging the tail.

Good Quality Television?

Evaluating the 'quality' of a television programme in terms of how it relates to your or your child's health is not a fine science. It also seems an odd and rather priggish way to consider an 'art form'. Nevertheless, because television is becoming a health issue, it is important to try and tease out some of the components of television programmes that can be described in terms of better or worse health.

While many people may think that the news or a documentary is better for you than a soap or 'daytime telly', this is not necessarily the case. For example, the news and documentaries also distort reality in ways that are often stranger than fiction. And the techniques and subject matter they use to arrest and hold your attention to maintain their ratings can be more extreme than any drama. All television is intended to arrest attention, and to do this hour after hour, broadcasters need to show a heightened version of reality. After all, reality television is a heightened version of reality.

These perhaps obvious points are something to think about when you are trying to make judgements about what you or your children watch. And if you take into consideration the findings presented in this book, there are some further themes that can help you to make decisions.

Continuity

Irrespective of the content of children's programmes there is the issue of the sheer speed of scene changes, which may damage their ability to pay attention. Programmes that you feel seem to have higher rates of editing and event changes, especially cartoons and music videos, are not good for young children. Lots of loud noises, colours and effects may arrest and hold a child's attention but should be avoided for the same reasons. For young children, the continuity of a story line and narrator's voice are two key things to look for. In this respect some of the classic children's films are best. This is not intended to appear old-fashioned for its own sake. *Noddy*, *Thomas the Tank Engine* and *Pingu* are good points of reference by which to judge others. There are also some modern examples such as the BBC's *Balamory*. Films such as *Chitty Chitty Bang Bang*, *Fantasia*, *Oliver*, *Annie* and *The Wizard of Oz* are good benchmarks.

There is an even greater number of adult films that appeal to children on a different and innocent level and are immensely entertaining. Adult musicals from *An American in Paris* to *Grease* are full of physical movement and can mesmerise children. And while adults assume *Carry On* films are full of smut and innuendo, this goes over younger children's heads because it is all implied, and children love the slapstick of it all. Moreover, pop music programmes and many children's cartoons, music videos and adverts are far more explicitly sexual than *Carry On* films; just take a look at the hip movements and sentiments that accompany them. *Laurel and Hardy* will make most children laugh.

Many parents may think that children shouldn't watch the same film again and again on different occasions. Not true. Children notice new elements of a good film each time they see it. There's also the element of a comforting familiarity. Of course, the film industry wants them to do the opposite so they can sell more films.

Diseased Role Models

Young girls are strongly influenced by the body shape of female cartoon characters as well as those of actresses and

children's television presenters. There is a link with dangerous dieting, body dissatisfaction and serious eating disorders
(see pages 199 and 204). Keep your children away from these
images, no matter how famous the 'personalities' are or
whether they are approved by CBBC or Nickelodeon.
Permarexic women on television are not only damaging their
own health; they're damaging your child's health as well.

Bad Points of Comparison

Learning to loathe yourself can be even easier if you watch a
lot of television awash with the beautiful people. The
research showing that beautiful images on television make
women feel worse about themselves should be taken seriously. It is not normal for such a high proportion of society
to feel as bad as they currently do about the way they look.
Your child is also susceptible to this, especially while they are
developing and forming reference points of what is normal
and possible in terms of their appearance. Some of the
cartoon channels also have characters which represent
powerfully unrealistic points of physical comparison. If you
want to retain some semblance of self-esteem, watch less of
this sort of television; in fact watch less television full stop.

Dissing

While most attention has been paid to violence on television,
its close relative, disrespect, has flourished. Many programmes
cultivate an inherent unhealthy equality with, or disrespect
towards, adults. Soaps in particular are immersed in this
imbalance, as are some children's drama series such as *The*

Story of Tracy Beaker, which may be contemporary, PC, urban and reflect social issues, but it won't get you much respect as an adult. *Grange Hill* enables young people to rule and affords viewers a sense of entitlement. In ordinary sitcoms broadcast during the early evening adolescents are often given cocky adult lines – great for a laugh if you're a hip urban scriptwriter, but if your kids start behaving this way it'll wipe the smile right off your face. Even more influential are famous football players swearing at the referee and putting two fingers up. Bear all of this in mind when your children want to watch television, as the cultivation of disrespect is insidious and cumulative.

Violence

Chapter 4 made it clear that violent television leads to more violence and/or the fear of it. What is more worrying is that indirect aggression isn't being considered. Soap operas such as *EastEnders*, *Coronation Street* and *Hollyoaks* and series like *The Bill* and *Holby City* have plenty of sneering, snarling, bitching and general confrontation. The subtle body language and attitude that the television role models provide rub off easily on children and adults. *EastEnders* may be contemporary urban art comprising lashings of 'social realism' but this has nothing to do with being good for the psyche or society: it's bad for your children. There are plenty of other things they can watch. Hip-hop videos and films, which make inner-city street urchins look somewhat user-friendly and falsely elevate them to the status of influential individuals, are peddling a fundamental lie which will influence boys' behaviour and attitude. Many black leaders deplore this media, so ask yourself

'If the hip-hop and gangsta role models were white...would our society be as accepting of this media?'

Nocturnal Viewing

Watching television before bedtime leads to poorer sleep for both children and adults (see Chapter 1 for the health implications). Children should not be watching 'bedtime' videos. Read to them, encourage them to read themselves or play them an audio book. Adults who complain about lack of sleep or difficulty sleeping often fail to consider that television – especially the kind you watch in the evening – is not conducive to sleeping well. In particular, many people feel they have to see the news in order to be visually informed of 'what's happening in the world'. Question this assumption! It is not necessary to watch the night-time news in order to be 'well-informed'. It can be argued that lots of stimulating pictures of bad things from around the globe may bathe you in snippets of information but actually leave you less well-informed than if you listened to *The World Tonight* on BBC Radio 4 or the BBC World Service, or your local speech radio station, or one of the infinite digital stations you can receive via the Internet from around the world. Or better yet, listen to it the next morning. And what about reading the newspaper? Television news changes mood by increasing anxiety and is bad for your sleep, so follow the same advice given to your children – read or listen to an audio book or gentle speech or music radio. If you have to see the news on a television screen then watch an earlier edition such as Channel 4 News at 7pm or BBC 24, long before your bedtime.

PCTV

If you feel your child is taking in values or social or political messages embedded within programmes that are contrary to your own, you need to undermine those messages. Comment on the aspects of the programme you disagree with and explain why the message is flawed. Better yet, explain how the programme is trying to socially engineer your child's attitudes and feelings, and enable them to become vigilant to it. This process can also be immensely educational by cultivating rational analysis as opposed to a bewildered herd mind-set.

Adverts

Don't assume your child is immune to adverts for sweets, toys, drinks, snacks, breakfast cereals or new television shows without your help. When your child asks for these 'as-seen-on-TV' things, explain what the adverts are trying to do – make people want things whether they need them or not. You can drastically reduce the number of adverts they see by watching public broadcasting stations, recording programmes leaving the adverts out, and hiring videos/DVDs and starting the film from the point after all the trailers for other films start.

If you use more videos and DVDs, including television programmes you record, then you will be controlling what your children see. This is ideal. While the video and film classification system doesn't take some of the medical issues in this book into consideration, it does issue age ratings on videos which can help rule out some bad ones. The Coalition for Quality Children's Media has a website with reviews of and suggestions for old and new children's programmes and videos/DVDs. Although they are a non-profit organisation, they do receive sponsorship from the television-related media (www.cqcm.org). Mediawatch-uk has a list of organisations that can provide some parental guidance for new children's television and videos/DVDs (www.mediawatchuk.org/NewLinks.htm).

Prescription Television

Television can be used for very selective purposes. Interestingly, scientists who study the biology of emotions and moods in the laboratory are now harnessing the effects of television and cinema films as a dedicated tool to create the specific emotions they need to examine: emotion elicitation with movie clips. In other words, men in white coats are verifying that we can use a television programme or a video to change our mood. And in the clinical arena, psychologists are now using the act of watching a programme or film as a helpful technique in resolving emotional issues. 'Cinema therapy' is an approach that uses film as an emotional prompt in psychotherapy. The therapists believe that exploring the effect of a film can enable them to gain access more easily to the emotionally charged themes and conflicts suffered by their patients.

For example, we have always self-administered comedy programmes to make us laugh without thinking too much about what the laughter is actually doing for us. But genuine laughter does, in itself, immediately change the way we feel for the better. The field of psychoneuroimmunology has charted the ways in which key aspects of our immune system change immediately in response to a good television-induced belly laugh. And so do our levels of stress hormones such as adrenaline and cortisol, calming us down and raising our spirits. An occasional good comedy may also provide an emotional holiday from our present concerns, and enable us to view them in a different light or from a different angle.

These recommendations may seem rather austere but all health issues need some general guidelines to be used only as ideals. We need some frame of reference in which to make judgements, and these recommendations are that frame of reference. If this comes across as medical fascism, then please read the evidence one more time.

In the United States, there's a very American 'can-do' approach to the problem – TV Turnoff Network (www.tvturnoff.org). It's a national non-profit organisation encouraging people to live the 'low-TV lifestyle', as they put it. It was founded in 1994 to encourage people 'to watch much less television in order to promote healthier lives and communities...we all have the power to determine the role that television plays in our lives. Rather than waiting for others to make "better" TV, we can turn it off and reclaim time for our families, our friends and for ourselves'. TV Turnoff is even endorsed by the circumspect, conservative American Medical Association, as well as US Surgeon General David Satcher.

And for those of us who want to get rid of our televisions altogether, there is a great deal of further rationale and persuasion offered by White Dot, the international campaign against television (www.whitedot.org). While the television industry would like to portray their stance as extreme, it's not at all. They offer, for example, practical advice on how to deal with children without using an electronic screen: 'Sixteen tips to manage toddlers – without resorting to television.'

Getting rid of your television should not be considered extreme. You are immediately doubling the amount of free time you have and, after a short period of time, you are very unlikely to miss it. Many people think they can be a discerning viewer, but simply can't, and this may well be the best solution.

But we also have to ask ourselves what we are actually doing, or going to do, with the untelevised waking hours of our lives.

ELEVEN
THE STATE FORMERLY KNOWN AS BOREDOM

In Praise of True Idleness and Little Stimulation

At a point when many people are preoccupied with finding ways to be happier and healthier, many of the options – while right in front of our noses – are not obvious. Yet as medicine finds fault with television, it offers praise for television's competitors, rediscovering tremendous benefits in many of the ways we could spend our time.

In surveying our own lives and our society's 'lifestyles', there are some illuminating points of comparison gleaned from recent research.

The last half-century has seen a dramatic retreat from silence and solitude. Unlike television-sponsored media studies researchers, the American philosopher Ralph Waldo Emerson would never receive funding today for thoughts such as these:

'Solitude, the safeguard of mediocrity, is to genius the stern friend...He who should inspire and lead his race must be defended from travelling with the souls of other men, from living, breathing, reading, and writing in the daily, time-worn yoke of their opinions.' (From *Conduct of Life*, 1860.)

Such heretical thinking nowadays flies in the face of the media marketplace, which needs us to shun solitude, introspection and independent thinking in favour of the opposite – watching the same screen as everyone else – with all of the health consequences that are coming to light. This retreat from solitude and silence goes hand in hand with our aversion to 'boredom'. People go to great lengths to avoid boredom. They try to protect their children from suffering it. Yet boredom is sadly one of the most misused and misunderstood terms. What passes for boredom nowadays is in fact withdrawal symptoms from a glut of stimulation brought to you by an attention economy. The fuel that keeps such economy running isn't oil – it's adrenaline laced with a dash of dopamine. After all, in order to make a commercial profit it's important to keep the bewildered herd stimulated.

While it's true that we are sensation-seeking organisms, our bent for a buzz has been hijacked. Once we settle for a certain level of variety, intensity and novelty we quickly become habituated and need a change and so it goes on...and on. It isn't just high-spice television programming but a cultural imperative to Go For It and never say 'dull'. Adrenaline is our new drug of choice. In describing time when we're not doing or actively experiencing something, some academics now refer to 'undesignated moments' because they have become such an exception. In a society where we are always 'ON', why would any industries in their right mind want us to turn off?

If we turn inward then we're not spending money or helping to increase the ratings for network television: there's little commercial profit to be found in promoting idleness and daydreaming, worst of all introspection. This is yet another case of truth belonging to those who commission it. Can you imagine being an academic and trying to get research money for a project. On the application form where it says 'Title of Proposed Research' you put: 'Investigating the Potential Intellectual and Emotional Benefits of Doing Nothing in Particular.' Don't give up your current daytime job.

Our need for real downtime couldn't be greater. While I'm not trying to portray boredom as the new sex, ensuring that we experience enough troughs within a life of peaks is necessary to enjoy those peaks. Describing this in chemical terms may seem an odd way to think about respite, but adrenaline and our overuse of it is very real. Adrenaline keeps you disconnected from your feelings, the very thing that defines what we experience as life. If children are brought up with too much stimulation and fail to learn how to experience and utilise downtime, it sets a precedent whereby their engine speed is unable to slow down and cruise intellectually and emotionally.

Our dependence on television is symptomatic of avoiding the deeply unfashionable state of being 'understimulated'. Yet there are sound reasons for a passionate celebration of bore-dom, daydreaming or, for the more earnest, introspection, especially for children. And there are compelling reasons why we shouldn't be filling our children's free time with 'stimulating' play activities. Psychologists now talk of the 'overbooked child' or 'overscheduled kid'. Boredom, not computers, is the single greatest gift to your child's intellectual and creative development. The developmental and clinical psychologist Professor Diane Ehrensaft writes of 'spoiling childhood', observing that many middle-class children in the United States 'have almost no "nothing time". They have no time to call on their own resources and be creative. Creativity is making something out of nothing, and it takes time for that to happen'. These same points apply to adults, especially considering the extent to which we complain of 'time poverty'.[1]

Boredom is the raw material used to build self-awareness. Children need time to read, write, draw, create, fantasise, think, build and explore their interests. This helps the child shape, clarify and identify who they are and what they are interested in. Children bathed in too many structured activities have little time for this type of self-generated development.

The Threat to Imagination and Creativity

While children today theoretically have many more opportunities to develop intellectually and emotionally, this has turned out to be a curse rather than a blessing.

Children need time to explore things in depth, yet our culture promotes the opportunity to skim myriad surfaces, to channel hop, surf the net, try different things out. Variety and diversity may sound contemporary but conceal a new generation sacrificing breadth for depth. Whether it's the number of television channels, toys or activities to choose from, the libertarian concept of choice is hardly liberating. Like today's consumer, today's child feels the burden of a tyranny of options brought upon them, drowning in a sea of alternatives. Choice as manifested today is retarding, and now the tangible effects on imagination and creativity are visible.

Television has been at the core of this change. And now researchers are merely confirming what many teachers have reported for years: children are becoming less imaginative because they watch too much television and their parents fill their leisure time with structured activities. For example, a British study analysed creative writing by 10- and 11-year-old children to assess whether their stories were influenced by television and videos. Dr Teresa Belton at the Centre for Applied Research in Education at the University of East Anglia found, after analysing more than 400 short stories about a 'face at the window', that it was more a case of a face on the television. Many children simply copied television plot lines. She commented, 'While it proved possible for screen material to set off fresh thinking, this firing of the imagination was a rare occurrence. Those stories that seemed the most imaginative, the most attractive...appeared to have no connection with the screen...television or video are now virtually always there to fill the gap, so that children are rarely without distraction and rarely find themselves having to initiate their own reveries or occupations.' And the conclusion of her study was unambiguous: '...the ubiquity and ease of access to television and videos perhaps robs today's children of the need to pursue their own thoughts and devise their own occupations ...'[2,3]

And in A-level exams, Shakespeare too has been subjected to the television touch. A study by the Assessment and Qualifications Alliance, the largest exam board in Britain, found that A-level students are increasingly using 'soap opera' phrases and 'shockingly inappropriate slang' in their English exams. In fact, they reported that some exam answers 'relied mainly on soap opera descriptions'. And there were many other examples from television that permeated the thinking of the examinees. The report said, 'There are many examples of psychobabble: both Hamlet and Leontes need to "move on" but they can be "comfortable around" Horatio and Paulina who are "always there" for them, while they seek "closure".' Other examples of television-derived prefabricated creativity from exam papers included:

'It's like yeah, Cleo is player'
(*Antony and Cleopatra*)

'So anyway, Viola's had it with Olivia and is fuming with her'
(*Twelfth Night*)[4]

Research into Boredom (not Boring Research)

Yet the infringement of television on creativity and imagination can be so easily prevented, and often reversed, by

reducing screen time and replacing it with other activities...
including boredom. One way of looking at this area of boredom and understimulation is to see what happens when you
artificially remove all external stimulation to someone. In the
Cold War 1950s, boredom had a bad reputation – so much
so that the military became interested in how it could be used
to brainwash. Boredom was a negative state, a disease to be
avoided or, better yet, harnessed as a weapon to make the
enemy talk. *Scientific American* published 'The Pathology of
Boredom'. Research on 'sensory deprivation' had been
started in 1951 at McGill University, Canada, by psychologist D.O. Hebbs, who recalls, 'The aim of the project was to
obtain basic information on how human beings would react
in situations where nothing was happening. The purpose was
not to cut individuals off from any sensory stimulation whatever, but to remove all patterned or perceptual stimulation,
so far as we could arrange it.' Life without a television screen
could be deemed a form of deprivation.

The 1950s also saw behaviourism growing in influence.
The behaviourist school of psychology considered the brain
as an organ, which needed outside stimulation to react to.
Little has changed when you look at the way parents embrace
this assumption today regarding their children's brains. But a
medical researcher, John C. Lilly, had a more favourable view
of boredom's potential. He conducted 'physical isolation'
experiments at the US National Institutes of Mental Health
Lab, minimising external stimulation. At this time, some
scientists were curious as to what would happen to the brain
and mind if all stimulation and interactions with the outside

world could be cut off. As the brain was thought to function by reacting to outside stimulation, they thought that if all outside stimuli were removed, the brain would essentially enter into a type of comatose state or 'dreamless' sleep. Others thought that in a state of extreme sensory isolation the brain would continue functioning and producing experiences. The main question was: does the brain need sensory stimulation to remain active, alert and alive?

Lilly published his findings in 1956 and they were pleasantly surprising. 'The mind does not pass into unconsciousness, the brain does not shut down. Instead, it constructs experience out of stored impressions and memories. The isolated mind becomes highly active and creative.'[5] So not only can the mind cope perfectly well without a television screen to stimulate it, it can become actively imaginative.

And 20 years later an academic paper, 'The Benefits of Boredom', heralded a greater acceptance that such isolation work could have a positive side. Subsequently, the term 'sensory deprivation' was thought to carry some unsavoury baggage and projected a rather punishing image. So in the adrenaline-flooded 1980s it re-emerged as 'restricted environmental stimulation' (RES). 'Flotation tanks' began to replace 'isolation chambers'. And now, if people's brains are in any way washed, it means cleared of the unwanted ubiquitous electronic distractions of today. The effects of restricting environmental stimulation are very revealing. In short, by giving people, including children, an enforced absence of stimulation, there are measurable improvements in a variety of things, from creativity to calmness. Tests of attention and reaction time also show improvements after restricting environmental stimulation. Even sporting performance in tennis, rowing, basketball and athletics has been found to improve as the result of lying down and being 'bored'. Watching television reduces your performance in these things.[6,7]

It seems that our reaction to restricted stimulation is to regain a sense of equilibrium which allows necessary things to happen rather invisibly. Perhaps this is why the middle classes are now paying in order to withdraw to a 'retreat'.

And perhaps this is why Edward Gibbon, the 18th-century British historian, felt 'Conversation enriches the understanding, but solitude is the school of genius.' It probably also has something to do with why he was able to write *The History of the Decline and Fall of the Roman Empire*.

Less is More

Aside from those few people who own flotation tanks in order to sell 'sessions' in them, there's little economic or academic future to be had investing in boredom and its attributes. I can't really see MTV running an ad campaign: Boredom – Check it Out. But in an age of stimulation abundance, less is proving to be more. For example, it's recently been found that reducing the number of toys young children have has significant intellectual benefits, as too much variety confuses and distracts them. This enables them to enjoy depth as opposed to breadth.[8] I somehow can't imagine that an industry exists to promote and publicise the need to reduce the number of toys we buy for our children.

Moreover, by not watching television, children will benefit tremendously from being allowed to learn how to stimulate themselves using their own imagination and resourcefulness. This fosters a form of emotional and intellectual self-sufficiency, skills that will provide them with enormous advantages in every area from school to marital relationships. And adults derive the benefits of greater concentration, clarity of thought, enhanced creativity and a greater resilience to anxiety and stress.

Again the problem is that there are no public health messages, daily reminders in the newspapers or advertisements on television prompting us to look away and do less in order to feel better and ultimately even achieve more. Who, aside from a few scruffy psychologists, would derive any benefit from dedicating their life to recommending a bit more daydreaming? The stuff can't be bottled. And politicians are hardly likely to initiate a public debate addressing questions such as: 'Is it really mindless to let our minds wander aimlessly, or is it the most productive yet undervalued strategy available to us?' No, boredom-for-all doesn't sound a particularly appetising entrée on a manifesto.

Unlike the rather feeble version of 'getting in touch with your emotions' promoted in endless self-help books, isn't allowing our minds time to file our feelings nothing more than sensible psychological housekeeping? And in this respect boredom is the perfect housekeeper.

Reducing the amount and intensity of stimulation we consume is one of the greatest challenges and achievements we could embark on. In an age of techniques, methods, hothousing and enriching, simply reducing stimulation as opposed to adding it is the greatest trick of all. It's just that the idea lacks funding because it can't be patented. Fortunately, it's free, and we can start by simply watching less television or computer screen and doing very little except thinking to ourselves. Given that we're spending between 28 and 40 hours a week voluntarily looking at a screen, trading in some of this time won't require a course in time management. This nouveau boredom can even be conducted while taking in a bit of free greenery. It's wholesome and simple, but the advantages are solid yet understated.

Small children most enjoy the timeless pleasures of a walk in the park and visiting grandparents. And it's often the grandparents who actually remember how to fire a child's imagination using books and stories as opposed to television. Children are being deprived of living circumstances that would expand their minds – they're being deprived of the right to be bored and, in turn, of learning the process to escape the boredom. It's the creative equivalent of preventing children from doing any physical exertion to the point that they become unfit. So if you love your children, give them the gift of boredom.

When I question the existence of television in children's lives and tell parents that I've recently stopped my own young children from watching television, allowing the occasional video, the response I often hear is 'But what do they do all day? How do you keep them busy?' Fortunately, much to my surprise, they keep themselves perfectly busy with little help from me. This was a child's default setting long before television was invented. Yet parents find it hard to believe in a child's innate ability to find interest and pleasure so intuitively and spontaneously.

It should be a great relief to parents that children adapt very quickly and easily to removing the television from their room. One of the benefits of being a child is your adaptability. Children are naturally nosy and their imaginations can be jump-started by leaving the intellectual space for them to begin the process. Whether it's scribbling, playing with cardboard or digging in the garden, they will naturally do things to stop any imagined pain you feel they might suffer at the hands of boredom. Whether they play hide and seek or doctors and nurses, the process driving it is their imagination and initiative. It's time we changed the public face of daydreaming and general idleness and reintroduced the lost art of taking it easy.

TWELVE
THE POTTING SHED EFFECT
How Greenery Counteracts Television's Effects

Beyond a new appreciation of boredom and 'undesignated moments', there is another timeless, free phenomenon offering extraordinary benefits at odds with television's effects: exposure to greenery. This is a timely issue. While unstructured outdoor playtime has decreased considerably during the past quarter of a century, childhood obesity and attention deficit disorders have risen dramatically. Researchers at the Children's Hospital of Philadelphia have issued a call to bring unstructured outdoor playtime back into children's lives as a matter of urgency.

Laudable as the green movement is, it has always been bedevilled by images of Swampy emerging from a hole in the ground and Prince Charles seeming unnaturally close to plants. The environmental movement, while rightly emphasising the importance of greenery for our world in a general sense, does not yet pander to people's selfish side: 'What will greenery do for me in the here and now, to make me happier and healthier?' But things are about to change. The new fields of environmental medicine and ecopsychology are coming into their own with research that neither the television nor pharmaceutical industry would have any reason to fund, or welcome for that matter.

The Benefits of Greenery for Attention

You may have noticed a recurring theme in this book is the way in which television affects our attentional skills: young children who watch more television may have a significantly increased risk of developing an attention deficit hyperactivity disorder (ADHD) (see Chapter 1), and there is also good reason to believe that early exposure to television subverts and damages other aspects of a child's attention. Watching television also affects adults' attentional state. Studying the link between television and attentional damage may in future actually reveal different types of attentional damage. Even if the effects of watching television on our ability to pay attention are temporary, if we are watching television and looking at other screens for hours every day, these 'temporary' effects will persist a great deal of the time. In fact, some scientists now report that modern activities and situations involving prolonged or intense use of our attention cause an attentional 'fatigue' to set in. Interestingly a study in the *American Journal of Public Health* reports '...it becomes increasingly difficult to pay attention and inhibit impulses; that is, the behavior and performance of individuals without ADHD temporarily take on many of the characteristic patterns of ADHD'.[1]

Like many discoveries in other areas of science, something rather ordinary is being reconsidered as unlocking some of the mystery surrounding attentional damage. The *American Journal of Public Health Study* has found that exposing children with ADHD to outdoor greenery significantly reduces their symptoms. The scientists evaluated the effects of 49 after-school or weekend activities conducted in green outdoor settings versus those conducted in both built outdoor and indoor settings. The results were highly impressive. And the effect was consistent across age, gender, socioeconomic status, type of community, geographic region and diagnosis. In fact, the greener the setting, the greater the relief from symptoms. The researchers also pointed to 'substantial research conducted' among people without ADHD showing that inattention and impulsivity are reduced after exposure to green natural views and settings.[1]

So, a growing number of scientists now believes that, for most of us, being exposed to greenery has general, widespread benefits for our ability to pay attention. Studies now report 'superior attentional functioning' and that 'the effect of nature on inattention is robust'.[2]

What Causes these Benefits?

But how can something as mundane as a tree or some grass exert any biological effects on people? The explanations seem to revolve around the way greenery effortlessly engages our attention, allowing us to attend without paying attention. This is profoundly different to the arresting effect of television on our attention. One theory is referred to as 'attentional restoration theory' whereby certain activities cause a temporary 'attention fatigue' which is corrected when our underlying attention system has an opportunity to rest. And natural green environments help in recovery from this attention fatigue, in part because they engage our mind effortlessly. So the sense of rejuvenation we often experience after spending time in natural settings may in part reflect a 'recharging' of some parts of our attentional system.[3] It's as if television, with its compelling images and fast editing, arrests our attention while greenery disengages or liberates it. Greenery offers us 'soft fascination' – holding our attention but leaving us ample opportunity to think about other things.

And nowadays there are precious few opportunities for experiencing this state of soft fascination. Modern forms of entertainment and recreation are indeed designed to arrest our attention. Our economy depends upon our 'arrest' and our culture is defined by it. We spend an increasing amount of our time and effort responding to the external distractions imposed on us. The information-processing demands of everyday life – traffic, telephones, email, television, conversations, problems at work, increasing consumer and lifestyle choices and associated decisions – take their toll on our intellectual and emotional resources. We increasingly pay attention to more than one thing at a time – 'multitasking' – and are encouraged to do so. Research shows that many children are now looking at more than one screen at a time, switching glances between the television and the Internet. That's why economists now talk in terms of the 'attention economy', as if our attention were a limited resource to be spent. And so our contact with greenery seems to provide some form of neurological respite from deliberately misspending our attention all day through too much screen time. The study in the *American Journal of Public Health* speculated on how the possibility of 'daily doses of "green time" might supplement medications and behavioral approaches to ADHD'.

In a completely different context, prescribing 'green time' is again being shown to improve concentration. A recent study looked at the effects of exposing women in their third trimester of pregnancy to nature settings. Several measures of concentration were taken before one group of women was prescribed spending 120 minutes each week outdoors surrounded by nature. When they were tested again later, these women had significantly fewer errors on the attention tests compared to the control group. Again, the conclusion was straightforward '...encouraging women to spend time in activities that involve nature...may help pregnant women improve their ability to concentrate and reduce errors'.[4]

And the effects of greenery run contrary to the effects of television in a number of other important ways.

❑ Unlike television, greenery improves children's mental abilities including perceiving, thinking, recognising and remembering. For example, children who move home to somewhere

293

surrounded by more greenery show increases in these capacities, and the greener the new surroundings, the higher their performance.[5]

❏ Watching television has been shown to cause social disengagement and worsening of mood and limited face-to-face contact within families, neighbourhoods and communities, not least because of the sheer amount of time people spend looking at a screen as opposed to one another.[6] Now large-scale research is finding that green space in residential areas 'fosters more face-to-face contacts among neighbors that lead to more social interaction'. Researchers found 83 per cent more people involved in social activities in green areas compared to barren spaces. This is a systematic positive link between the greenness of a neighbourhood and the number of people involved in activities. They interpret this as central to the 'social cohesion and vitality of a neighbourhood'. This is the exact opposite of what television does to communities.[7,8]

Effects on Self-discipline

In addition to affecting our ability to concentrate, television has been strongly criticised for cultivating a sense of entitlement to instant gratification and the fulfilment of impulses – giving permission to our id (the part of the personality driven by raw impulse and desire). But in a complete inversion of this effect, scientists at the University of Illinois say 'views of green help girls foster life success'. In their study, they randomly assigned 169 inner-city girls and boys to 12 architecturally identical high-rise buildings with varying levels of nearby greenery in view. (As boys spent less time at home and played elsewhere the results did not apply to them.) They found that the greener and more natural a girl's view from home, the better she scores on tests of concentration, impulse inhibition and delayed gratification. They see this as happening through an improvement in 'self-discipline – a predictor of delinquency, drug abuse, poor school grades, teenage pregnancy'.[9] Again, this is the exact opposite of what television is being found to do to these potential behaviours. It's as if greenery reinforces the more responsible parts of the psyche, the ego and superego, enabling these departments to deal more assertively with the reckless, selfish id.

Self-discipline requires your attention. So when your attentional system becomes tired your self-discipline declines, but when your attention is revived by exposure to greenery, your self-discipline improves again. If the medium of television alone causes your attention to become tired, leading to a decline in your ability to delay your need for gratification, the content of television – especially advertising – makes matters worse by stoking up your selfish urges intentionally.

Plant Power

Freud called our experiences of nature 'oceanic'. Unlike man-made recreation, greenery provides a sense of coherence. It is devoid of negative feedback – it does not offer bad news, disturbing images or criticism – and therefore reinforces our self-esteem. While modern recreation – television and computer games in particular – stimulates the stress-producing sympathetic nervous system, greenery activates the opposite parasympathetic nervous system, which calms and relaxes us. Greenery can wean us off the need for the constant high stimulation of television images and other sources of the buzz. It's even used to help treat drug addiction. And neither the indoors nor urban landscapes possess the attribute of mystery that satisfies our need to explore, television even less so. While promoting Mother Nature may seem earnest, holistic and woolly, this new scientific line of enquiry is certainly not. For most of us, horticulture's effects on our well-being are perhaps accepted but thought of in vague terms. Yet the study of plants and trees truly is a new domain of medicine; it's just that unlike pharmaceuticals, Mother Nature doesn't have a benefactor to lobby on her behalf. As a point of comparison with television, here are some examples:

❑ While both violent and non-violent television has been consistently linked to increased aggression and violence, exposure to greenery is being found to diminish it within neighbourhoods. All things being equal, the greener the surroundings, the less 'wife beating' occurs and fewer crimes are committed against people and property. Greenery seems to help people to relax and renew, reducing aggression. And greenery also increases social interaction and cohesion. The message to urban planners is: block planning permission for large television screens in public places and make those spaces greener.[10]

❑ Further research is looking at the way plants have a powerful effect on people's ability to cope with poverty. Poor people with a slightly green view were found to be much better able to manage major life issues. A researcher remarked, 'It is striking that the presence of a few trees and some grass outside a 16-storey apartment building could have any measurable effect on an individual's capacity to manage the most important issues in her life, with an effect size comparable to that of major factors such as health and age.'[11] Yet again, greenery's effect on attention is cited as the main factor. A study published by the British Medical Association finds that people in cities live longer and are healthier when they are exposed to greenery.[12] This is everything that television works against. Not only does television erode attentional resources but the content of television makes viewers feel even more deprived. It seems that exposure to greenery enables people to cope and make decisions more effectively.

Beyond our mere exposure to greenery is the hands-on type of relationship – gardening.

❑ The British love of gardening is actually saving people's lives and extending them. Not only is gardening now considered to be of medical benefit in terms of exercise, it also involves contact with plant life, increasing the benefits even further. For example, an hour of gardening a day can reduce your risk of dying prematurely by 28 per cent and help reduce coronary heart disease and other chronic illnesses. Even 30 minutes of gardening a day on most days of the week that doesn't produce a noticeable improvement in your physical fitness will protect you from certain chronic diseases.[13,14] In comparison, even one-and-a-half to two hours of television is being linked with an array of well-established risk factors for serious illness later in life and premature death.[15]

❑ While television is making people fatter, greenery can do the opposite. The Early Learning Centre has found that nearly nine in ten children spend almost the whole weekend stuck indoors, most in front of a television screen, at a time when the Royal College of Physicians is concerned that the UK has the lowest level of physical activity for children in Europe. Luring us away from passive indoor electronic distractions to gardening or the outdoors is vital.

❑ Just thinking about plants affects our physiology for the better. Simply visualising images of nature scenes induces significantly greater relaxation, including a lower heart rate. Television does not do this.[16,17]

❑ Caring for plants has often been found to be so engrossing that people lose track of time: soft fascination at work. There has been an enormous interest in 'boosting', 'building' or simply 'giving' children higher self-esteem. Television erodes both adult and child self-esteem in a wide variety of ways. A study of 120,000 children found that gardening increases their self-esteem and reduces the degree of stress they experience.[18]

❑ And while television feeds disregard, entitlement, instant gratification and impatience, through watching the development of their plant, children learn caring, responsibility and the ability to defer gratification by thinking in the longer term. Gardening enables you to focus on one thing – a live plant – something undeniably wholesome, and to gain a sense of control and completion by doing one thing well – planting and caring for it. In a globalised world of multimedia, where we may feel a sense of learned helplessness over events beyond our control, the simple act of gardening can restore our locus of control, helping us put things in perspective. And perhaps a revival of the escapist potting shed is what every couple needs for a happy marriage.

An RDA for Greenery?

As a counterpart to the time limits suggested for the amount of television we watch (see page 262), there is a minimum amount of exposure we should have to greenery every day. A conservative minimum is 20 minutes a day. A £1.7 million part EU-funded campaign has recently been launched urging people in the UK to increase their involvement with plants and exposure to greenery. I was involved in reviewing the research and helping to come to this recommended minimum figure.[19] One of the scientists involved, Dr Ross Cameron of the University of Reading, reported 'A human being needs some exposure to plants or other green space for at least a couple of hours each week...depriving ourselves of it could lead to increased stress levels, low concentration, lower productivity – even feeling physically a bit below par. Realistically, it's not a huge effort to get involved with plants for 20 minutes a day.' When you think that people stare at an indoor screen for more than 28 hours a week, with all the effects this entails, sacrificing a fraction of this time for the benefits of greenery is effortless.

Science aside, gardening for children also gives them a magical experience that we may take for granted. Gardens seem more enchanted when you're a child. Buying them miniature tools and taking them to a garden centre to choose plants is money well spent.

It's a shame to think that we live in a time when scientific evidence has to be provided in favour of something our grandparents took for granted: being outdoors in greenery is good for you while staying indoors and watching a lot of television isn't.

Stressing the need for more exposure to something we enjoy anyway but never considered a health practice is nice for a change. Studying the effects of greenery has caused us to stumble upon a new insight into how television is affecting our brains and minds, and how these effects can be redressed. By acknowledging our need to reconcile television's attention-arresting hard fascination with our perpetual need for soft fascination, we'll now be able to watch television more selectively while avoiding its effects.

THIRTEEN
THE DAYS OF OUR LIVES VERSUS THE DAZE OF OUR LIVES
Better Alternatives to Television

It is important to consider the enormous benefits that can be derived from activities that do not involve a television screen. These are benefits that most people, particularly children, are currently missing out on. These involve activities that on the surface may be fun but have profound effects on your brain, intellect and body – effects that in many cases last for life. So, in surveying our own lives and our society's 'lifestyles', here are some points of comparison.

Reading to Children
Here's yet another reason to read to children. A study by a Canadian professor, Daniela O'Neill, finds that helping

children to develop their storytelling abilities may contribute to their success in maths years later. This is a good example of how a child's brain often benefits from one form of stimulation, later enhancing skills you would normally assume come from a completely different form of stimulation. She sees the ease with which her results can be applied in our homes tonight: 'It is also a nice finding, I think, because storytelling is something every parent can easily do and foster with their children, without the need to buy any fancy toys or materials.'[1]

Music

Another Canadian study of six-year-olds provides the first solid evidence that the studying of music promotes a child's intellectual development, increasing their IQ in all areas of an IQ test. The researcher, Glenn Schellenberg, believes the effect lasts for up to five years. What's more, he says that 'music has to be a good way to get them away from the TV'. Listening to music at any age also taps directly into our innate pleasure systems. Abstract pleasures such as music or art stimulate the brain's opioid and dopamine circuits. The emotional 'chills' we get from music activate the same brain regions as euphoria-inducing things, such as food, sex and recreational drugs.[2]

Games and Puzzles

Good old board games, chess, cards and doing puzzles have been found to provide significant social, intellectual and even neurological advantages for those who play them, whether they're five years old or seventy-five years old. A study in the *New England Journal of Medicine* concludes that they even prevent or minimise memory loss and the development of Alzheimer's disease.[3] Another study, of primary school children, finds that '…playing board games has a notable effect upon the academic achievement and visual perceptual skills of children…board games develop a child's ability to make use of anticipatory images. Playing board games develops a child's strategic and visual thinking skills by training them to pay attention to detail'. The study goes on to recommend board games in schools to help children develop important skills, such as attention to task, team building and the ability to categorise things.[4]

Television has just the opposite effect of board games, chess, cards and doing puzzles. In fact, a good point of comparison has recently been provided by a study in *The Proceedings of the National Academy of Sciences*. This study reports that television is the only mid-life recreation positively linked to developing Alzheimer's disease. The author says 'use it or lose it' when it comes to the brain between the ages of 20 and 60: 'I think it is bad for the brain to watch four hours of television a day…When you watch TV, you can be in a semi-conscious state where you really are not doing any learning.'[5]

Many traditional games involve cooperation, eye-to-eye contact, talking, negotiation, longer-term strategic thinking, taking turns and delayed, cumulative gratification.

Exercise
If Monopoly is too static for you, physical activity can also develop your intellect and more.

❑ Physically active people – whether they're children or adults – are happier than those who sit in front of the television, and they're less prone to depression and suicide. And it does seem that it is actually the exercise alone that produces these effects. For example, depressed patients prescribed exercise improved just as well as those prescribed antidepressants, but their relapse rate was only a third of the pill-poppers.[6]

❑ Exercise also has both an immediate and long-term effect on your mental performance. Aerobic-type exercise makes us mentally sharper at any age. When inactive people become active, their ability to focus on important things and filter out distractions improves significantly. You also become better at switching from one task to another. Even your memory improves...while watching television is linked with Alzheimer's disease and dementia.

❑ Exercise enlarges not only muscles but brain structures as well. A study in *Nature* found that people who took up juggling for only 90 days caused the part of the cortex that processes motion to become physically bigger. Exercise increases a neurochemical that helps brain cells multiply and form new connections.

❑ Combining physical activity with informal children's games such as tag or 'it', stuck in the mud or a group skipping rope provides children

with some of the benefits of traditional games
mentioned above – cooperation, eye-to-eye
contact, talking, negotiation, taking turns and
delayed, cumulative gratification – plus the
benefits of exercise.

And there are some additional effects of exercise that parents
may want to keep to themselves...

If we watch television we become less physically active.
This is now found to have a direct negative effect on our sex
drive. It's a case of tune in, turn off. But the opposite is also
true. A medical report in the *Archives of Sexual Behaviour*
describes how a large sample of unfit 50-year-old men was
made to take up physical exercise. The results were explicit:
their improvement in fitness was directly correlated with
them having more sex, experiencing less impotence and
having more powerful and satisfying orgasms.[7] Making such
men sit down every evening to watch *Coronation Street* does
not have this effect. One reason has just been put forward by
the Georgia Institute of Technology. Scientists identified a
substance called anandamide in the brains of those who exercise.[8] And as anandamide comes from the same family as
tetrahydrocannabinol, the active ingredient in cannabis,
which is known to make us libidinous, it is quite possible that
exercise triggers sex-inducing drugs. And then there are the
effects of endorphins to consider as well.

Biologists at Harvard University studying fit swimmers
in two age-groups (40s and 60s) are finding that sexual
activity is three times the rate normally expected for these

age groups.[9] Another study involving 8,000 women in California by the Society for the Scientific Study of Sexuality has revealed that 40 per cent of the women felt an immediate increase in libido after aerobic exercise. And the long-term effects are even more pronounced with a third of the women having sex more often, a full 40 per cent reporting a significant increase in their ability to become sexually aroused, and more than a quarter experiencing an increase in their ability to climax. In fact, one in twenty noted that their orgasms were actually more intense. And unlike the contrast effect caused by watching television (see page 178), 90 per cent of the women reported an increase in their sexual confidence.[10] Canadian researchers have now discovered (using a vaginal photoplethysmograph) that it is actually the physical activity alone causing physiological changes in the sympathetic nervous system that produces this increased sexual arousal.[11,12]

Exercise is a miracle worker, which like greenery and daydreaming is overlooked as a mind-expanding pastime. Most of us are vaguely aware of the way exercise causes the release of endorphins – morphine-like substances that not only dull pain but also make you relaxed and slightly high. Even 10 minutes of exercise can increase your endorphin levels for an hour. If children are introduced to these natural opioid drugs early on and exercise becomes habit-forming, nothing could be better.

We are hardwired to take risks as opposed to passively watching someone else do it on a screen. Taking risks makes you feel alive. It's interesting that as our culture becomes more safety conscious with helmets, seat belts and health and safety regulations, adventure sports and holidays are booming. People can get an adrenaline buzz from something they are actually doing themselves rather than trying to experience it vicariously. Pick your poison and, if you survive, there are always other things to do. Like sit and talk.

Talking

Technology isn't all bad. Despite the veneration of email, the ingenious invention of the land-line telephone has been taken for granted. While email is in many respects merely a jumped-up version of the telegram, it is actually the telephone that is far more advanced and sophisticated, even though it was invented almost 100 years earlier. You are actually receiving two messages simultaneously: what the speaker is saying, along with the second dialogue of voice inflection, how he is saying it. Both adults and children can reinforce their friendships and family relationships by talking to people on the telephone instead of watching so much television. Furthermore, at a time when children are found to lack verbal skills, the telephone will give them more practice, and again they are having to paint pictures using sound. And unlike the term 'interactive' as applied to television, talking on the telephone actually is interactive. I say 'land-line' telephone because the sound quality is much better than a mobile telephone so there is a greater sense of intimacy. You have a sense of being geographically closer to the person you're talking to, without the same radiation risks. Radio can also force your child to paint pictures with sound, and aside from music radio there is, for example, BBC7, a digital radio station with stories, dramas and news for children.

During your leisure time, as a rough guide, you and any children should spend more time per day:

❑ Being physically active and reading, rather than watching television;

❑ OR engaging in activities that require you to paint pictures with your imagination: listening or telling stories including audio books, painting, playing and reading;

❑ And, in particular, fostering your child's innate ability to entertain him- or herself and play with others.

And, as we will see in Chapter 14, doing things other than watching a screen doesn't merely benefit us as individuals.

FOURTEEN
IN REAL TIME
The Medical Benefits of Real Shared Experiences

When I first visited London in the 1970s, the first of many eccentricities I remember was seeing British people queuing in the rain in order to stare through a small shop window. The shop was rather unremarkable and it wasn't in Soho; it was Radio Rentals on Edgware Road and the orderly English queue was gazing at the BBC test card on a colour television. There were only three stations at that time, broadcasting started at 6pm, and *Crossroads* was a compelling reason for a nation of shopkeepers to close by half past five.

By the beginning of the next decade, video for all was on the horizon. It was predicted that cinemas would all but disappear because people would be able to circumvent all that queuing up and the noise of other people eating popcorn and watch 'home cinema' instead. And some television people have been predicting that as recording technologies become more sophisticated and the number of channels grows even more, younger generations will drift away from sharing a common experience through watching the same programme at the same time, and just watch something on their own. But it's interesting how resilient this ritual is today despite our ability to watch what we want when we want. At a time of innumerable channels to watch and DVDs to rent, to think that 12 million people – a fifth of the British population – can watch a single episode of a soap opera on an average Monday night is perversely reassuring.

Our dependency on television is part of our need to share a common experience with the rest of society. We don't just watch *Coronation Street* at half past seven; we watch it in the vague knowledge that as we watch it millions of other viewers are joining us. But is it a true sense of mutuality or a virtual one? Having simultaneous but separate experiences is not the same as sharing a common experience. Even misery deserves real company.

And real company is not as easy to come by as it used to be. In the 1960s, people watched less television; and with only two or three channels, a high proportion of people watched and then talked about the same few programmes. Television was, at least on the surface, more of a communal activity. Today, the multiplicity of channels available has changed this. People now have to watch even more programmes to share this common television experience. Furthermore, in the 1960s and 70s, many programmes were intended to be relevant to the viewer; some even changed national legislation. A British television 'classic', *Cathy Come Home* directed by Ken Loach in 1966, was a 'drama-documentary' and led directly to the housing action charity

'Shelter' being formed, along with changes in housing laws. In contrast, the nature of today's programming has an overwhelming emphasis on lifestyle, celebrity or escapist themes.

Societies I've seen where people share more common experiences appear healthier, and individuals who share more common experiences are happier and healthier. It may seem an obvious point but when people are connected and compelled to interact, they are more accountable and considerate, and they think more collectively because they routinely engage with the collective. This is the basis of any community and society deserving of these terms.

Television Inhibits Shared Experiences

On the other hand, high levels of television viewing prevent and inhibit real shared experiences: the connection between people. Study after study finds that 'television reduces social involvement' and leads to a decline in people's social circles. This is plain to see in any country where television sets become more commonplace in homes, huts or public places. People-watching and simple interactions between people decline and social cohesion weakens. Even scientists who study the effects of television for a living are not impervious to its grip. Percy Tannenbaum of the University of California at Berkeley has written, 'Among life's more embarrassing moments have been countless occasions when I am engaged in a conversation in a room while a TV set is on, and I cannot for the life of me stop from periodically glancing over to the screen. This occurs not only during dull conversations but during reasonably interesting ones as well.'[1]

Television erodes the consideration we have for our own geographically real communities by deceiving us into feeling that we are in some abstract way part of a larger world community, connected within a more important scheme of things. Furthermore, this new sense of omnipresence – events and images of people, values and lifestyles which we have little connection with and even less control over – adds to an ever-growing sense of impotence and inadequacy.

Television's endless novelty and unsettling news, entertaining and fascinating as it is, accentuates our sense of the world changing quickly. It makes us feel as if our world and lives are not under our control. Yet it is a sense of *real* shared experience and connection closer to home that buffers us against the effects of rapid change our culture is undergoing. I notice that the foreign cultures that fare best in the face of change are those that retain distinct elements of constancy. Ballet dancers say the way they prevent dizziness and nausea while they pirouette is to keep sight of one point. This constant reference point enables them to cope with the rapidly spinning and changing landscape before their eyes. The same is true of us in a more general sense.

Reinforcing various forms of shared or common experience and preserving our sense of place provides a feeling of control over our lives. The need to maintain and reinforce our sources of common experience is, in effect, a social medicine with hard scientific evidence to support the medical benefits. Watching *Match of the Day* or *Songs of Praise* is not the same as going to a local football match or church. Another part of the prescription involves identifying and nurturing the aspects of our home life, community routines and rhythms that provide us with a sense of constancy, re-establishing our locus of control away from the remote control.

What is Common Experience?

To put this in perspective it's useful to look at some concrete examples of what constitutes the rather hazy notions of 'common experience', 'social cohesion', 'social support' and 'sense of place', and to understand how these concepts actually affect us in practice. In 1970, Dr Ruth Mock wrote that television is the one influence, common to us all today, that has replaced the social, religious and political meetings and festivals that were important expressions in the past. To pick up where Mock left off is to find a whole new generation of studies which are actually beginning to measure the precise biological and psychological benefits of common experiences, 'the social, religious and political meetings and festivals' she referred to.

Religious Worship

As a devout agnostic, I've noticed that the British seem to feel it is in some way rather unfashionable to go to church. Organised religion is considered uncool and oppressive. This in turn has given rise to what I see as closet Christians, those believers who practise their faith rather discreetly. A secular society is seen as a more modern, enlightened society. The Church of England has been described as 'dying on its knees' because it has a poor 'market share'.[2] Only 1.1 million

Britons regularly attend its services each week. Far more British people shop or go to the pub on a Sunday...or watch television in a pub on a Sunday. However, as the importance of religion has been declining in developed countries, scientists are finding a consistent pattern emerging which shows that going to church regularly confers significant health advantages.

A study in the *International Journal of Psychiatry in Medicine* has shown that people who regularly attend religious services appear to have a healthier immune system than those who don't. They say the mechanism behind this effect remains unclear, and the results may not apply to people who live in regions where religious participation is not a major cultural force. Those people who attended services at least once a week were about half as likely as non-attenders to have elevated levels of interleukin-6 (IL-6), an immune system protein involved in a wide array of age-related diseases. This effect continued even when researchers accounted for factors like depression, chronic illness and negative life events that were likely to weaken their immune systems. The researchers speculate that religion may enhance our immune system by enabling us to cope better, along with 'psychosocial factors' and the mechanisms by which organised religions promote positive thoughts and behaviours. The lead author of the study, Harold Koenig, commented: 'Perhaps religious participation enhances immune functioning by yet unknown mechanisms, such as through feelings of belonging, togetherness, even perhaps the experience of worship and adoration... Such positive feelings may counteract stress and convey health effects that go far beyond simply the prevention of depression or other negative emotions.'[3]

Koenig says the study results are the first scientific proof of actual physical evidence that those with a strong religious conviction and regular weekly church attendance really do have better health. He advises, however, that simply showing up at church to 'warm the pew' will not assure you of good health and long life. There is something about the connection between the people who go to church that is important, and the authors suggest the results may represent, in part, a regional influence. Participants in the study are from the 'Bible Belt' south in the United States, where they said religion is 'ingrained in the social fabric of the community'. This is the same social fabric that the television screen wears so very thin.

The same research team and others have now found a connection between attendance at religious services and lower death rate.[4,5]

It's worth pausing for a moment to compare these results with the type of effects that watching television has on our physiology. One example is a study that monitored 22 women and 18 men watching two five-minute clips from the movie *Sleeping With the Enemy* and two five-minute clips from *Falling Down*. The violent scenes on television raised their blood pressure and increased the level of stress hormones in their bodies. The researchers also measured urine levels of the three stress hormones – adrenaline, noradrenaline and cortisol. Women had higher levels of cortisol, the most damaging of the three stress hormones. Cortisol suppresses the immune system and prolongs the negative effects of the other two stress hormones, while high blood pressure taxes the heart muscle. Presumably visiting God's house wouldn't do this to you.

Religion also has a highly beneficial link with our mental health. A study of 7,000 Californians found that West Coast worshippers who took part in church-sponsored activities experienced markedly less stress over money, health and other daily concerns than those who didn't participate.[6] And while television overtakes church attendance and is linked to depression, north of the border, the *Canadian Journal of Psychiatry* reports that psychiatric patients who worship more frequently have significantly lower levels of depression, a shorter stay in hospital, higher satisfaction with life, and lower rates of current and lifetime alcohol abuse.[7] Owning a television or worshipping a television personality not only fails to offer any health benefits – it causes a decline in your physical and mental health as well as your quality of life.

Other Beneficial Common Experiences

Those irreverent people who find all this talk of worship and faith too much to bear can be reassured that vice, too, has its place in promoting social cohesion and health. Greed can be good. In a study published in the *American Journal of Psychiatry*, epidemiologists at Yale University Medical School found that older recreational gamblers seemed to be healthier than non-gamblers. And like a congregation in a house of worship, it is likely that the *social* activity involved in gambling in the den of iniquity was the factor that maintained health, rather than the gambling itself.[8] Watching television together doesn't offer these benefits.

What studies of vice or religious virtue are showing us is that common experience with real people, in a variety of different contexts, is translated into important biological changes. For instance a study published in the *British Medical Journal* found that in people over 65, social and cultural activities such as book clubs had the same impact on life span and general health as physical fitness programmes.[9]

And the fuzzy concept of 'social support' is being examined for its actual medical benefits. People with the most types of social bonds are the least susceptible to the common cold. Those who had one to three types of social relationships were over four times more likely to develop a cold than those with six or more types – a rather crude way of looking at the benefits of having friends and families. By the way, people with six or more televisions have no particular immunity to colds. Professor Sheldon Cohen, who led the study, found a similar negative effect on health when he looked at loneliness or when people's actual social networks didn't meet their expectations. He found that people who scored high on measures of loneliness produced substantially less protective antibodies in the weeks following a flu vaccine compared with people who were less lonely. Cohen feels strongly that in designing health strategies, health professionals should take advantage of people's 'natural networks' of support – their friends and family, their colleagues, people they go to church and volunteer with.[10]

And there's a further positive twist to the practice of social support – it could be even better to *give* it than to receive it. The University of Michigan's Institute for Social Research looked at 400 older married couples and found that those who provided social support to their spouses, or practical support such as transport and childcare to relatives and friends, reduced their chances of dying by between 40 and 60 per cent in a five-year period. The authors thought the effects of these altruistic acts were surprisingly powerful and that there could be an as yet unidentified evolutionary advantage gained from helping others.[11] Furthermore, not only will you live longer, but you'll feel happier for being on the giving end. The act of giving is being found to provide more longstanding good feeling than an act of hedonistic pleasure. The author of the study explains 'You can take drugs, masturbate a lot or engage in mindless entertainment' (such as watching television), which is described as the 'fidgeting until death' syndrome. But an engagement in family life, work, and a sense of meaning through devotion to an institution or a cause greater than yourself ultimately rewards us with a better feel-good factor.[12] The prescription suggests that you turn off the television more frequently, savour your time with your children and find a way to give to others, whether they are needy strangers or your own relatives.

□

Socially connected people are less prone to stress. Social support seems to keep increased heart rate, blood pressure and stress hormones from running amok. Professor Shelley E. Taylor believes our need for social contact is so fundamental that what drives us towards people has to be somewhat biologically based. And in this respect, women have a natural advantage in social support and giving. American women, on average, live seven-and-a-half years longer than men. New biological evidence in animal and human subjects suggests that, unlike men, when women experience stress it activates hormones and neurotransmitters associated with attachment and care-giving: the hormone *oxytocin* which is associated with female nurturing and reproduction, and feel-good *opioids*. Men find it easier to languish in the classic 'fight or flight response' to stress and they die young.[13]

Far away from the health-giving gambling parlours and churches, lack of social cohesion is levying its influence in the deleterious effects of sex, drugs, rock'n'roll and violence. Paediatric researchers are now measuring 'students' connectedness to school' and confirming that '...when adolescents feel like a part of their school, they are less likely to use substances, engage in violence, or initiate sexual activity at an early age'.[14,15,16]

And at a time when more than half of dinners are taken in front of the television set, eating together in real time is found to prevent depression in children. A new study at Columbia University suggests that children who eat dinner with at least one parent have better grades and fewer emotional problems than those who dine on their own.[17]

So, just to drive the real-time point home, television actually reduces social contact, social support, social cohesion, our sense of connectedness and genuine common experience. These are all rather vague, earnest and worthy concepts, which none the less are being found to boost everything from your immunity to disease to your spirits and ultimately your life span. Watching television, on the other hand, will only boost the networks' ratings.

CONCLUSION
TUNE IN, TURN ON – OR DROP OUT?

Thousands of miles away from the Los Angeles location set of *Desperate Housewives* in the seaside town of Hastings, East Sussex, I'm standing in Queen's Arcade at the entrance to the attic where John Logie Baird, the inventor of the world's first 'seeing by wireless machine', conducted his early experiments. Struggling for years to convince a sceptical scientific world he had invented a seeing-by-wireless machine, Baird wrote '...I felt I was doing something worthwhile'. He never finished his autobiography nor lived to see what television would eventually become. While many people today might gasp in horror, wondering what people actually did with themselves before Baird's box arrived, what would Baird himself make of television becoming far more popular than shopping or going to the pub, church and library combined? More popular than reading? That more people would 'vote' for a figure in a contest on the screen than for the Prime Minister and his entire party in a general election? Would he ever have believed that the average person would spend twelve-and-a-half full years of 24-hour days doing nothing else but watching his invention? And what would he think if he was told that his little box had such power over people that someone would pay nearly $5 million per 58 seconds for their frozen peas to be advertised on his seeing-by-wireless machine?

Would he believe that people's bodies could instantly be altered physiologically, while watching television, by hormones, neurotransmitters, metabolism and blood pressure? And that they could be made to cry, eat more and even commit murder as the direct reaction to what they saw on his screen? That natives living in huts in far-off lands would, within months of seeing images on his screen, change their body language and form of dancing and singing? That girls in the remote islands of Fiji would suddenly make themselves vomit because they didn't look like the figures on his screen? And how would he react if he saw the Prince and Princess of Wales each telling the world, through his little screen, of their extramarital relationships? Or to the vision of the President of the United States wagging his finger through the screen while declaring he hadn't had a sexual relationship with his assistant? I suspect Baird would, at the very least, have a double whisky.

That our single main activity, taking up at least half the time that we're not sleeping or working, has eluded a comprehensive scrutiny is nothing short of extraordinary.

And the fact that the medical examination of television's effects has such little coverage and impact is inexcusable. We make more of a fuss about the contents of bottled water than we do about the effects of television, and we filter the running water entering our homes in ways we wouldn't filter the television transmissions entering our children's bedrooms.

The response often heard by those defending television is that millions of children and adults enjoy watching it. This contemporary habit of using the 'people power' card may work wonders in terms of ingratiation, but surely ratings and audience preferences tell us about entertainment value, not about health value. In fact, it is often the hedonistic folly of the majority that is the main concern of our health authorities. The television industry has used this 'they enjoy it, therefore it must be good' logic to discourage criticism of television as a medium. This, by the way, is a very different point to saying: therefore what is not good should not be enjoyed. People will decide for themselves how much and what type of television they and their children watch – but they must now have the necessary information to make an informed decision. And they have to be aware that watching television is even something that requires making a decision about.

It is imperative for our society to adopt a better-safe-than-sorry position towards watching the amount and type of television that we have been, and we need to be decisive now. We should also learn lessons from the way the tobacco and sugar industries have influenced debates on health. There's too much at stake to accept the views of academics receiving even the most indirect funding from television, computer or software companies. And even the broadcast 'authorities' and 'commissions' are themselves ultimately part of the media.

Any future consideration of the effects of television should be carried out in the way we consider new medicines, new cars or even plane flights: they are not automatically assumed to be safe, so the burden is on the provider to convince the authorities that they are. Given the evidence now emerging, the same should be required of those who claim television is merely a benign, discretionary leisure activity. The burden of proof should now be on proponents of television to demonstrate that the way we use it – watching four hours a day – is harmless. Television executives and culture ministers are now faced with some difficult questions. And they'll need more than an Autocue to come up with the answers.

We also need to adopt a far more suspicious and hostile attitude to those who say we should treat this new evidence about television 'with caution', that we should 'keep an open mind', and that those who warn of the dangers of television are over-reacting, or in some way extreme. The scientists whose studies I have reported in this book are, if anything, rather cautious and conservative. And the respected peer-reviewed medical journals that have published their studies are most certainly so. The picture their numerous studies have painted of television is a far more credible one than that offered by those who say television isn't really harmful.

Furthermore, many of the newspapers and magazines that report on this issue are owned by or own television networks. If you discovered that McDonald's, Burger King or

KFC owned your newspaper, wouldn't you see their coverage of debates on fast food in a rather different light?

Television should be considered something powerful and special. Perhaps its status should be reinstated to nearer that of home cinema.

There is a now a wonderful solution to the growing trend of televisions in all types of restaurants, bars, cafés and public places. It's called TV-B-Gone and it's a special tiny remote control that will turn off any normal television anywhere 'because a TV that is powered On is like second-hand [cigarette] smoke. Why should you be exposed to TV just because someone else is addicted to it? TV-B-Gone is capable of turning off virtually any remotely controlled TV. Since a TV that is powered On fills the room with its sights and sounds, impinging on everyone in the room, it is similar to a smoker who fills a room with smoke. Some people may like breathing in someone else's smoke, but that's not for everyone. Similarly, not everyone wants to be disturbed with someone else's media. If someone were smoking a cigar in a public place and you were disturbed by it, you would probably either leave, or you would ask them if they would mind putting it out. Similarly, if someone is filling your space with disturbing sights and sounds of a TV, you have the same choices'.[1]

Italy has recently had its first nationwide television viewers' strike. Under the subtle slogan 'Television is Nasty and Bad', the organisers urge viewers to turn up between Friday and Sunday with their remote control, and in return offer them discounts at museums, galleries, theatres, bars, restaurants, stately homes and parks from the foothills of the Alps to the straits of Messina. The initiative, from the Milan Cultural Association, wants to promote live events and personal, as opposed to vicarious, electronic experiences to counter 'modern media-induced alienation'.

At the very least, I hope this book has prompted you to ask: what role do I really want television to play in my life or the lives of my children?

In the end, perhaps, it won't be the hundreds of scientific studies that determine how you think of your television set. So this question, inspired by White Dot, might help: if you were on your deathbed and someone could give you back those missing twelve-and-a-half years to be with people you loved, and maybe do things differently, would you take their offer? Or would you say, 'No, thanks. I'm glad I spent that time watching TV'?

REFERENCES

Introduction: This Is Your Life

1. Audience Research Board, 12 January 2004
2. Time Use Survey, 15 July 2004, Office for National Statistics
3. Key Note market analysts, report on subscription television, 12 May 2004
4. Poussaint, A., Linn, S. 'SAY NO TO TELETUBBIES', www.family education.com
5. Klesges, R.C. et al. 'Effects of television on metabolic rate: potential implications for childhood obesity', *Pediatrics*, 1993; 91 (2) 281–6
6. Robinson, T.N. 'Television Viewing and Childhood Obesity', *Pediatric Clin. North Am.*, August 2001; 48 (4) 1017–25
7. Ma, G.S. et al. 'Effect of Television Viewing on Pediatric Obesity', *Biomed. Environ. Sci.*, December 2002; 15 (4) 291–7
8. Dietz, W., Director of Division of Nutrition and Physical Activity for the Centers for Disease Control and Prevention, speaking at American Medical Association press briefing in New York, 18 March 1999
9. Centerwall, B.S. 'Exposure to television as a risk factor for violence', *American Journal of Epidemiology*, 1989; 129, 642–52
10. Centerwall, B.S. 'Television and Violence: The Scale of the Problem and Where to Go From Here', *Journal of the American Medical Association*, 1992; 267 (22) 3059–63
11. The WHO World Mental Health Survey Consortium. 'Prevalence, Severity, and Unmet Need for Treatment of Mental Disorders in the World Health Organization World Mental Health Surveys', *Journal of the American Medical Association*, 2004; 291, 2581–90
12. Kubey, R., Csikszentmihalyi, M. 'Television Addiction is No Mere Metaphor', *Scientific American Special Addition*, 2004; 14 (1) 48–55
13. Large, M. 'No TV for Children Under Three', *Guardian*, 21 July 2004
14. 'The Trouble with Sugar', *Panorama*, BBC1, 10 October 2004

1: Arrested Developments

1. Preston, P. 'Television: a modest proposal', *Guardian*, 29 November 2004
2. American Academy of Pediatrics Committee on Public Education. 'Media Education', *Pediatrics*, 1999; 104, 341–3
3. Taylor, E. 'ADHD: Does the evidence answer the controversies?' Delivered at British Association Festival of Science Symposium, 8 September 2004
4. Christakis, D.A. et al. 'Early Television Exposure and Subsequent Attentional Problems in Children', *Pediatrics*, 2004; 113 (4) 708–13
5. Davenport, T.H., Beck, J.C. *The attention economy: understanding the new currency of business*, Harvard Business School Press, 2001
6. Sigman, A., Phillips, K.C., Clifford, B. 'Attentional concomitants of hypnotic susceptibility', *British Journal of Experimental and Clinical Hypnosis*, 1985; 2 (2) 69–75
7. Sigman, A., Phillips, K.C., Clifford, B. 'Unpackaging "attention": a reply', *British Journal of Experimental and Clinical Hypnosis*, 1985; 2 (2) 86–8
8. Struss, D.T. et al. *Neuropsychology*, October 2002, 16 (4)
9. Amen, D.G. 'Healing ADD: Identifying and Treating 6 Types of ADD', *Amen Clinic News* and Information Articles
10. Chan, A. et al. 'Music Training Improves Verbal Memory', *Nature*, 12 November 1998
11. Reeves, B. et al. 'EEG Activity and the Processing of Television Commercials', *Communication Research*, April 1986; 13 (2) 182–220
12. Richards, J.E., Anderson R.E. 'Attentional Inertia in Children's Extended Looking at Television'. *Advances in Child Development and Behavior*, 2005
13. Hawkins R.P. et al. 'What Holds Attention to Television?: Strategic Inertia of Looks at Content Boundaries', *Communications Research*, 2002; 29 (1) 3–30
14. Lang, A. et al. 'The Effects of Arousal, Attention, and Memory for Television Messages: When an Edit is an Edit can an Edit be too Much?', *Journal of Broadcasting & Electronic Media*, 2000; 44 (1) 94–109
15. Koolstra, C.M. et al. 'The Formal Pace of *Sesame Street* Over 26 Years', *Perceptual and Motor Skills*, 2004; 99, 354–60
16. Hooper, M.L., Chang, P. 'Comparison of Demands of Sustained Attentional Events Between Public and Private Children's Television Programs', *Perceptual and Motor Skills*, 1998; 86, 431–4
17. Mailer, N. 'One Idea', *Parade*, 23 January 2005; 4–6
18. Johansen, E.B., Sagvolden, T. 'Response disinhibition may be explained as an extinction deficit in an animal model of attention deficit/hyperactivity disorder (ADHD)', *Behavioural Brain Research*, 2004; 149, 183–196
19. Sagvolden, T. et al. 'A dynamic developmental theory of Attention-Deficit/Hyperactivity Disorder (ADHD) predominantly hyperactive/

impulsive and combined subtypes'. *Behavioural and Brain Sciences*, 2005
20. Koepp, M.J. et al. 'Evidence for striatal dopamine release during a video game', *Nature*, 1998; 393, 266–8
21. Volkow, N.D. et al. 'Evidence that methylphenidate enhances the saliency of a mathematical task by increasing dopamine in the human brain', *Am. J. Psychiatry*, July 2004; 161 (7) 1173–80
22. Healy, J.M. 'Early Television Exposure and Subsequent Attentional Problems in Children', *Pediatrics*, 2004; 113 (4) 917–18
23. 'Zero to Six: Electronic Media in the Lives of Infants, Toddlers and Preschoolers', study by Kaiser Foundation, 28 October 2003
24. Shin, N. 'Exploring pathways from television viewing to academic achievement in school age children', *J. Genetic Psychology*, December 2004; 165 (4) 367–81
24a. Zimmerman F.J., Christakis D.A. 'Children's television viewing and cognitive outcomes: a longitudinal analysis', *Archives of Pediatric Medicine*, 2005; 159:619-625
24b. Borzekowski D.L.G., Robinson T.N. 'The remote, the mouse, and the no. 2 pencil: the household media environment and academic achievement among third grade students', *Archives of Pediatric Medicine*, 2005; 159:607-613
24c. Hancox R.J. et al. 'Association of television viewing during childhood with poor educational achievement', *Archives of Pediatric Medicine*, 2005; 159: 614-618
25. 'What Children Watch: an Analysis of Children's Programming Provision', Broadcasting Standards Commission and the Independent Television Commission, June 2003, reported in the *Guardian*, 10 June 2003
26. Hancox, R.J. et al. 'Association Between Child and Adolescent Television Viewing and Adult Health: a longitudinal birth cohort study', *Lancet*, 2004; 364, 257–62
27. Ludwig, D.S., Gortmaker, S.L. 'Programming Obesity in Childhood', *Lancet*, 2004; 364, 226–7
28. 'Cut Kids' TV "to protect health"', news/bbc.co.uk. health.print, 15 July 2004
29. McGinn, Daniel. 'Guilt Free TV', *Newsweek*, 11 November 2002
30. Mokhiber, R., Weissman, R. *Why Newsweek is Bad For Kids*, Society for the Eradication of Television, 12 November 2002
31. Burke, D., Lotus, J. *Get a Life!*, Bloomsbury, 1998
32. Nowak, R. 'Blame lifestyle for myopia, not genes', *New Scientist*, 10 July 2004
33. Sadeh, A. et al. 'The Effects of Sleep Restriction and Extension on School-Age Children: What a Difference an Hour Makes', *Child Development*, 2003; 74 (2) 329–646
34. Wiggs, L. 'Children and Sleep', University of Oxford Section of Child and Adolescent Psychiatry report with ICM, Borkowski UK, March 2004

35. Van den Bulck, J. 'Television viewing, computer game playing, and Internet use and self-reported time to bed and time out of bed in secondary-school children', *Sleep*, February 2004; 1, 27 (1) 101–104

36. Wong, M. et al. 'Sleep Problems in Early Childhood and Early Onset of Alcohol and Other Drug Use in Adolescence', *Alcoholism: Clinical & Experimental Research*, 2004; 28 (4) 578–87

37. Carskadon, M.A. 'Sleep Difficulties in Young People', *Archives of Pediatric Medicine*, 2004; 158, 597–8

38. Johnson, J.G. et al. 'Association Between Television Viewing and Sleep Problems During Adolescence and Early Adulthood', *Archives of Pediatric Medicine*, 2004; 158, 562–8

39. Sephton, D., Speigel, D. 'Circadian disruption in cancer: a neuroendocrine-immune pathway from stress to disease?' *Brain, Behavior, and Immunity*, 2003; 17 (5) 321–8

40. Nelson, R., Predengast, B. *Proceedings of the Royal Society of London: Biological Sciences*, 8 November 2001

41. Van den Bulck, J. 'Text messaging as a cause of sleep interruption in adolescents, evidence from a cross-sectional study', *Journal of Sleep Research*, 2003; 12 (3) 263

42. Lange, T. et al. 'Sleep Enhances the Human Antibody Response to Hepatitis A Vaccination', *Psychosomatic Medicine*, 2003; 65, 831–5

43. Herman-Giddens, M.E. et al. 'Secondary Sexual Characteristics and Menses in Young Girls Seen in Office Practice: A Study from the Pediatric Research in Office Settings Network', *Pediatrics*, 1997; 99, 505–12

44. Herman-Giddens, M.E. 'Early Puberty', Women's Health Matters Forum and Expo., Toronto, January 2002

45. Early Puberty, conference, Washington, DC, 7 February 2001

46. The National Center on Substance Abuse at Columbia University. 'The Formative Years: Pathways to Substance Abuse Among Girls and Young Women Ages 8–22', 2005

47. 'Ever-Younger Puberty Puzzles Researchers', Early Puberty, conference, Washington, DC, 7 February 2001

48. 'TV is Here to Stay', Conference of National Literacy Trust, London, 15 March 2004

49. Op. cit. Introduction, reference 4

50. Basic Skills Agency study and conference, Warrington, 8 January 2003

51. Statement by Chief Inspector of Ofsted, 31 August 2003, reported in *Sunday Telegraph*

52. Sewell, Dr Tony. 'Gold chains and no brains: popular culture and low educational aspirations', Council for the Advancement and Support of Education, Europe Annual Conference, University of Hertfordshire, 8 September 2004

53. Social Values Research, MORI, 20 August 2002

54. Scase, Richard, interviewed by *BBC News*: 'What makes you feel working class?' and *Daily Mail*: 'The Middle Classes who say they are now Working Class', 21 August 2002

55. Honey, John, author of *Does Accent Matter*, Faber and Faber, 1989, speaking at the Annual Meeting of the Queen's English Society, 18 October 1997

56. Markley, Diane, Cukor-Avila, Patricia. 'Study of Discrimination and Accent', University of North Texas Resource News Brief, 2000, www.unt.edu/resource

57. Gerbner, G. 'Learning Productive Aging as a Social Role: The Lessons of Television' in Bass, S.A., Caro, F.G., Chen, Y.P. (eds.) *Achieving a Productive Aging Society*, Greenwood Publishing Group, 1993

58. Winston, Professor Robert. 'The damning proof that TV DOES corrupt our young', *Daily Mail*, 9 January 2004

59. NOP Study, 3 September 2003

60. 'The Most Expensive Room in the House', Study by AXA, 4 December 2003

61. 'Generation M: Media in the Lives of 8–18 Year-olds', Kaiser Family Foundation, 9 March 2005

2: Walking The TV Walk, Talking The TV Talk

1. *Bolivia 4*, Lonely Planet Publications, 2001

2. Scott-Clark, Cathy, Levy, Adrian. 'Fast Forward into Trouble', *Guardian*, 14 June 2003

3. Becker, A.E. et al. 'Eating behaviours and attitudes following prolonged exposure to television among ethnic Fijian adolescent girls', *Br. J. Psychiatry*, June 2002; 180, 509–14

4. Norman, Philip. 'Lay Down Your Arms!', *Daily Mail*, 6 August 2002

5. 'Well off is the new poor', news/bbc.co.uk, 5 September 2003

6. Hamilton, C. *Growth Fetish*, Pluto Press, 2004

7. Sardar, Z., Wyn-Davies, M. *American Dream, Global Nightmare*, Icon Books, 2004

3: Visual Voodoo

1. Schuster, M.A. et al. 'A National Survey of Stress Reactions after the September 11, 2001, Terrorist Attacks', *New England Journal of Medicine*, 2001; 345, 1507–12

2. Kettl, P., Bixler, E. 'Changes in Psychotropic drug use after September 11, 2001', *Psychiatric Services*, November 2002; 53, 1475–6

3. Wilson, N. et al. 'Events of 11 September 2001 significantly reduced calls to the New Zealand Quitline'. *Tobacco Control*, 2002; 11, 280

4. Op. cit. Chapter 1, reference 31

5. *Dallas Morning News*, June 2004

6. Fiser, J. et al. 'Small modulation of ongoing cortical dynamics by sensory input during natural vision', *Nature*, 30 September 2004, 431, 573–8

7. Deaner, R.O. et al. 'Monkeys Pay Per View: Adaptive Valuation of Social Images by Rhesus Macaques', *Current Biology*, 2005; 15, 543–8

8a. Interviewed for BBC Radio 4 documentary 'Look Into My Eyes', written and presented by Aric Sigman, broadcast 21 August 2002

8b. Sigman, A. 'Hypnotic and Feedback Procedures for Self-Regulation of Autonomic Nervous System Functions' in Heap, M. (ed.) *Hypnosis: Current Clinical, Experimental and Forensic Practices*, Croom Helm, 1988

9. Krugman, Herbert E. 'Brain Wave Measures of Media Involvement', *Journal of Advertising Research*, 1971; 11.1, 3–9

10. Op. cit. Introduction, reference 12

11. Gazzaniga, M.S. 'The Split Brain Revisited', *Scientific American*, special edition, 2002; 12 (1) 27–31

12. Williams, T.M. *The Impact of Television: A Natural Experiment in Three Communities*, Orlando, Florida, Academic Press, 1986

13. Douglas, D.M., Sutton, R.M. 'Right about others, wrong about ourselves?', *British Journal of Social Psychology*, 2004; 43, 581–602

14. Pulford, B. 'Not Immune to Media Messages', *The Psychologist*, 2005; 18 (1) 39

15. Kawashima, R. et al. reported in *World Neurology*, September 2001, 16 (3) 3

16. Sigman, A. 'An Assessment of the Methodological Standard of Current Research in Psychosurgery', M.Sc. dissertation, 1982

17. I have been unable to trace the source of this phrase and suspect it may have been a comment made by the cultural historian Raymond Williams.

18. Freeman, J. et al. 'Immersive Television', *The Psychologist*, 2001; 14 (4) 190–94

19. Postman, N. *Amusing Ourselves to Death*, UK: Methuen, New York: Penguin, 1985

20. Ravaja, N. et al. 'Suboptimal exposure to facial expressions when viewing video messages from a small screen', *Journal of Experimental Psych Applied*, 2004; 10 (2) 120

21. Whalen, P.L. et al. 'Human Amygdala responsivity to masked fearful eye whites', *Science*, 2004, 306, 2061

22. 'The Telly Belly Research', Norwich Union Healthcare studies, 13 November 2002 & 21 April 2005

23. Collins, R.L. et al. 'Watching Sex on Television Predicts Adolescent Initiation of Sexual Behavior', *Pediatrics*, September 2004, 114 (3) e280–89

24. Van Den Bulck, J., Damiaans, K. 'Cardiopulmonary resuscitation on Flemish television: challenges to the television effects hypothesis', *Emergency Medicine Journal*, 2004; 21 (5) 565–7

25. McIlwraith, R. 'Television addiction', annual meeting of the American Psychological Association, Boston, August 1990, as interviewed in 'How Viewers Grow Addicted to Television' in *New York Times*, 16 October 1990

26. Charles Winick's study described in Introduction, reference 12

27. Op. cit. Chapter 1, reference 20

28. Volkow, N.D. et al. 'Activation of orbital and medial prefrontal cortex by methylphenidate in cocaine-addicted subjects but not in controls: relevance to addiction', *Journal of Neuroscience*, 2005; 25 (15) 3932–9

29. Op. cit. Chapter 1, reference 21

30. Koepp, M.J. et al. 'Evidence for striatal dopamine release during a video game', *Nature*, 1998; 393, 266–8

31. Perry, B.D. 'The Neuroarcheology of Childhood Maltreatment: The Neurodevelopmental Costs of Adverse Childhood Events' In Geffner, B. (ed.) *The Cost of Child Maltreatment: Who Pays? We All Do*, Haworth Press, 2000

32. 'Back to the Beginning', *Observer*, 20 January 2002

33. Baudouin, C. 'Suggestion and Autosuggestion', George Allen and Unwin, 1920

34. Various national news reports throughout 2003

35. 'See you at the Big Screen', BBC Charter Review Update, February 2005

36. Comments made in advance of Bafta conference on 'media literacy', *The Times*, 21 January 2004

37. Dahl, Roald. *Charlie and the Chocolate Factory*, Penguin, 1964

4: Amusing Ourselves To Death

1. Anderson, C.A. et al. 'The Influence of Media Violence on Youth', *Psychological Science*, 2003; 4 (3) 105

2. Interview with Richard Rhodes, American Booksellers Foundation for Free Expression

3. Op. cit. Introduction, reference 9

4. Op. cit. Introduction reference 10

5. Op. cit. Chapter 3, reference 12

6. Johnson T.N. et al. 'Television Viewing and Aggressive Behavior During Adolescence and Adulthood', *Science*, 2002; 295, 2468–71

7. Ozmert et al. 'Behavioral Correlates of Television Viewing in Primary School Children Evaluated by the Child Behavior Checklist', *Archives of Pediatrics and Adolescent Med.*, 2002; 156, 910–14

8. Zimmerman, F.J. et al. 'Early Cognitive Stimulation, Emotional Support, and Television Watching as Predictors of Subsequent Bullying Among Grade-School Children', *Arch. Pediatr. Adolesc. Med.*, April 2005; 159, 384–8

9. Television 'could create child bullies', news/bbc.co.uk, 4 April 2005

10. Robinson J.G. et al. 'Effects of Reducing Children's Television and Video Game Use on Aggressive Behavior, *Arch. Pediatr. Adolesc. Med.*, 2001; 155, 17–23

11. Humphries, John. 'First Do No Harm', MacTaggart Lecture, Edinburgh International Television Festival, 27 August 2004, reported in his essay 'TV's Great Betrayal', *Daily Mail*, 28 August 2004

12. Gentile, D.A. et al. 'Media violence as a risk factor for children: A longitudinal study', paper presented at the American Psychological Society 16th Annual Convention, Chicago, May 2004

13. Coyne, S.M. 'Indirect Aggression on Screen: A Hidden Problem?', *The Psychologist*, 2004, 17 (12) 688–90

14. Coyne, S.M., Archer, J. 'The relationship between indirect and physical aggression on television and in real life', *Social Development*, 2005

15. Kidd, David, Chairman of the Incorporated Association of Preparatory Schools, quoted in the *Daily Mail*, 7 March 2005

16. Cook, D.E. et al. Joint Statement on the Impact of Entertainment Violence on Children for a US Congressional Public Health Summit, 26 July 2000

17. Browne, K.D., Hamilton-Giachrisis, C. 'The Influence of Violent Media on Children and Adolescents: a public-health approach', *Lancet*, 2005; 365, 702–10

18. Anderson, C.A., Bushman, B.J. *Science*, 2002; 295, 2377–8 and reported by *Washington Post*, 29 March 2002

19. Murray, J.P. 'TV Violence and Brainmapping in Children', *Psychiatric Times*, 2001; XVIII (10)

20. Mathews, V.P. 'Violent video games trigger unusual brain activity in aggressive adolescents', 88th Scientific Assembly and Annual Meeting of the Radiological Society of North America, Chicago, 2 December 2002

21. Mathews, V.P. et al. 'Media Violence Exposure and Frontal Lobe Activation Measured by Functional Magnetic Resonance Imaging in Aggressive and Nonaggressive Adolescents', *Journal of Computer Assisted Tomography*, May/June 2005; 29 (3) 287

22. Statement of Joanne Cantor before the US Senate Commerce Committee Subcommittee on Science, Technology and Space, Washington, DC, 10 April 2003

23. Roberts, Paul William. *The Demonic Comedy: Some Detours in the Baghdad of Saddam Hussein*, Farrar Straus Giroux, 1997

24. Rilling, J.K. et al. 'A Neural Basis for Social Cooperation', *Neuron*, 2002; 35 (2) 395–405

5: Meet The Telly Tubbies

1. Krebs, Sir John, Food Standards Agency chairman, reported by *Observer* and news/bbc.co.uk, 9 November 2003

2. Olshansky, S.J. et al. 'A Potential Decline in Life Expectancy in the United States in the 21st Century', *New England Journal of Medicine*, 17 March 2005, 352 (11) 1138–45

3. Eurostat, Luxembourg, 28 July 2004

4. NOP World, June 2005

5. Op. cit. Introduction, reference 5

6. Stroebele, N., de Castro, J.M. 'Television viewing nearly adds an additional meal to daily intake'. Under review. *Nutrition*, 2004

7. Wansink, B. *The Annual Review of Nutrition*, 2004, 24, 455–79

8. Epstein, L.H. et al. 'Allocation of Attentional Resources during habituation to food cues', *Psychophysiology*, 1997; 34 (1) 59–64

9. Volkow, N.D. et al. '"Nonhedonic" food motivation in humans involves dopamine in the dorsal striatum and methylphenidate amplifies this effect', *Synapse*, 2002; 44, 175–80

10. Stubbs, R.J. et al. 'A Decrease in Physical Activity Affects Appetite, Energy and Nutrient Balance in Lean Men Feeding ad libitum', *American Journal of Clinical Nutrition*, 2004, 79 (1) 62–9

11. Dunstan, D.W. et al. 'Physical Activity and Television Viewing in Relation to the Risk of Undiagnosed Abnormal Glucose Metabolism in Adults', *Diabetes Care*, 2004; 27, 2603–9

12. 'TV Linked to Diabetes', *Diabetes Australia NSW*, 8 May 2003

13. Reilly, J. et al. 'Total Energy Expenditure and Physical Activity in Young Scottish Children: Mixed Longitudinal Study', *Lancet*, 2004; 363 (9404) 211–12

14. Francis, L.A. et al. 'Parental Weight Status and Girls' Television Viewing, Snacking and Body Mass Indexes', *Obesity Research*, 2003; 11, 143–51

15. Giammattei, J. et al. 'Television Watching and Soft Drink Consumption: Associations with Obesity in 11-to-13-year-old Schoolchildren', *Archives of Pediatric and Adolescent Medicine*, 2003; 157, 882–6

16. Vorona, R.D. et al. 'Overweight and Obese Patients in a Primary Care Population Report Less Sleep than Patients with a Normal Body Mass Index', *Archives of Internal Medicine*, January 2005; 165, 25–30

17. Taheri, S. et al. 'Short Sleep Duration Is Associated with Reduced Leptin, Elevated Ghrelin, and Increased Body Mass Index', *Public Library of Science Med.*, December 2004; 1 (3) e62

18. Speigel, K. et al. 'Brief Communication: Sleep Curtailment in Healthy Young Men Is Associated with Decreased Leptin Levels, Elevated Ghrelin Levels, and Increased Hunger and Appetite', *Ann. Intern. Med.*, December 2004; 141, 846–50

19. Batty D., Thune, I. *British Medical Journal*, 9 December 2000; 321, 1424–5

20. Chong, D.L., Blair, S.N. 'Cardiorespiratory fitness and smoking-related and total cancer mortality in men', *Medicine & Science in Sports & Exercise*, May 2002; 34 (5) 735–9

21. Lagerros, Y.T. et al. 'Physical activity in adolescence and young adulthood and breast cancer risk: a quantitative review', *European Journal of Cancer Prevention*, 2004; 13 (1) 5–12

22. Rintala, P., Pukkala, E., Laara, E. et al. 'Physical Activity and Breast Cancer Risk Among Female Physical Education and Language Teachers: A 34-year follow-up', *International Journal of Cancer*, 2003; 107, 268–70

23. Hernandez, B. et al. 'Association of obesity with physical activity, television programs and other forms of video viewing among children in Mexico city', *International Journal of Obesity Related Metabolic Disorders*, 1999; 23 (8) 845–54

24. Op. cit. Introduction, reference 7

25. Op. cit. Introduction, reference 6

26. Op. cit. Introduction, reference 8

27. Bazar, K.A. et al. 'Obesity and ADHD may represent different manifestations of a common environmental oversampling syndrome: a model for revealing mechanistic overlap among cognitive, metabolic, and inflammatory disorders', *Medical Hypotheses*, 16 May 2005

28. Chester, G. June 1998, Co-op supermarket, West Yorkshire

29. Drummond, Professor Colin. Statements made 18 January 2005 and debate reported in House of Commons *Hansard* Debates for 25 January 2005 (pt 8)

30. Hansen, A. 'The portrayal of alcohol and alcohol consumption in television news and drama programmes', a research report for Alcohol Concern, 2003

31. 'Underage Drinking: A Major Public Health Challenge', US Government National Institute on Alcohol Abuse and Alcoholism, April 2003, no. 59

32. Suter, P.M. et al. 'The effect of ethanol on fat storage in healthy subjects', *New England Journal of Medicine*, 1992; 326 (15) 983–7

6: Sexual Stealing

1. *Evening Standard*, London, 3 December 1997

2. Fletcher, J. 'New Floor Plans Provide Peace, Quiet and Privacy', *The Wall Street Journal Online: Guide to Property*, 7 April 2004

3. Bourdain, A. *Kitchen Confidential*, Bloomsbury USA, 2001

4. Kahneman, D. et al. 'A Survey Method for Characterizing Daily Life Experience: The Day Reconstruction Method', *Science*, December 2004; 3, 1776–80

5. Kraut, R. et al. 'Internet Paradox: A Social Technology That Reduces Social Involvement and Psychological Well-Being?', *American Psychologist*, September 1998; 53, 9, 1017–103

6. Geary, D.C. *Male, Female: The Evolution of Human Sex Differences*, American Psychological Association, 1998

7. Taylor, S.E. et al. 'Biobehavioral Responses to Stress in Females: Tend-and-Befriend, Not Fight-or-Flight', *Psychological Review*, 107, 411–29

8. Zerjal, T. et al. 'The Genetic Legacy of the Mongols', *American Journal of Human Genetics*, 2003; 72, 717–21

9. Andrianni, A. 'Sex Positions – Rear Entry', www.allsexguide.com

10. Platell, A. 'Women on top? No thanks!' *Daily Mail*, 15 February 2005

11. *Prima*, 6 August 2004

12. Warburton, D. *The National Enjoyment Report*, Associates of Research into the Science of Enjoyment, Reading University, 1999

13. Greeley, A. *Sex: The Catholic Experience*, Thomas More Press, 1995

14. Op. cit. Chapter 1, reference 31

15. Gutierres, S.E. et al. 'Beauty, Dominance, and the Mating Game: Contrast Effects in Self-Assessment Reflect Gender Differences in Mate Selection', *Personality and Social Psychology Bull.*, 1999; 25, 1126–34

16. Levine, Michael, Marano, Hara Estroff. 'Why I Hate Beauty', *Psychology Today*, July/August, 2001

17. Slater, A. Paper presented at the British Association Festival of Science, University of Exeter, September 2004

18. Satoshi, K., Still, M.C. 'Teaching May Be Hazardous to Your Marriage', *Evolution and Human Behavior*, 2000; 21, 185–90

7: Shiny Happy People
1. Op. cit. Introduction reference 11
2. Ayuso-Mateos, J.L., Vázquez-Barquero, J.L., Dowrick, C. et al. 'Depressive disorders in Europe: prevalence figures from the ODIN study', *British Journal of Psychiatry*, 2001; 179, 308–16
3. Singer. 'Viewing preferences, symptoms of psychological trauma, and violent behaviours among children who watch television', *J. Am. Acad. Child. Adolesc. Psychiatry*, 1998; 37, 1041–8
4. MARS OTC/DTC Pharmaceutical Study, Multimedia Audience Research Systems, 2002
5. Roger, Derek. Director of Stress Research Unit, York Univ., as reported in *Independent*, 30 May 1999
6. Smail, D. 'The Origins of Unhappiness', HarperCollins, 1993
7. Adler, N.E. et al. 'Relationship of Subjective and Objective Social Status With Psychological and Physiological Functioning: Preliminary Data in Healthy White Women', *Health Psychology*, 2000; 19, 6
8. Argyle, M. *The Psychology of Social Class*, Routledge, 1994
9. Argyle, M. Interview regarding his book *The Psychology of Leisure* (1996), for the London *Evening Standard*, 21 February 1996
10. Op. cit. Chapter 6, reference 5
11. Lutgendorf, S. et al. 'Religious Participation, Interleukin-6, and Mortality in Older Adults', *Health Psychology*, September 2004; 23 (5) 465–75
12. Johnson, W., Davey, G. 'The psychological impact of negative TV news bulletins: the catastrophizing of personal worries', *British Journal of Psychology*, February 1997; 85
13. Amichai-Hamburger, Y. et al. 'The Effects of Learned Helplessness on the Processing of a Persuasive Message', *Current Psychology – New Brunswick*, 2003; 22 (1) 37–46
14. Burdette, H.L., Whitaker, R.C., Kahn, R.S., Harvey-Berino, J. 'Association of maternal obesity and depressive symptoms with television-viewing time in low-income preschool children', *Arch. Pediatr. Adolesc. Med.*, September 2003; 157 (9) 894–9
15. 'Causes of Suicide: The Media', report by the South East Health Board of Ireland, 2003
16. Pirkis, J., Blood, R.W. 'Suicide and the Media', *Crisis*, 2001; 22 (4) 146–69
17. Zahl, D.L., Hawton, K. 'Media influences on suicidal behaviour: An interview study of young people', *Behavioural and Cognitive Psychotherapy*, 2004; 32, 189–98
18. Cameron, E.M., Ferraro, F.R. 'Body satisfaction in college women after brief exposure to magazine images', *Percept. Mot. Skills*, June 2004; 98 (3 Pt 1) 1093–9

19. Winkler, Christopher, Rhodes, Gillian. 'Perceptual adaptation affects attractiveness of female bodies', *British Journal of Psychology*, 2005; 14, 141–54

20. Groesz, L.M., Levine, M.P., Murnen, S.K. 'The effect of experimental presentation of thin media images on body satisfaction: a meta-analytic review', *Int. J. Eat. Disord.*, January 2002; 31 (1) 1–16

21. Shirao, N. et al. 'Gender differences in brain activity generated by unpleasant word stimuli concerning body image: an fMRI study', *British Journal of Psychiatry*, 2005; 186, 48–53

22. Cafri, G., Thompson, J.K. 'Evaluating the convergence of muscle appearance attitude measures', *Assessment*, September 2004; 11 (3) 224–9

23. Leit, R.A. et al. 'The media's representation of the ideal male body: a cause for muscle dysmorphia?', *Int. J. Eat. Disord.*, April 2002; 31 (3) 334–8

24. Pope, H.G. Jr., Gruber, A.J., Mangweth, B., Bureau, B., deCol, C., Jouvent, R., Hudson, J.I. 'Body image perception among men in three countries', *Am. J. Psychiatry*, August 2000; 157 (8), 1297–301

25. Pope, H.G. Jr., Katz, D.L. 'Psychiatric effects of exogenous anabolic-androgenic steroids' in Wolkowitz, O.M., Rothschild A.J. (eds.) *Psychoneuroendocrinology for the Clinician*, American Psychiatric Press, 2002

26. Eating Disorders Association, 2005

27. 'Eating Disorders', factsheet, the US Department of Health and Human Services Office on Women's Health, February 2000

28. I calculated the mortality rates from the information the Eating Disorders Association provided me with on 28 January 2005: that of the 1.15m people they cite as having an eating disorder, 40 per cent are anorexic and 60 per cent bulimic. The mortality rates they cite (13–20 per cent) apply to cases of **anorexia**: people 'diagnosed or receiving treatment'. All of these estimates are conjecture and vary widely because, for example, many anorexics stop treatment and cut off contact. Also, the literal cause of death through anorexia may be, in order of prevalence, suicide, heart failure, renal failure and pneumonia. Starvation through anorexia is not often cited as the actual cause of death, even though it ultimately is. Therefore, 40 per cent of 1.15m people with eating disorders suffer from anorexia: this is 460,000 people. Subtract 10 per cent of sufferers who are supposedly male and the figure is 414,000 females. Even if one takes the lowest mortality rate of 10 per cent (from US Department of Health and Human Services), this comes to 41,000 dead women. And even if one accepts that only a tiny percentage of these fatal cases of anorexia were directly triggered by the influence of television – for example 5 per cent – this still leaves a figure of 2,070 women dying as a result of seeing television images.

29. 'Domestic violence: a national report', Home Office, 2005

30. 'HIV and other Sexually Transmitted Infections in the United Kingdom in 2003', Health Protection Agency, Annual Report, November 2004

31. Harris, G. et al. British Psychological Society's annual conference, Oxford, 13 September 1996

32. Hill, A. British Associations' Annual Science Festival, Birmingham University, 13 September 1996
33. Op. cit. Chapter 2, reference 3

8: Living in a Tellytocracy

1. Bonneville Communications, 2005
2. Sabido, M. *The tone, theoretical occurrences, and potential adventures and entertainment with social benefit*, National Autonomous University of Mexico Press, 2002
3. Goebbels, Joseph. *Der Kongress zur Nürnberg*, Zentralverlag der NSDAP, Frz. Eher Nachf., 1934
4. Goebbels, Joseph. *Erkenntnis und Propaganda Signale der neuen Zeit. 25 ausgewählte Reden von Dr. Joseph Goebbels (1928)*, Zentralverlag der NSDAP, 1934
5. Fifth annual report card, National Latino Media Council Reports Limited Progress on Network Television, 18 November 2004
6. 'TV for millions misses the minorities', CRE press release of executive summary of report entitled 'Top Ten TV' by the Commission for Racial Equality, 2 April 2001
7. '2001 Decline in SAG Minority Roles', Screen Actors Guild, 2002
8. 'Missing In Action: Latinos In and Out of Hollywood', Screen Actors Guild, 1999
9. 'The Latino Television Study', The National Latino Media Council, 4 February 2004
10. 'Multicultural Broadcasting: concept and reality', Broadcasting Standards Commission and Independent Television Commission report, November 2002
11. 'UK Broadcasters Report Strong Year for Cultural Diversity', BBC press release, 15 December 2004
12. 'Row Over Black TV Stars', *BBC News*, 26 September 2003
13. Sewell, T. 'Sorry, We Can't Just Blame Racism for Black Boys' Failings', *Daily Mail*, 8 March 2005
14. Trevor Phillips interviewed on *Inside Out*, BBC1, 7 March 2005
15. 'Victims of Racial Crime (England and Wales)', UK Government National Statistics, 12 December 2002
16. 'The Voice of Britain: Britain beyond Rhetoric. Study for the Commission for Racial Equality conducted by MORI Social Research Institute, 2002
17. Presentation made by MORI director Ben Page, reported by Mark Easton, BBC *Ten O'Clock News*, 25 January 2005
18. Ispas, A. 'Repairing Historical Rifts: Is collective guilt the answer?', *The Psychologist*, 2004; 17 (7) 396–8
19. Sowell, T. *The Vision of the Anointed*, Basic Books, 1995
20. Speech by Gavyn Davies to the Westminster Media Forum, 13 March 2002

21. Greg Dyke interviewed on *The Mix*, BBC Radio Scotland, 7 January 2001

22. Talk by Greg Dyke, 'Insight with Greg Dyke', 25 January 2005, reported in the *Daily Mail*, 3 February 2005

23. Gomez-Pena, Guillermo. 'The New Global Culture: Somewhere Between Corporate Multiculturalism and the Mainstream Bizarre (a border perspective)', *The Drama Review*, Spring 2001; 45, 1

24. Dennis, D. 'Priming the Pump of War: Toward a Post-Ethnic, Post-Racial Fascism', *Journal of Theory, Technology, and Culture*, 11 June 2002

25. Amato, P.R., Cheadle, J. 'The long reach of divorce: Divorce and child well-being across three generations', *Journal of Marriage and Family*, February 2005; 67, 1, 191–206 (16)

26. Deborah Moggach interviewed by Angela Levin in 'Hot and Spicy', *Weekend* magazine, *Daily Mail*, 2 April 2005

27. Brady, J.V. et al. 'Avoidance behavior and the development of gastro-duodenal ulcers', *Journal of Experimental Analysis of Behavior*, 1958; 1, 69–73

28. Baird, M. *Television and Me*. Mercat Press, 2004

29. Shaw, Michael. 'Teens wait for Becks-style break', *The Times Educational Supplement*, 16 January 2004

30. Chris Humphries, director general of the City and Guilds qualification board, evidence given to Commons education select committee, 12 January 2004

9: Fade To Grey

1. Levy, Becca R., Slade, Martin D., Kunkel, Suzanne R., Kasl, Stanislav V. 'Longevity increased by positive self-perceptions of aging', *Journal of Personality & Social Psychology*, August 2002; 83 (2) 261–70

2. Linley, A. 'Age Concern?', *The Psychologist*, 2002; 15 (10) 530

3. Levy, B.R., Slade, M.D., Kasl, S.V. 'Longitudinal benefit of positive self-perceptions of aging on functional health', *J. Gerontol. B. Psychol. Sci. Soc. Sci.*, September 2002; 57 (5) 409–17

4. Levy, B.R., Myers, L.M. 'Preventive health behaviors influenced by self-perceptions of aging', *Preventative Med.*, September 2004; 39 (3) 625–9

5. Sagansky, Jeff, CBS Entertainment Chief. *The Tampa Tribune*, 5 October 1993, cited in Tupper, Meredith, 'The Misrepresentation of Elderly Persons in Prime Time Television Advertising', masters thesis, University of South Florida, 1995

6. *Ten Years Younger*, Channel 4, 9 February 2005

7. *How Soaps Changed the World*, Channel 4, 17 July 2004

8. 'Age in the Frame', Age Concern, 1999

9. Dail, P.W. 'Prime-time television portrayals of older adults in the context of family life', *The Gerontologist*, 1988; 28, 700–706

10. 'Employment Statistics Decline in SAG Minority Roles', Screen Actors Guild, 2002

11. Ryan, Nigel. 'Age before beauty – the Americans teach us a lesson', *Sunday Times* News Review, 8 September 2002
12. Bakewell, Joan. *Daily Mail*, 9 September 2004

10: Controlling the Remote

1. Op. cit. Chapter 4, reference 1

11: The State Formerly Known as Boredom

1. Ehrensaft, D. *Spoiling Childhood*, Guilford Press, 1997 (as quoted in interviews)
2. Belton, T. 'The "Face at the Window" Study: a fresh approach to media influence and to investigating the influence of television and videos on children's imagination', *Media, Culture and Society*, 2001; 22, 629–43
3. Belton, T. 'Television and imagination: An investigation of the medium's influence on children's story-making', *Media, Culture and Society*, 2001; 23, 799–820
4. Report by Chair of Governors, Assessment and Qualifications Alliance, 2003, report by Chair of Governors, Edexcel, 2003. Reported in Henry, Julie, 'Low marks for pupils who use soap opera slang in their exams', *Sunday Telegraph*, 12 October 2003
5. Lilly, J.C. 'Mental Effects of Reduction of Ordinary Levels of Physical Stimuli on Intact, Healthy Persons', *Psychiat. Res.*, 1956, Report 5, American Psychiatric Assn.
6. Suedfeld, P., Borrie, R.A. 'Health and Therapeutic Applications of Chamber and Flotation Restricted Environmental Stimulation Therapy (REST)', *Psychology and Health*, 1999; 14, 545–66
7. Wagaman, J., Barabasz, A. 'Flotation REST and Imagery in the Improvement of Collegiate Athletic Performance: Basketball', *Clinical and Experimental Restricted Environmental Stimulation: New Developments and Perspectives*, Springer-Verlag, 1993; 87–92
8. National Center For Infants, Toddlers and Families, Zero to Three, 2005

12: The Potting Shed Effect

1. Kuo, F.E., Taylor, A.F. 'A potential natural treatment for attention-deficit/hyperactivity disorder: evidence from a national study', *American Journal of Public Health*, 2004; 94 (9) 1580–86
2. Taylor, A.F., Kuo, F.E., Sullivan, W.C. 'Views of Nature and Self-Discipline: Evidence from Inner-City Children', *Journal of Environmental Psychology*, 2001; 21
3. Kaplan, S. 'The restorative benefits of nature: toward an integrative framework', *J. Environ. Psychol.*, 1995; 15 169–82
4. Stark, M.A. 'Restoring Attention in Pregnancy: The Natural Environment', *Clinical Nursing Research*, 2003, 12 (3) 246–65

5. Wells, N.M. 'At home with nature: effects of "greenness" on children's cognitive functioning', *Environ. Behav.*, 2000; 32, 775–95

6. Op. cit. Chapter 6, reference 5

7. Sullivan, W.C. et al. 'The Fruit of Urban Nature: Vital Neighborhood Spaces', *Environment and Behavior*, 2004; 36 (5) 678-700

8. Kuo, F.E. 'Making an Impact: From Research to the Real World' in Bechtel, R. (ed.), *New Handbook of Environmental Psychology*, Sage, 2005

9. Op. cit. Chapter 12, reference 2

10. Kuo, F.E., Sullivan, W.C. 'Aggression and violence in the inner city: impacts of environment via mental fatigue', *Environ Behav.*, 2001; 33, 543–71

11. Kuo, F.E. 'Coping with poverty: impacts of environment and attention in the inner city', *Environ. Behav.*, 2001; 33, 5–34

12. Takano, T. et al. 'Urban residential environments and senior citizens' longevity in megacity areas: the importance of walkable green spaces', *J. Epidemiology & Community Health*, 2002; 56 (12) 913–18

13. Kushi L.H. et al. 'Physical Activity and Mortality in Postmenopausal Women', *Journal of the American Medical Association*, 1997; 277, 16

14. American Heart Association, 2005, Scientific Position: Physical Activity

15. Op. cit. Chapter 1, reference 26

16. Ulrich, R. 'View Through a Window May Influence Recovery from Surgery', *Science*, 1984; 224, 420–21

17. Ulrich, R.S. 'Effects of gardens on health outcomes: Theory and research', in Cooper, M.C., Barnes, M. (eds.), *Healing Gardens: Therapeutic Gardens and Design Recommendations*, John Wiley & Sons, 1999

18. Waliczek, T.M. et al. 'Using a web-based survey to research the benefits of children gardening', *Horticultural Technology*, 2000; 10, 71–6

19. Sigman, A. 'A Plant a Day Keeps the Doctor Away', review for the Plant for Life Campaign, 2004

13: The Days of our Lives Versus the Daze of our Lives

1. O'Neill, D.K. et al. 'Preschool Children's Narratives and Performance on the Peabody Individualized Achievement Test – Revised: Evidence of a Relation between Early Narrative and Later Mathematical Ability', *First Language*, 2004; 24, 149–83

2. Schellenberg, Glenn. *Psychological Science*, 2004; 15 (8), reported in *New Scientist*, 183, (2457)

3. Verghese, J. et al. 'Leisure activities and the risk of dementia in the elderly', *New England Journal of Medicine*, 2003; 348 (25) 2508–16

4. Thompson, K.P. 'An investigation of self-esteem, academic achievement and visual perception of abstract stimuli amongst urban elementary school children who participated in the use of board games in developing strategic

and visual thinking skills as utilized in the Mente program', Dissertation Abstracts International Section A: Humanities and Social Sciences, 2001; vol. 62 (1-A): 85, US: Univ. Microfilms International

5. Friedland, R.P. et al. 'Patients with Alzheimer's disease have reduced activities in midlife compared with healthy control-group members', *Proceedings of the National Academy of Sciences*, 2001; 98 (6) 3440–45

6. Babyak, M. et al. 'Exercise Treatment for Major Depression: Maintenance of Therapeutic Benefit at 10 Months', *Psychosomatic Medicine*, 2000; 62 (5) 633–8

7. White, J.R. et al. 'Enhanced Sexual Behavior in Exercising Men', *Archives of Sexual Behavior*, 1990; 19 (3) 193–209

8. Sparling, P.B. et al. 'Exercise activates the endocannabinoid system', *Neuroreport*, 2003; 14 (17) 2209–11

9. Whitten, P., Whiteside, E.J. 'Can Exercise Make You Sexier?' in Rader, B.G. 'The Quest for Self-Sufficiency and the New Strenuosity: Reflections on the Strenuous Life of the 1970s and the 1980s', *Journal of Sport History*, 1991; 18 (2)

10. De Villers, L. National Conference of the Society for the Scientific Study of Sexuality, 1989, reported in *American Health*, January/February 1990

11. Meston, C.M., Gorzalka, B.B. 'The effects of sympathetic activation on physiological and subjective sexual arousal in women', *Behaviour Research and Therapy*, 1995; 33, 651–64

12. Meston, C.M., Gorzalka, B.B. 'The effects of immediate, delayed and residual sympathetic activation on sexual arousal in women', *Behaviour Research and Therapy*, 1996; 34, 143–8

14: In Real Time

1. Op. cit. Introduction, reference 12

2. 'Dr Carey's departure can be the cue to separate church and state', *Independent*, 9 January 2002

3. Koenig, H.G. 'Attendance at Religious Services, Interleukin-6, and Other Biological Parameters of Immune Function in Older Adults', *International Journal of Psychiatry in Medicine*, 1997; 27, 3

4. Larson, David B., Larson, Susan S. 'Spirituality's potential relevance to physical and emotional health: A brief review of quantitative research', *Journal of Psychology and Theology*, 2003; 31 (1) 37–51

5. Op. cit. Chapter 7, reference 11

6. Strawbridge, W.J. et al. 'Religiosity buffers effects of some stressors on depression but exacerbates others', *Journals of Gerontology Series B: Psychological Sciences and Social Sciences*, 1998; 53 (3) S118–26

7. Baetz, M. et al. 'Canadian psychiatric inpatient religious commitment: An association with mental health', *Canadian Journal of Psychiatry*, 2002; 47 (2) 159–66

8. Desai, Rani A. 'Health correlates of recreational gambling in older adults', *American Journal of Psychiatry*, 2004; 161 (9) 1672–9

9. Glass, T.A. et al. 'Population based study of social and productive activities as predictors', *BMJ*, August 1999; 319, 478–83

10. Cohen, S. APA Distinguished Scientific Contributions Award address, American Psychological Association Annual Convention, Honolulu, 2004

11. Brown, S. et al. Minnesota Board on Aging, 2003

12. Peterson, C., Seligman, M.E.P. *Character Strengths and Virtues: A Handbook and Classification*, Oxford University Press and the American Psychological Association, 2004

13. Op. cit. Chapter 6, reference 7

14. McNeely, C.A., Nonnemaker, J.M., Blum, R.W. 'Promoting school connectedness: evidence from the National Longitudinal Study of Adolescent Health', *J. Sch. Health*, 2002; 72 (4) 138–46

15. McNeely, C.A., Falci, C. 'School connectedness and the transition into and out of health-risk behavior among adolescents: a comparison of social belonging and teacher support', *J. Sch. Health*, 2004; 74 (7) 284–92

16. Wilson, D. 'The interface of school climate and school connectedness and relationships with aggression and victimization', *J. Sch. Health*, 2004; 74 (7) 293–9

17. Luthar, S.S., Latendresse, S.J. 'Children of the Affluent. Challenges to Well-Being', *Current Directions in Psychological Science*, 2005; 14 (1) 49–53

Conclusion: Tune In, Turn On – or Drop Out?

1. www.TV-B-Gone.com

INDEX